In Cod We Trust

*From Sea to Shore, the Celebrated Cuisine
of Coastal Massachusetts*

Heather Atwood

Photography by Allan Penn

Globe
Pequot

GUILFORD, CONNECTICUT

**Globe
Pequot**

An imprint of Rowman & Littlefield

Distributed by NATIONAL BOOK NETWORK

Copyright © 2015 by Heather Atwood
All photography copyright © 2015 by Allan Penn
Text design: Nancy Freeborn
A Hollan Publishing, Inc. Concept

British Library Cataloguing in Publication Information Available

Library of Congress Cataloging-in-Publication Data Available

ISBN 978-1-4930-0403-4 (hardcover)
ISBN 978-1-4930-2236-6 (e-book)

∞™ The paper used in this publication meets the minimum requirements of American National Standard for Information Sciences—Permanence of Paper for Printed Library Materials, ANSI/NISO Z39.48-1992.

Contents

Introduction

For all of you who think coastal Massachusetts cuisine starts with salt pork and ends with cream, watch out. Watch for gorgeous chunks of golden fried cod slathered with garlic whipped potatoes. Watch for quahogs stuffed with chourico, Cohasset Chocolate Mousse Cake, and bronze, rich-as-Croesus loaves of Massa Sovado, a delicious Portuguese sweet bread. Did you know the Portuguese in New Bedford serve loaves of this bread beside a bowl of daffodil-yellow rice pudding called Arroz Doce? New Bedford children dream about spoonfuls of this creamy *pudim*. What a breakfast!

Some of the coastline's most beautiful dishes are being prepared by the Portuguese in kitchens from New Bedford to Newburyport. Portuguese Caldeirada consists of layers of fish, potatoes, and vegetables that simmer for hours and create a bourguignon-like richness. The Portuguese and Azorean tomato sauce called Molho de Tomate, is a ragout of tomatoes, crushed red pepper, red wine, vinegar, garlic, and parsley that simmers on the stove for half a day. Poach eggs in this finished masterpiece, or dip crusty Portuguese Broa in it, and have yourself a bold Massachusetts breakfast.

Across Buzzards Bay to Martha's Vineyard, farmers are heroes; the cuisine built around local ingredients there dazzles. Cavatappi with Nasturtium Pesto is what's for dinner tonight! Let's begin with a Rhubarb Cocktail, and then we'll share some Za'atar Seasoned Kale Chips, and a Smoky Eggplant and Fresh Tomato Platter. The flavors in an Aquinnah Salad—a ravishing composition of local greens, roasted butternut squash, and red onion, topped with wild blueberries and toasted sunflower seeds—reflect all the colors and tastes of this sacred Wampanoag land on a late summer day.

The Wampanoag influence is seen in our cuisine even today. Sobaheg is the powerful Native American stew made with coastal Massachusetts ingredients and thickened with toasted sunflower seeds. Made with venison or chicken, this stew is surprisingly light and vegetable fragrant; it's a soulful weeknight dinner, but would also be a perfect way to begin a Thanksgiving feast.

There is so much that is not dull about the coast of Massachusetts! On Nantucket, old recipe boxes are filled with ways to pickle limes and make inky, black gingerbread. Pickled limes were once so common in Massachusetts that in Louisa May Alcott's *Little Women* the schoolteacher reprimands May for bringing them to school. Pickled limes—the combination of tart citrus with molasses, vinegar, and clove—is a natural. Yes, a well-roasted chicken would love a pickled lime beside it, but when you taste the old Nantucket recipe for Beebe Gingerbread you taste the affinity molasses has for the sweet citrus. Yes, Beebe Gingerbread with Pickled Limes is historic, but it also packs such a wallop of flavor that it never goes out of style.

In Cape Cod's West Barnstable, the older Finnish families remember shining loaves of fragrant *joululimppu*, a Finnish spice bread brushed with molasses. Perhaps someone in a West Barnstable kitchen right now is also stirring a fruit soup. The Finns there and in Gloucester love fruits and berries and use them to make soups, which become cherished meals. I've come to love having a jar of dried fruit soup in the refrigerator. With no sugar, just jewel-like cooked fruit, it makes an ambrosial instant lunch topped with yogurt. The Finns make a beautiful rice pudding, also, one that cooks very slowly and almost caramelizes the milk. A few tablespoons of the apricot-, orange-, and cardamom-scented fruit soup over a small bowl of warm rice pudding is a dessert that needs a better name than "soup" or "pudding"; it's sublime enough to impress a king.

Finns settled into both capes—Cape Cod and Cape Ann—carrying to each variations on their homeland's cuisines: soufflé-like pancakes that puff to cumulus heights, and then descend to a bowl broad enough to fill with berries; creamy casseroles of turnips and rutabagas in steaming nutmeg clouds. The Finns have taught us to love their golden braids of cardamom-laced bread, the beloved *nisu*, meant to resemble a young Scandinavian girl's tress of hair.

The Massachusetts coast, a gnarled, glacier-shredded 1,500 miles of peninsulas and islands, is as gloriously various as the coast of France. Like strewn pearls along these tidal marshes and granite promontories, fishing villages from New Bedford to Newburyport hold distinctively different culinary treasures.

When people think of dock-side dining in Massachusetts, they imagine buttery toasted lobster rolls, steaming bowls of creamy fish chowder, and porcelain scallops piled with bread crumbs. All this is true, and some of that is in this cookbook, but there is so much more to the coast of Massachusetts.

History is everywhere and it need not be dull. Buttercup Stew, for instance, turkey and fresh corn braised inside a buttercup squash, is a recipe that reflects what Myles Standish learned from Massasoit—pumpkins and squash make fine pots and pans. Better than the history lesson, this recipe is about hot wedges of blistering sweet squash tumbling with turkey and vegetables, proving that roasting inside a pumpkin is not a gimmick, it's brilliant.

And then there's chowder, which no one would be making if not for the Wampanoag lessons. But the history of chowder is for another book; this is about offering recipes for the best chowder being served on the coast of Massachusetts. And we can start with the Wampanoag version, still being made in Plymouth and Aquinnah. It's a heavenly home-made fish broth thickened with nothing but cornmeal. Oysters and young spinach are added at the end and heated just enough to plump the shellfish. This combination makes an elegant soup, far more sophisticated than the word "chowder" suggests. The Portuguese in Provincetown brought their own clam-as-stew variation to America; loaded with cumin, saffron, and fresh tomato—that's the way the Portuguese like their quahogs "chowdered."

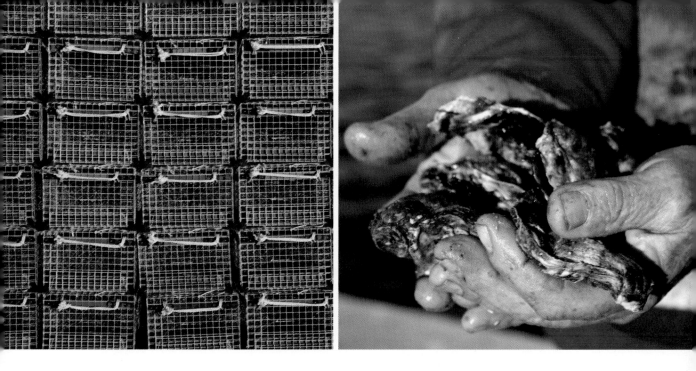

There is South of Boston Chowder, made with quahogs, and North of Boston Chowder, made with soft-shell clams. Both use evaporated milk. These chowder experts agree evaporated milk is critical. Laurie Lufkin, from Essex, is an expert. Her North of Boston recipe, the Essex translation of this classic, includes floating a homemade cracker on top.

Portuguese, Sicilian, Finnish, and English recipes can all be served on the same Massachusetts sideboard these days. My favorite example of this evolution is watching a young visitor recently trying her first fried clam. She tasted one, and then reached for the Portuguese red pepper sauce, Pimenta Moida, on the table.

"Wow!" she said after dipping a crispy fried clam in the pepper sauce. "They're really good with this!" That's the new Massachusetts—Portuguese red pepper sauce, indispensable in New Bedford, beside the tartar sauce at the clam shack.

Here's a note from a 1930's cookbook author in Provincetown. She, too, shared my concern that outsiders will think Massachusetts cuisine isn't sexy.

I fear a Cape Cod recipe makes uninspiring reading.
The recipes of other regions, the recipes of different nations, read like a novel, a best seller.
Here on Cape Salt Cod our recipes, they are so bare! They have not glamourous ingredients. Have no sumptuous seasonings. No provocative directions. Our Salt Fish Hash will lure you when and only when you have tasted it before.
BUT. If you have tasted it before—then, then, then, then certainly it will lure you.

The Salt Fish Hash recipe is included in this book, and it makes a fabulous breakfast that is not just the same old thing at all. On her advice and mine, make it.

Almost every community on the Massachusetts coast has a great recipe including salt cod, which was once Massachusetts' most abundant resource.

In recent years, the cuisine and culture of coastal Massachusetts have been celebrated in national media. From articles in *Food & Wine* and *Bon Appétit* about local restaurants to major motion pictures such as *The Perfect Storm* and the Discovery Channel's runaway hit TV show *Wicked Tuna*, the Massachusetts seacoast has captured the national imagination in a way few regions do. The range of breathtaking scenery, colorful history, and eclectic culture makes coastal Massachusetts—like France—one of the world's most fascinating shorelines.

And as the proud bumper stickers on fishermen's trucks proclaim here in Massachusetts, "In Cod We Trust."

Some Names and Ingredients

This book is meant to explore recipes from the wonderful communities that call the Massachusetts coastline home, and the way their cultures shaped the shore. Sometimes recipes from a distant homeland created a whole new market for Massachusetts ingredients, the way the Finns substituted cranberries for their native lingonberries when they arrived. Sometimes people came to Massachusetts following the ingredients—or natural resources—the way Portuguese and Italians followed the cod to New Bedford, Province-town, and Gloucester. Sometimes recipes from the old country were so perfect they leapt from family recipe boxes and permeated the culture already here, the way Clams Bulhao Pato and Caldo Verde are now served in almost every restaurant—Portuguese or not—on the Massachusetts south coast.

Some of the Massachusetts coastline dishes are just too insouciant to believe there was ever a pious Pilgrim living here: Blueberry Grunt, Rhubarb Slump, Apple Pandowdy, and Hog's Back Son of a Seacook, for example. Mostly these are simple dishes that depend on quality ingredients; maybe that's the fun of them—they're easy to make, easier to say.

About that salt pork—there is a lot of it on the coast of Massachusetts. I recommend you embrace it. Niman Ranch sells salt pork from pigs fed a vegetarian diet with no hor-mones and no antibiotics. Once you know that you're dealing with a well-raised source of salt pork, you should be not just comfortable with this source of fat, but ecstatic about it.

The best part about cooking with salt pork is the unparalleled way it mysteriously unites the flavors in a dish without demanding center stage. It is the shy conductor of taste, the umami of Massachusetts. Think about the mild fish that have made this coastline rich and famous: cod, haddock, whiting, and hake. These fish need salt pork. If cod and salt pork were school kids, salt pork would be the one quietly letting cod copy her homework. Cod gets all the credit, but salt pork is doing the work of creating flavor.

Perhaps the most famous ingredient on the coast of Massachusetts that no one knows about is salt cod, also known as bacalhau, baccala, bacalao, and the dried version: stokkfisk, or stockfish. Once considered the beefsteak of the sea, a reliable source of calories and pro-tein, salt cod fueled Europeans' cross-Atlantic exploration; it built fortunes, as Europeans found hungry markets for the stuff in Spain, Italy, Portugal, and the tropics, where salt cod fed the slave trade. Literally hundreds of acres of Massachusetts coastline were blanketed in "flakes," wooden racks for drying fish. People in Provincetown, Marblehead, and Gloucester recall how every inch of their cities was covered in these racks; buildings and roads were the only space free from drying fish.

In France, Spain, and Italy, there is no word for fresh cod; who needs it?—they say. While these culinary giants adore their salted fish, they consider the fresh stuff watery and insipid. Their salt cod recipes stack high.

The Massachusetts coast has a fine salt cod repertoire of its own. Poach it (after soak-ing it in milk), or lightly fry it. Better yet, layer the pieces in a tomato and pepper sauce that has stewed for hours, then put all that in the oven with a cover of bread crumbs, and you have Bacalhau com Molho Tomate, and you know why the Portuguese in New Bedford refuse to let go of this emblematic fish.

Or, layer the pearly chunks in a casserole with cream, a little salt pork, and potatoes for a luxurious baked Finnish dish called Kalalaatikko that Finns in Gloucester and on Cape Cod still savor on a winter night.

In northern Gloucester, a Brahmin artist declares her salt cod cakes "very superior fish cakes." Creamy and light, not "whiskery," Fish Cakes from Lobster Cove are indeed superior. Whipped together with potatoes, they resemble a lightly fried version of the famous French salt cod dish, Brandade du Morue.

You must not close the book on salt cod until you have tried the West Indies–inspired fish cakes made with salt cod and butternut squash, seasoned with lime and cilantro.

If we can learn to embrace salt cod again—and the only hitch is remembering to soak it—a rich repertoire of recipes awaits. Look for salt cod fillets in Italian and Portuguese grocery stores. Look for one-to-two-pound fillets with thick, meaty centers. Avoid large pieces of the thin end of a fillet, the thicker the better. These will rehydrate to white, moist flakes of cod. I know the wooden box is cute, but resist those little crates near the seafood section of your grocery store. You can't see the product inside; when I've used it the fish has been shriveled planks that soften to the same.

When I first began to prepare traditional Portuguese and Azorean dishes from New Bedford and Fall River, I learned that many of the recipes called for something called Pimenta Moida, a "crushed pepper sauce," as some recipes undersold it. The Azorean Islands are considered the Portuguese colonies with less fertile land and fewer resources. Spice and heat were the tools Azoreans employed to enliven their limited cuisine. Pimenta Moida is the Azorean ace, a fermented red pepper paste that contributes a magically complex combination of spice, heat, flavor, and salt. Pimenta Moida is as important to the Azorean people as fish sauce is to the Vietnamese.

In New Bedford and Fall River in the autumn, Azorean families still purchase truckloads of Shepherd peppers, the huge, fleshy red pepper even larger than a bell. The families spend an entire day if not a weekend cleaning the peppers of seeds and their white ribs, crushing them, and curing them with salt in great plastic buckets. At the end of the weekend, all the members of the family return home with enough Pimenta Moida for the year.

As I realized how critical—and probably irreplaceable—Pimenta Moida was to all these Azorean dishes, I thought I would have to make it myself or find a specialty store in New Bedford that might carry it. With little confidence, I began to consider substitutes—Tabasco? Sriracha? On a whim, I looked in my grocery store, a regular old grocery store, Shaw's. There it was. Pimenta Moida is as available in most Massachusetts grocery stores as ketchup; some stores even stock more than one brand.

This speaks to how many people are familiar with the powers and virtues of Pimenta Moida. It comes in a tall, round glass jar, with lots of pulpy pepper visible. The sauce is not too spicy, not too hot, and made complex by that fermentation. It's delicious on eggs, on meats, on every kind of fish, or stirred into Caldo Verde or Kale Soup. Drizzle it on butternut squash soup, and you make a straight New England standard colorful and complex. It's even delicious added to clam chowder, yes, even fried clams are improved with a touch

of Pimenta Moida. Try to find it, but if you must substitute the Portuguese sauce with a more common hot sauce the recipe will not be compromised.

Here's a note on linguica and chourico. While chourico can be found fresh, in these recipes I refer to the smoked, cured sausage usually seasoned with garlic and pimeton. People claim that chourico is spicier than linguica, also a smoked, cured sausage seasoned with paprika, but the two are mostly interchangeable. Both sausages have a papery casing that needs to be peeled away before using, but feel free to substitute one product for the other.

CHAPTER ONE

The South Coast

From the Rhode Island border arcing up to the Cape Cod Canal, the coast of Massachusetts looks like a ragged hemline, coattails of land shredded by a passing glacier millions of years ago.

Against the green and azure landscape, the gritty cities of New Bedford and Fall River have been calling people—Azorean, Cape Verdean, Portuguese, and French Canadian—to work for centuries, first to the whaling industry and then to the mills. Thus South Coast cuisine has a dissonance—urban/rural, gritty/pastoral. It's much more willing to be spicy, robust, and complex; it's almost unrecognizable as "New England" when one imagines the cornmeal, molasses, salt pork standard. Clams Bulhao Pao, clams steamed with garlic and cilantro, are an appetizer on almost every South Coast menu, as is kale soup; there's a variation of kale soup for almost every day of the year. Linguica and chourico lay down with eggs for breakfast far more often than bacon around here. A classic Azorean light meal, eggs poached in a spicy tomato sauce and served with toasted Bolos Levedos—the sweet Portuguese breads cooked on a bare cast-iron skillet—has become standard New Bedford.

The best example of the culinary riches that define New Bedford can be seen in August, at the Feast of the Blessed Sacrament, the largest Portuguese feast in the world.

There, racks of spicy grilled beef, Carne de Espeto, lay over coals for yards. Hundreds of Cacoil, the Portuguese version of a pulled pork sandwich, made sweet and hot with paprika, are served. Bacalhau com Molho Tomate, a traditional salt cod and slow-cooked tomato sauce beneath a golden layer of buttered breadcrumbs, causes the Italian guests to forget their beloved Chicken Parmesan. Stewed favas—meaty legumes in a delicious garlic, vinegar, and red pepper sauce—are served on the side or savored on their own; they are like baked beans on a date with the devil.

The fava beans and all these spicy, hearty Portuguese and Azorean foods have been in Massachusetts so long—not only in New Bedford, but also in Provincetown and Gloucester—that these dishes can justifiably now be called "Massachusetts traditions."

Vinegar, red wine, cumin, and Pimenta Moida are the trademarks of Portuguese and Azorean dishes. So is salt cod, which the Portuguese refuse to give up. In Gloucester and Provincetown, where acres and acres of drying cod once blanketed the cities, salt cod in fish cakes is just a memory. But in New Bedford and Fall River this cured fish is still a cherished ingredient. Many consider its firmer texture to have more character than fresh. To this day, in France, Spain, and Italy, there is no word for fresh cod. These cultures claim they have no purpose for what they consider the insipid fresh stuff.

While the Portuguese and Azorean cuisines appear the same to a non-Mediterranean, on the streets of Fall River and New Bedford people know the differences. In general Portuguese dishes have an urbanity to them; they are milder and less rustic. The Azorean Caldo Verde, for example, rumbles with big chunks of potatoes, large leaves of kale, and generous chunks of chourico. The Portuguese recipe is thinner, creamier, with ribbons of kale, and a restrained portion of chourico. (In the Cape Cod chapter you will find a complex, hearty, Azorean-style kale soup called Sopas do Espirito Santo, or Holy Ghost Soup, rich with beef bones, stew beef, and chourico; in this chapter I've included the refined Portuguese version from Chef Fernando Dovale, one of New Bedford's most revered Portuguese chefs.)

The Azores are an archipelago, a cluster of islands southeast of Portugal. With scant natural resources, people of the Azores embraced spice to make their country food more bracing. Piripiri, the small pepper from North Africa, is used liberally. Pimenta Moida, the fermented red pepper sauce, is added to everything. A roast chicken

in an Azorean kitchen is a bronze bird shining in paprika and lemon, resting on a glistening mound of onions, carrots, and potatoes, appointed with hot peppers and chunks of chourico.

When many Azoreans came to this country, they could not read or write, so they did not imitate their neighboring immigrants—they did not open restaurants. Many Azorean recipes remained in kitchens, told to the next generation, reserved for the family tables. Many of these dishes are treasures.

And the desserts?! New Bedford and Fall River are dotted with fabulous Portuguese and Azorean bakeries piled to the pressed-tin ceilings with bread and pastry selections. In many of these bakeries you can also buy house-made Portuguese cheeses. There are tables and coffee service, and the places fill up in the afternoon with Portuguese men and women having their coffee and sweet moment. It's easy to think you're still in Porto.

The overwhelming selection of golden, egg-rich custards and custard-filled pastries begs the question, "Why?" Why so many eggs in Portuguese pastries? The answer charms: Apparently in Medieval times, convents were the main producers of pastries in Portugal. The nuns had chickens and used copious amounts of egg whites to starch their wimples; something had to be done with the remaining yolks!

Westport, the last coastal town before Rhode Island, is postcard-pastoral. Still crisscrossed with two-hundred-year-old stone walls, Westport calls itself "The Coastal Agricultural Resource Community of New England." Fourteen dairy farms once grazed their cows on the sweet Westport grasses, buffed by sea breezes and fingered by the east and west branches of the Westport River. Today only two farms are left, but one,

Shy Brothers Farms, produces beautiful yeasty cheeses from that terroir. Pair Shy Brothers thimble cheeses, called "Hannahbells" with some warm Johnny Cakes, and pour a glass of Westport Rivers Winery's Blanc de Blancs, and you have a South Coast tapas, as elegant as any European experience. Westport Rivers Winery has earned international recognition. Perhaps those early-morning, sea spray–infused fogs rolling across the ripening grapes account for their success.

The way water cuts into land on this coastline makes a kind of Eden. South Coast sweet corn and New Bedford chourico make the best stuffed quahogs, or "stuffies," you'll ever taste. Macomber turnips, grown only in Westport, are served here with beautiful pearl-white sea scallops. Fishermen in New Bedford land thousands of pounds of glistening ivory scallops a week.

To walk along the fishing pier in New Bedford is to say, "So this is where fishing in America is." Miles of impressively rigged commercial fishing boats line up like a row of magnificent beasts along the pier. The scallop industry has rebounded in New Bedford, declaring it the largest fish landing in the country. The shellfish from which the goddess Aphrodite was hatched has done for New Bedford what whaling did when Herman Melville, in *Moby Dick,* wrote this about the south coast city:

The town itself is perhaps the dearest place to live in, in all New England. It is a land of oil, true enough: but not like Canaan; a land, also, of corn and wine. The streets do not run with milk; nor in the spring-time do they pave them with fresh eggs. Yet, in spite of this, nowhere in all America will you find more patrician-like houses; parks and gardens more opulent, than in New Bedford. Whence came they? how planted upon this once scraggy scoria of a country?

Go and gaze upon the iron emblematical harpoons round yonder lofty mansion, and your question will be answered. Yes; all these brave houses and flowery gardens came from the Atlantic, Pacific, and Indian oceans. One and all, they were harpooned and dragged up hither from the bottom of the sea.

The South Coast Index

Caldo Verde
(Shredded Kale Soup)

If you live in New Bedford, or even on the south coast of Massachusetts, you know that Caldo Verde, a light chicken broth crisscrossed with ribbons of kale and dotted with chourico, is not ordinary kale soup. Kale soup is a more imposing stew-like dish thick with beans, large chunks of linguica, and, of course, kale. Caldo Verde is a smoother, more elegant edition of kale meeting broth. Almost every restaurant south of Westport includes a Caldo Verde on its menu, and for good reason: it's luxuriantly satisfying. You could say it's "dining room" kale soup.

This delicious version, as hearty as it is smooth and subtle, is from Fernando Dovale, chef and owner of Fernando's, considered the finest Portuguese restaurant in New Bedford before it closed.

SERVES 6

2 quarts chicken broth

2½ pounds potatoes, peeled and quartered

5 garlic cloves

1 Spanish onion, chopped

¾ cup extra virgin olive oil

1 pound piece of chourico, whole, casing removed

Salt and pepper to taste

Red pepper flakes to taste

10 ounces, or about 4 cups, kale, tough middle stalk removed, thinly shredded

Juice of 2 lemons

In a large stockpot, put chicken broth, potatoes, garlic, onion, olive oil, whole chourico, salt, pepper, and red pepper flakes. Bring to a simmer, and cook until potatoes are very soft, about 45 minutes.

In a separate saucepan, bring 2 cups water to a boil. Add kale, and cook until tender, about 20 minutes. Reserve.

When all ingredients in the large pot are cooked, remove the chourico and set aside. Puree the remaining ingredients with an emulsion blender.

Add the kale and its water to the soup.

Reserve some of the chourico to use as a garnish, but slice the rest into ¼" rounds, and add to the soup.

Just before serving, stir in the lemon juice. Serve soup hot with reserved chourico, a last squeeze of lemon, and a few drops of olive oil.

Clams Bulhao Pato

Bulhao Pato was a nineteenth-century Lisbon poet, but everyone seems to remember only his clam recipe. If his verse was as simple and succinct as his clams, it, too, might be famous. Clams Bulhao Pato is straightforward, with exactly just what is needed to make shellfish wonderful—a little garlic, a little hot chili, a little lemon juice, and cilantro. It is clam poetry.

SERVES 6 AS A FIRST-COURSE

48 little neck or "mahogany" clams, about 5 pounds

4 tablespoons olive oil

4 tablespoons minced garlic

3–4 dried hot chilies, crumbled, or 1 teaspoon red hot pepper flakes

Juice from 3 lemons, or 6 tablespoons lemon juice

1 small bunch fresh cilantro, washed, dried, and loosely chopped

Scrub clams clean under running water. Then place in a large bowl of salted water to sit for ½ hour. This helps eliminate some of the sand inside.

Heat olive oil in a large skillet to medium high. Add garlic and chilies, and let cook until soft. Be careful not to burn the garlic, which at this temperature can happen quickly.

As soon as garlic is slightly yellow, add clams, and cover. Lower heat to medium.

Cook for about 10 minutes, lifting the lid occasionally to watch for doneness. Smaller clams take longer to open than larger ones.

When all the clams are completely opened, pour lemon juice over all. Cover pan again, and let sit for 1 minute, shaking the pan a bit to distribute the juices.

Ladle clams into individual heated bowls, distributing the broth evenly into all the dishes. Sprinkle with cilantro, and serve immediately.

Portuguese Spicy Shrimp

Consider this recipe an introduction to Pimenta Moida, which makes even more delicious everything we already love about shrimp marinated in garlic and cooked in a little white wine. In just 1 or 2 tablespoons, this potent sauce adds a little heat, a little spice, a little vinegar, and a little sweetness. The result may just be the best shrimp appetizer you've ever eaten.

Pimenta Moida is not a hard-to-find ingredient; just look carefully in the ethnic section of your grocery store. Once you understand its effect, you, too, will have a back-up jar in your pantry.

SERVES 2 AS AN ENTREE, 4 AS AN APPETIZER

6 tablespoons olive oil, divided

12 garlic cloves, minced

½ teaspoon smoked paprika

2 tablespoons Pimenta Moida

1 pound shrimp, peeled and deveined

Salt and pepper to taste

½ cup white wine

2 tablespoons lemon juice, plus lemon wedges for serving

Fresh cilantro for garnish

In a medium bowl mix together 4 tablespoons olive oil, garlic, paprika, and Pimenta Moida. Add shrimp and toss gently. Cover and chill in refrigerator for 1–3 hours.

Heat a large skillet to medium high. Add remaining 2 tablespoons olive oil. When oil is hot, add shrimp, making sure not to crowd the pan.

When shrimp begins to turn pink, add salt and pepper to taste, and white wine.

Turn shrimp over, and cook for 3–5 minutes, or until shrimp are cooked through. Add lemon juice.

Serve with the broth poured over the shrimp. Garnish with fresh cilantro.

Hake Molho de Vilhao

(Villain's Sauce)

Molho de Vilhao, or "Villain's Sauce," is the Portuguese way to brighten a coastal classic, not unlike the way the British do by adding vinegar to their fish and chips. Sharp, light, and piquant, this sauce adds all the right notes to a simply prepared fried fish. Subtract the sweet jab of tartar sauce, add the fresh, piquant taste of Molho de Vilhao, and a fried hake (or haddock) becomes a light, sophisticated dinner. Put your Hake Molho de Vilhao on two pieces of toasted Portuguese Corn Bread for a light and interesting fish sandwich. The components here are simple, but the taste is anything but.

MAKES 4 SANDWICHES

For the sauce:

2 onions, finely chopped

2 cloves garlic, minced

2 tablespoons chopped parsley

½ cup oil

¼ cup white vinegar

½ teaspoon salt

⅛ teaspoon pepper

For the sandwich:

1¼ pounds hake, not more than ½-inch thick

½ cup all-purpose flour

½ teaspoon salt

¼ teaspoon freshly ground black pepper

½ teaspoon paprika

4 tablespoons vegetable oil

8 slices Portuguese Corn Bread, toasted

In a small bowl whisk together the sauce ingredients. Set aside. Sauce may be prepared a few hours in advance.

To make the sandwich, cut the fish into pieces a bit larger than the bread slices. Combine the flour, salt, pepper, and paprika on a plate. Dredge the haddock in the seasoned flour, shaking off the excess.

Divide the oil between two medium-to-large skillets over medium-high heat. When the oil is hot but not smoking, add the fish and cook, turning once, until golden brown and crisp on both sides and just cooked within (the fish will flake easily when tested with a fork), about 2 minutes per side.

Lay the fish on the bread. Drizzle a liberal tablespoon of sauce over the fish, and top with the second piece of cornbread.

Carne de Porco a Alentejana
(Pork and Clam Stew from Alentejana)

Beloved, emblematic, more symbolic than a Portuguese flag, this dish is Portuguese soul food. Made with cubes of marinated pork, crispy fried potatoes, and briny clams, Carne de Porco a Altentejana is truly one of the world's great stews, an extraordinary synthesis of flavors and textures.

SERVES 4–6

¾ cup extra virgin olive oil, plus ¼ cup for browning potatoes and pork

2 cups white wine, divided

5 garlic cloves, crushed

3 bay leaves

2 tablespoons Worcestershire sauce

½ teaspoon dried cumin

2 teaspoons piri-piri sauce or dried red chilies

1 teaspoon Pimenta Moida (pg. 29) or hot sauce

1 teaspoon salt

1 teaspoon pepper

1 tablespoon Spanish paprika

3 pounds pork tenderloin, cut into 1-inch cubes

2½ pounds Yukon gold potatoes

24 hard-shell clams (little necks or cherrystones)

Grape seed oil (or olive oil) for frying potatoes

1 medium onion, cut in wedges

Olive oil

Lemon wedges

Black olives

Fresh cilantro, chopped

In a small bowl stir together ¾ cup olive oil, 1 cup wine, garlic, bay leaves, Worcestershire sauce, cumin, piri-piri, Pimenta Moida, salt, pepper, and paprika.

Place pork in sealable plastic bag, or a large bowl, and cover with the marinade. Let it sit, turning occasionally, for 3 hours.

Peel potatoes and cut into ½-inch cubes.

Rinse clams well, and place in a bowl with 1 teaspoon salt, placing them in refrigerator for ½ hour. This helps release their sand.

Heat a large skillet to medium high. Add grape seed oil, and heat. Pat dry the potatoes and place them carefully in the oil, frying them until crispy. Work in batches if necessary. Drain on paper towels and reserve.

Heat a large dutch oven to medium high. Add ¼ cup olive oil and heat. Add onions, and cook until softened, about 10 minutes.

Add the pork, and brown the meat in batches, cooking each batch for 5–10 minutes, or until meat begins to brown. Do not crowd the pan.

Return all the meat to the pan.

Rinse and pat dry the clams, and add to the pork with 1 cup wine and the leftover marinade. Cover and cook over medium heat until the clams open, about 10 minutes. Taste for salt.

Divide the crispy potatoes among the bowls. Ladle pork and clam stew over the potatoes. Garnish with a drizzle of good olive oil, a squeeze of lemon, a few black olives, and chopped cilantro.

Cod a Braz

(Fresh Cod with Eggs and Crispy Potatoes)

Cod a Braz is a fascinating Portuguese dish that demonstrates the culture's affection for a pile of crispy potatoes. Cooked cod is mixed with a warm pile of delicate homemade french fries, and then scrambled with a batch of eggs, resulting in a fabulous culinary study in texture. Probably born from a hungry fisherman with too many eggs on his kitchen counter, Cod a Braz has become a classic in Portuguese cuisine.

In this recipe a "salsa" of roasted cherry tomatoes, lemon, olives, and parsley adds a fresh garden finish to the dish. The gleaming vegetables on a mountain of golden eggs, cod, and potatoes look magnificent. The soft texture of fish and egg mixed with the satisfying crispness of the potatoes is wonderful, and not something our often segregated plates of meat, vegetable, and starch usually offer.

This recipe was originally made with salt cod, or bacalau, but fresh cod is substituted for convenience here. The recipe is so delicious, and the principals of the composition so interesting, that it would be a shame not to make it because one is daunted by soaking fish. That said, if you have the time and inclination to prepare this with the salt cod, the textures and flavors are wonderful in a new way.

SERVES 4

For the roasted cherry tomato sauce:

2 cups cherry tomatoes

4 tablespoons olive oil, divided

1 large or 2 small lemons, sliced

3 tablespoons chopped fresh parsley

½ cup pitted black olives

1 tablespoon lemon juice

Sea salt and freshly ground black pepper to taste

For the cod, potatoes, and eggs:

Peel of 1 lemon

Salt

½ teaspoon black peppercorns

1 bay leaf

1 pound fresh cod

5 tablespoons olive oil (more if needed)

3 large baking potatoes, peeled and cut into thin strips like very skinny french fries

1 large onion, thinly sliced

1 teaspoon oregano

8 large eggs

Pepper

1 teaspoon red pepper flakes

1 tablespoon parsley

To make the roasted cherry tomato sauce:

Preheat oven to 400°F. Toss tomatoes in 3 table-spoons olive oil, and spread in a baking dish. Roast for fifteen minutes, or until just beginning to crack and brown. Remove from oven, and allow to cool a bit. Toss into a medium-size bowl, and mix in about 6 lemon slices, remaining olive oil, parsley, olives, lemon juice, salt, and pepper. Stir gently together and set aside.

To make the cod, potatoes, and eggs:

Fill a shallow skillet with 1 inch of water. Bring to a simmer and add lemon peel, 1 teaspoon salt, pep-percorns, bay leaf, and fish. Cover and simmer for 7–10 minutes, or until fillets begin to flake. Remove fish from broth and cool. Flake the fish, checking for bones.

Heat 4 tablespoons olive oil in a large skillet and fry potatoes in batches until brown and crispy.

Drain on paper towels, sprinkle liberally with salt, and start the next batch, adding more oil if necessary.

When all the potatoes are done, drain that oil, but then return 1 tablespoon of fresh olive oil to the same pan. Add the onion and sauté until golden brown, about 10 minutes. Stir in the oregano, a sprinkle of salt, and reduce the heat to low.

Gently stir in the flaked fish and fried potatoes, reserving at least a cup of potatoes for garnish.

Whisk together the eggs with salt and pepper, red pepper flakes, and parsley. Pour the eggs over the fish, onions, and potato mixture, and stir very gently until the eggs are cooked, about 3 minutes. Do not let them stick to the bottom of the pan and brown.

Serve hot with a healthy spoonful of tomato mix-ture piled on top, and the reserved fried potatoes on the side.

Bacalhau com Molho de Tomate

(Baked Salt Cod with Portuguese Tomato Sauce)

The first taste of steaming Bacalhau com Molto de Tomate is like this: golden, pillowy squares of fried cod nestled within a winey, old-world, patiently simmered tomato sauce. Bacalhau com Molho de Tomate is a miscellany of textures. There's the velvety alabaster that only salt cod, or bacalhau, can become. There's the laciness of fish rolled in rice flour and fried in olive oil, the melting plumpness of onions and tomatoes that have cooked gently for hours on the back of a stove, and the comforting crunch of a toasted bread crumb and Parmesan cheese, the perfect coda to so much.

These are the parts of Bacalhau com Molho de Tomate, a Portuguese dish that adds up to a brilliant orchestration of garden and sea. There are many steps, but none of them difficult, and the sauce, which cooks for 1–2 hours, can and should be made in advance.

SERVES 4–6

1½ pounds salt cod

Milk for soaking

1 cup olive oil

1 cup rice flour

2 cups Molho de Tomate (Portuguese Tomato Sauce) (page 20)

2 teaspoons minced garlic

⅓ cup chopped pimentos

½ cups bread crumbs

1 teaspoon Pimenta Moida or Tabasco, or more to taste

Freshly ground black pepper to taste

1 cup grated Parmesan cheese

1 cup panko crumbs

Fresh cilantro for a garnish

Prepare the salt cod by soaking it for 24–36 hours, refreshing the water often. In the last 4 hours, remove the fish from the water and soak in milk to cover.

When ready to prepare the dish, drain the cod, and cut into 2-inch squares. In a medium saucepan, heat 3 inches of water, drop in cod, and simmer for 10 minutes. Once done, remove cod, drain, and pat it dry. This can be done a day in advance. Keep covered in the refrigerator.

In a large skillet, heat olive oil. Toss cod pieces in the rice flour, and fry in the hot oil, turning pieces until golden brown on both sides, about 4 minutes per side. Remove to baking racks to drain.

Preheat oven to 350°F.

Mix the tomato sauce with the garlic, pimentos, bread crumbs, hot sauce, and pepper.

Spread half the mixture into the bottom of an ovenproof casserole or glass baking dish. Lay the cod pieces in one layer on top of the sauce. Cover with the remaining sauce.

Toss the Parmesan cheese and panko crumbs together, and sprinkle generously over the dish.

Bake for 30 minutes, or until the fish is hot and the breadcrumbs browned. Garnish with fresh cilantro and serve immediately.

Portuguese Codfish Cakes with Garlic and Fresh Herbs

These fish cakes are as comfortable in a Lisbon restaurant as in a New Bedford kitchen. These cakes would make a great summer dinner, or, made in 1-inch size, a gutsy appetizer beside a bowl of olives. Pour the Vinho Verde.

SERVES 4

1 pound salt cod

Milk for soaking

2 cups day-old Portuguese or Italian bread, crusts removed and coarsely crumbed

¾ cup olive oil, divided

1 tablespoon finely chopped fresh mint

1 tablespoon finely chopped fresh parsley

2 tablespoons paprika

Freshly ground black pepper to taste

2 cloves garlic

Lemon wedges

Paprika

Prepare the salt cod by soaking it in cold water for 24-36 hours, refreshing the water 3–4 times. In the last 4 hours, remove the fish from the water and soak in milk to cover.

When ready to prepare, place drained cod in a saucepan and cover with fresh water. Simmer for 10 minutes, or until fish flakes easily.

In a large bowl combine the bread crumbs and ½ cup olive oil. Beat them together vigorously with a wooden spoon until the oil is completely absorbed. Add fish, mint, parsley, paprika, and pepper. Continue to mix well, using your hands if necessary, so that everything is completely incorporated.

Shape into round cakes about 3 inches in diameter and ½-inch thick (or smaller if using as an appetizer).

Heat remaining olive oil in a wide skillet to medium. Add garlic cloves, tossing until they begin to brown. Discard garlic and add the fish cakes. Cook over medium heat until each side is golden brown. Serve with wedges of lemon and a shake of paprika on top.

Caldeirada de Raia e Tamboril

(Portuguese Fish Stew with Monkfish and Skate)

Caldeirada, a basic fish stew, is produced in almost every Portuguese and Azorean home, but each in its unique way. The scaffolding is always potatoes, tomatoes, and onions layered with at least two kinds of fish (one oily, one white, some insist). There is usually lots of white wine and olive oil involved, and the stew is simmered long and low. (Azorean dishes typically cook for a long time at very low temperatures, another way to build those wonderful flavors.)

This recipe, from chef Fernando Dovale, includes monkfish and skate, two flavorful fish with textures that melt beautifully into the stew after an hour of slow cooking. But the Portuguese practicality invites almost any fish in; I particularly love the texture of dogfish, if you can find it, but tuna or swordfish combined with hake, haddock, or pollock would also be delicious.

The fish here becomes almost meaty, thus like a good bourguignon, the flavors improve with time and reheating; it's almost better the next day.

SERVES 8

2 white onions, cut in ¼-inch rings

3 pounds potatoes, peeled and cut in ⅓-inch slices

2 pounds ripe tomatoes

½ red pepper, cut in ¼-inch rings

½ green pepper, cut in ¼-inch rings

2 pounds monk tail, cut in medallions

2 pounds skinless skate wings, cut in 1-inch cubes

4 garlic cloves, sliced

½ bunch flat parsley, finely chopped

2 teaspoons tomato paste

¾ cup extra virgin olive oil

1¼ cups white wine

2 bay leaves

1 teaspoon paprika

1 teaspoon salt, more to taste

1 teaspoon freshly ground pepper

Lemon for garnish

Chopped parsley for garnish

Hot sauce to taste

In a large covered skillet or a large covered casserole dish, layer ⅓ of onions, ⅓ of potatoes, ⅓ of tomatoes, ⅓ of peppers, and ⅓ of fish on the bottom. Repeat this sequence for two more layers.

Layer garlic, parsley, and tomato paste on final layer. Pour olive oil and white wine over all. Tuck in bay leaves, and season with paprika, salt, and pepper. Cover casserole.

On a low simmer, cook dish covered for 1 hour, or until fish and vegetables are cooked through. (Do not stir; shake the pot if necessary.)

Serve from the pot at the table. Garnish bowls with fresh lemon, parsley, and hot sauce.

Cacoila
(Classic Spicy Portuguese Pork Stew)

No discussion of Portuguese cuisine is complete without a recipe for Cacoila, the pulled pork of Portugal. Every Portuguese feast and celebration includes great pots of this spicy pork stew simmering away. It is then ladled out onto fresh Bolos Levedos or "Pops," the simple Portuguese rolls, or paired with a Portuguese Salad or rice. Cacoila is served in Portuguese homes for lunches the way other families make ham and cheese sandwiches. This spicy marinated pork, cooked very slowly, is one of the world's most perfect combination of flavors; if you haven't grown up in New Bedford or the Azores, you may not know the alchemical combination of paprika, red wine vinegar, cinnamon, and garlic. Drink gutsy Portuguese wines from the Douro with this.

Note: The festival and feast version of this dish is "pulled" or shredded pork. This recipe is more like the original, which was always a stew.

SERVES 4–6

3 pounds pork butt, cut in 1-inch cubes

2 tablespoons hot sauce or 1 tablespoon red pepper flakes

1 cup white wine

2 tablespoons paprika

1 teaspoon salt

1 tablespoon red wine vinegar

2 bay leaves

4 garlic cloves, finely chopped

1 tablespoon cinnamon

½ cup olive oil

1 cup chopped onion

In a large container, add cubed pork, hot sauce, wine, paprika, salt, vinegar, bay leaves, garlic, and cinnamon. Mix everything together, making sure the pork is covered well in the marinade. Marinate for 24 hours.

Remove pork from marinade, reserving the marinade.

In a large dutch oven, heat olive oil to medium high. Add chopped onion, and cook for 5 minutes, or until they begin to soften.

Add pork to pan, and allow to brown, turning the pieces occasionally. You may have to do this in batches; it gets a little complicated because the onions may brown too much. If that happens you can remove the onions while you brown the meat, or be less fussy about browning the meat. It will all still taste wonderful.

Once all your meat is browned, add reserved marinade. If liquid does not quite cover the meat, add wine or chicken broth. Lower heat to a very low simmer, and cook for 3–5 hours, or until the meat falls apart and is very tender. If the dish gets too dry, add white wine, broth, or water to keep it simmering. You want the meat to melt. Serve hot over rice or open face on a Portuguese roll.

Molho de Tomate

(Portuguese Tomato Sauce)

Portuguese tomato sauce is a lot like the classic Italian Sugo di Pomodoro, but at the same time it isn't anything like it at all. There are simpler versions of Molho de Tomate, such as the one in which eggs are poached for Ovos com Molho de Tomate, but this version, which cooks slowly for 1–2 hours is something you can keep in your freezer. A wowing combination of flavors—from garlic to red wine to cumin to a splash of vinegar—this sauce is like a ticket to far-away places. It is the sauce used in the sublime Bacalhau com Molho de Tomate. Served with chicken, meat, or simply over rice, this sauce makes a very special dinner.

MAKES APPROXIMATELY 1 QUART

½ cup olive oil

2 medium onions, halved and sliced thinly

2 teaspoons minced garlic

½ cup chopped parsley

1 (28-ounce) can whole plum tomatoes

1 green pepper, sliced

1 cup red wine

1 cup water

2 tablespoons vinegar

1 tablespoon sugar

1 teaspoon powdered cumin

½ teaspoon red pepper flakes

Salt and freshly ground black pepper to taste

Heat olive oil to medium in a large saucepan. Add onions and sauté for 5 minutes. Add garlic. Cook until onion and garlic are soft but not brown, about 10 minutes. Add parsley.

With your hands or scissors, squeeze or loosely cut tomatoes in their can. Add them to the onions, garlic, and parsley along with the remaining ingredients.

Heat to medium high and simmer vigorously for 1 minute, just to incorporate the ingredients.

Turn heat down to very, very low, and simmer the sauce for 1–2 hours, stirring occasionally to prevent sticking.

Use this sauce in the Bacalhau com Molho de Tomate or simmer shrimp in the sauce and serve over rice for a vibrant dinner. Clams also marry beautifully with the bit of vinegar and spice here; throw a dozen littlenecks into a shallow pan of simmering Molho de Tomate, cover until the clams open, and serve over a bowl of hot pasta. The sauce's acidity also makes it a wonderful condiment for grilled meats.

Freeze remaining sauce in plastic containers; it's a priceless find in your freezer!

Bolos Levedos

These lightly sweet, egg-rich "pancakes" may be one of the more delicious and significant culinary gifts the Massachusetts coastline has received from the Portuguese community. Looking like a larger, more yellow English muffin, Bolos Levedos come in bundles of six in grocery stores up and down the Massachusetts coast. Their unique flavor and texture—as delicate as brioche—make them perfect for breakfast, slathered with butter, marmalade or honey, used as a sandwich with everything from peanut butter to Portuguese barbecued pork, or simply by themselves beside a hot bowl of Caldo Verde. Even the Mrs. Cabots and Mrs. Lodges of the North Shore tuck them into their grocery carts.

The commercial variety is good, but this homemade, baked-on-your-own-skillet version is divine. They take time, but if you ever make homemade bread, you know the rewards are outstanding. Making this dough in your own kitchen, with good eggs and sweet milk, just magnifies all that is delicious about these little round loaves.

MAKES ABOUT 24 4-INCH ROUNDS

1½ packages active dry yeast (3½ teaspoons)

1½ cups plus 1 tablespoon sugar

½ cup lukewarm water

6 eggs

8–10 cups all-purpose flour

1 cup whole milk

½ cup (1 stick) butter, melted

1 tablespoon grated lemon rind

2 teaspoons salt

Dissolve yeast and 1 tablespoon sugar in lukewarm water. Set aside to proof for 10 minutes.

In a mixing bowl, add eggs and remaining 1½ cups sugar. Beat until color is light and consistency creamy, 5–7 minutes.

In a separate large bowl, add flour and make a well in the center with a wooden spoon. Carefully pour milk, melted butter, lemon rind, and salt into the well. Stir, bringing the flour down from the sides into the wet ingredients. Add creamed eggs and mix well. If dough gets stiff you can begin to work it with your hands.

Finally, add the proofed yeast and knead for 10 minutes, or until the dough is shiny and soft.

Lay the dough in a lightly buttered bowl, turning it so it is lightly coated with butter. Cover with a dishcloth and let rise in a warm place until double in bulk, about 2 hours.

After the dough rises, pull apart into 3-ounce pieces (about the size of a golf ball). With floured hands roll each piece of dough into a ball.

Lay the balls on a floured towel or cookie sheet. Dust the tops with flour, and cover with a towel. Let rise a second time, about 4 hours.

When balls have risen, pat them down to ½-inch "pancakes."

Preheat oven to 350°F.

Heat a large, ungreased skillet to medium low. Lay the cakes in the pan, leaving at least a ½-inch space between them. Brown them on the bottom, about 4 minutes, but watch carefully so they don't burn. Lower the temperature if they are browning too quickly. Flip them over and brown the other side. If both sides are a nice dark color but the cake is still uncooked inside, place it on a cookie sheet and finish in the oven for 5–10 minutes. Cakes will be firm and slightly puffed in the center when they are completely cooked.

Cool on wire racks. The cakes are obviously heavenly served fresh, but will keep for up to a week securely wrapped. They freeze well stored in a heavy duty plastic bag, which makes it easy to remove one or two for breakfast.

Broa

(Portuguese Corn Bread)

Varying qualities of brioche-like Portuguese sweet bread are sold in grocery stores up and down the Massachusetts coast. This round, shiny loaf is so ubiquitous that it's easy to think Portuguese communities have only that sweet, eggy bread to butter, but the Portuguese and Azorean communities have many choices in their local bakeries, including this delicious corn bread.

Made with corn flour, Broa is a small, low, rounded loaf, whose shape is just an opportunity for more of that wonderful crust. With a gentle toasty flavor of corn, Broa has a texture and character all its own. It's not sweet, and it's not cakey. It's firm and crusty, an Old World cornbread delicious toasted in the morning with jam, or thickly sliced for dinner and served beneath a slice of Fried Haddock Molho de Vilhao.

MAKES 1 ROUND LOAF

1½ cups corn flour, or white cornmeal pulverized until fine

1½ teaspoons salt

1 cup boiling water

1 tablespoon olive oil, plus more for the pan

¼ cup lukewarm water

1 package active dry yeast

1 teaspoon sugar

2 cups flour

Combine 1 cup cornmeal, salt, and boiling water and blend until smooth. Stir in tablespoon of olive oil and let the mixture cook until lukewarm.

In a separate bowl, add the ¼ cup lukewarm water, stirring in yeast and sugar until they dissolve. Set aside in a warm place until the yeast has doubled in volume. When ready, stir this into the cornmeal mixture.

Gradually add the remaining cornmeal and 1 cup flour, stirring well. Form dough into a ball, place in a greased bowl, and cover with a towel. Set in a warm place and allow to double in bulk.

Coat a 9-inch pie pan with olive oil.

Turn the dough onto a floured surface and punch down, kneading for 5 minutes. Add as much of the remaining flour as you can, until dough is firm but not stiff.

Shape into a round, flattened loaf. Place in the pie pan, cover with a towel, and allow to double in bulk again.

Preheat oven to 350°F and cook bread for 40 minutes or until the top is golden.

Cool on a wire rack. This is a wonderful bread to make for breakfast or dinner that day, but is best toasted if you are having it later in the week; store remaining loaf in a paper—not plastic—bag. I don't recommend freezing this loaf, as the wonderful cornmeal crumb does not hold up.

Massa Sovada

(Portuguese Sweet Bread)

This is the gorgeous, golden hillock of a loaf of bread that crowns each Portuguese holiday table. A wealth of eggs, butter, and sugar, Massa Sovada smells like a special occasion when it's baking. It is often on the dessert table close to the Arroz Doce, or sweet rice pudding. The thought of a fluffy slab of Massa Sovada topped with this creamy rice pudding, while not a sophisticated combination, sends many South Coast adults straight back to their grandmother's kitchen in Fall River or Provincetown with happy hearts.

With a bowl of fresh pineapple, Massa Sovada and Arroz Doce make a wonderful special occasion breakfast on a slow Sunday morning.

MAKES 2 LOAVES

3¼-ounce package dry yeast

3 cups plus 2 tablespoons sugar

1 cup warm water

1½ cups (3 sticks) butter

2 cups milk

Zest from 1 lemon

8 large eggs, plus 1 egg for wash

1 teaspoon salt

10 cups flour (2½ pounds)

In a medium bowl, proof the yeast with 2 tablespoons sugar and 1 cup warm water. Set aside until foamy, about 10 minutes.

In a large saucepan, heat the butter, milk, and lemon zest over low heat, stirring to encourage butter to melt. Set aside to cool.

In the bowl of an electric mixer, beat 8 eggs, 3 cups sugar, and salt until creamy and light.

Add yeast mixture and cooled milk and butter, and mix well.

Slowly, about ½ cup at a time, add the flour, beating well until everything is mixed, about 15 minutes.

Place the dough in a large buttered bowl, and cover with a cotton towel. Let rise until double in bulk, 2–3 hours.

Liberally grease 2 9-inch cake or pie pans.

Punch down the dough, and knead briefly. Divide into 2 loaves, and shape each into a ball. Place in pans, and cover with a cotton towel. Let rise until double in bulk again, 2–3 hours.

Preheat oven to 325°F.

Using scissors, make 2 snips in the center of the dough, one snip across the other to make a cross. Beat the egg for the wash, and brush the loaves well with it. Bake for 45 minutes. The bread is done if a toothpick inserted comes out clean. Avoid over-baking because it can easily get too dry.

Cool on racks, and remove from pans after 20 minutes. Cool completely before serving.

Cavacas
(Glazed Portuguese Popovers)

Everyone needs to taste these revelatory popovers at least once. Cavacas in Portuguese and Azorean homes mean it's a birthday, a holiday, or someone special is coming for dinner. Not one of the elaborate Portuguese pastries produced in bakeries, Cavacas are what Portuguese and Azorean moms bake to make everyone happy. Made with lots of olive oil and good eggs, these rise up and become slightly hollow but eggy inside, just like a popover. While still warm, they are dipped in a lemony glaze. Cavacas are crisp, like an eggy pastry, and not too sweet. The tops become rough, almost tiled looking. Sometimes they collapse, and the glaze runs into the hollow center. All this is normal, and just makes Cavacas even more novel and delightful! You could be traditional and serve them as dessert with fresh fruit or ice cream, but they would also make a sweet start to a special day beside a well-made latte.

MAKES 24

For the popovers:

2 cups flour

Pinch salt

8 eggs

¾ cup olive oil

For the glaze:

1 cup confectionary sugar

Zest from 1 lemon

2 tablespoons milk

Preheat oven to 350°F. Use cooking spray to grease 2 muffin tins (24 muffins). Spray the tops, also, as the popovers rise over the edge.

Mix together the flour and salt.

Using a mixer, beat the eggs and olive oil together for a few minutes. Add the flour, and beat for 20 minutes. Fill the muffin tins halfway up, no higher.

Bake for 50 minutes on the middle rack of the oven, or until golden brown.

While they are baking, put together the glaze. Using the mixer, beat the confectionary sugar, zest, and milk together until thick and smooth. Use more milk if necessary.

When popovers are done and still warm, dip the tops of each one into the glaze to lightly cover. Set the popovers to dry on racks, and let the glaze drip down the sides. Enjoy while warm if you can!

Queijadas de Leite
(*Milk Tarts*)

Custards, pastry, custard in pastry, Portuguese desserts are a sweet study in milk and eggs. The theme of sweetness and church funnels down to an extremely practical if not fascinating history: The origins of these complex pastries lies in Portuguese convents and monasteries of the Middle Ages. The nuns needed lots of egg whites to keep their habits starched, and thus found themselves with a regular surplus of egg yolks; religious orders became Portugal's leading producers of extravagant commercial pastries. Bakeries in New Bedford—and there are many of them—their cases piles high with pastries called *barriga de freiras,* or "nun's belly," reflect that history.

But there is also a long tradition of family-baked desserts in the Portuguese and Azorean homes—equal celebrations of egg yolks, but with perhaps fewer layers of pastry. Queijadas de Leite are beloved little tarts, baked in muffin tins, which boast a sweet custardy flan-like filling with a crispy, caramelized exterior. They make a delicious, uncomplicated dessert; their lightness and texture are an interesting alternative to crème caramel.

This recipe makes a lot, but they tend to be eaten by the fives. Milk Tarts would be beautiful stacked on a platter for a brunch.

MAKES 3 DOZEN TARTS

3 cups milk

Zest from 1 lemon

1½ cups sugar

1 cup (2 sticks) butter (at room temperature)

5 large eggs

3 cups flour

2 teaspoons vanilla

Confectionary sugar for dusting

Preheat oven to 350°F. With cooking spray, generally grease 2 cupcake pans (24 cupcakes).

In a small saucepan, heat milk with lemon zest. When bubbles begin to form around the edges, remove from heat, and set aside.

In the bowl of a mixer, cream the sugar and butter together until light colored and creamy. Add the eggs, and mix well. Add the flour ½ cup at a time.

Remove the lemon zest from the milk, and add the milk to the mixing bowl with the vanilla. Beat well for 3–5 minutes, or until everything is well incorporated. The batter will be runny.

Fill the cupcake tins ¾ full, and bake for 40–45 minutes or until the tops are golden brown.

Remove from pans immediately, and let cool on racks. Serve with a dusting of confectionary sugar.

Pimenta Moida

This is a loose recipe for the sauce that is critical to so many Azorean dishes. Ironically this spicy cured pepper sauce that arrived in Massachusetts with the Azorean immigrant population is exactly the right thing to season so many traditional Massachusetts dishes. A drizzle on a traditional clam chowder adds just the right sweetness and heat to complement the cream and brine. The same goes for a golden crusty fried clam—it's delicious lightly dipped in Pimenta Moida. While you're welcome to make your own with this recipe, you should also know that it's fairly easy to find Pimenta Moida in the imported section of many grocery stores. Although many Azorean families in New Bedford still make a gigantic batch of this in the fall when peppers are ripe, most are happy with the grocery store edition. Whether homemade or store bought, a few jars of this essential sauce are always available in their pantries.

Red chilies (preferably Shepherd peppers, but a mix of hot and mild is fine)

Coarse sea salt

Olive oil

Wash the peppers and blot them dry. Cut them in half and deseed.

Layer all the peppers in a ceramic bowl or baking dish, sprinkling each layer liberally with sea salt, using about 1½ tablespoons to cover 6 pepper halves.

Cover the bowl with something like a pot lid or tray, and store in a cool, dark place for 2–3 weeks. They do not need to be refrigerated; the salt is preserving them.

The peppers are basically "cured" after 2–3 weeks. Some of them may turn dark or soft, but that is normal. You can set some halves aside to use as garnish for dishes throughout the year, but to make the sauce, put the peppers into a food processor, or pass them through a grinder. Let the sauce "rest" for a day or so. Then pour it into sterilized jars if you think you are not going to use it soon. Pour a teaspoon of olive oil over the top of the sauce in the jar to preserve even better. Seal the jars. This will keep indefinitely.

New Bedford Scallops with Macomber Turnip Puree

This is a wonderful, uber-minimal something to do with turnips, and a nice way to show off the very Massachusetts Macomber or Eastham turnips if you can find them. It makes a light, velvety dip that is delicious with a glass of cold rosé.

But then, if you sauté some New Bedford sea scallops to a caramel brown, and lay them on top of the turnip puree with a squeeze of lemon, a wisp of cilantro, and a little Pimenta Moida, you have a quintessential South Coast appetizer.

SERVES 4 AS AN APPETIZER

For the turnip puree:

About 1 pound of turnips (Macomber or Eastham are ideal, but don't make this with old woody turnips)

1 tablespoon good quality olive oil

1 garlic clove, finely minced

Sea salt and freshly ground black pepper to taste

For the New Bedford scallops:

12 large sea scallops, about 1 pound, rinsed and tough tendon removed

Salt and freshly ground black pepper

2 tablespoons vegetable oil

2 tablespoons melted unsalted butter

Juice of 1 lemon

Minced cilantro for garnish

Hot sauce (optional)

To make the turnip puree:

Peel turnips, and chop into rough pieces, about 1 inch.

Set turnips on a steaming rack over boiling water, and steam until very tender, 15–20 minutes. Let cool slightly.

Meanwhile, warm olive oil in a small pan. Add garlic, and heat very gently until just softened, about 1 minute. Do not brown.

With a food processor or an emulsion blender, puree turnips. Add garlic, olive oil, salt, and pepper, and beat so the turnips are very light.

To make the New Bedford scallops:

Rinse scallops well and then blot with paper towels to make sure they are very dry. Let them sit on paper towels for a few minutes, making sure to absorb as much water as possible.

When ready, season scallops with salt and pepper. In a large cast-iron skillet, heat oil to medium-high, not quite smoking. Add scallops in a single layer and cook, without moving, until nicely browned, 2–3 minutes.

Reduce heat to medium. Add butter and swirl it around. Using tongs, gently turn the scallops. If they stick to the pan, just let them cook a little longer. They are cooked perfectly when they turn easily.

Using a large spoon, baste the scallops with melted butter as you tilt the skillet and continue

to cook the scallops until opaque, 30–90 seconds. Smaller scallops will cook more quickly than larger ones.

Have four small plates ready. Spoon some of the turnip puree onto each plate, spooning a hollow into the center for the scallops. Transfer 3 scallops to the center of the each puree. Pour the butter and juices from the pan over each serving. Squeeze lemon over each, garnish with cilantro, and add just a touch of hot sauce to each scallop if desired.

Back Eddy Stuffies

The Back Eddy Restaurant is lodged on a Westport dock, if not permanently embedded in the Westport terroir. For a bunch of years it's been translating the freshest South Coast seafood and the wealth of local produce into its own signature cuisine. "Stuffies," stuffed baked quahogs, are all South Coast when made with sweet local corn and New Bedford chourico. Any stuffed quahog is a labor of love, but all the love comes back to you with this sweet and spicy version. Do your best to use Portuguese bread for the crumbs, and have a small jar of Pimenta Moida ready to dab on top.

MAKES 12

12 large quahogs, scrubbed

1 tablespoon olive oil

½ pound ground chourico (casings removed, pulse chourico in food processor to grind)

1 large onion, finely chopped

1 tablespoon chopped garlic

1 cup corn kernels (cut from 2–3 ears or thawed frozen corn)

½ cup coarsely ground toasted Italian or Portuguese bread, plus additional if necessary

¼ cup chopped fresh oregano

1 teaspoon dried sage

6 tablespoons unsalted butter

Salt and pepper to taste

12 lemon wedges for garnish

In a large pot, bring 1 inch of water to a boil. Add clams, and return to a boil. Reduce heat to medium, and cook, covered, until the shells open, 5–10 minutes. Remove clams with a slotted spoon and cool, reserving the cooking broth. Working over a bowl to catch the juices, scrape clam meat out of the shells. Set juice aside. Reserve 12 shells, and clean them well. Pulse the clam meat in a food processor until finely chopped.

In a large skillet, heat the oil. Add chourico and onion, and cook over medium heat, stirring frequently, until meat is lightly browned, about 5 minutes.

Add chopped clams, garlic, and corn, and cook for 5 minutes. Pour reserved clam juices through a strainer, and add them to the pot with 1 cup cooking broth. Bring to a boil, and cook until liquid is reduced by about half.

Remove from heat, and stir in bread crumbs, oregano, and sage. If mixture is dry, add a couple of tablespoons more of reserved cooking broth. If too wet, add more bread crumbs. Season to taste with salt and pepper.

Loosely pack stuffing into cleaned shells. (This can be done a day ahead and refrigerated.)

When ready to bake, preheat oven to 400°F.

Arrange stuffed quahogs on a baking sheet. Place ½ tablespoon pat of butter on each quahog. Bake uncovered until tops are crusty and lightly browned, about 7 minutes. Garnish with lemon and serve.

Warm Hannahbells Springtime Salad

Westport's Shy Brothers Farms makes unique thimble-size cheeses called Hannahbells, named for the brothers' mother. Hannahbells are made in four flavors: shallot, lavender bud, classic French, and rosemary. The origins of Hannahbells are French; to save their family dairy, the Santos brothers turned to cheesemaking. Looking for a cheese produced in conditions that might match Westport's, they traveled to Burgundy, France, where they found *boutons de coulottes*, or trouser buttons. A novel shape and an easy bite, Hannahbells may seem like a playful addition to a cheeseboard, but the flavors are serious. Mold-cured, complex cheeses, Hannahbells soften with heat, but retain most of their darling shape and all of their nutty flavor. They make this 1980s version of salad with rounds of warm artisanal cheese new again—and easy!

SERVES 4

1 head Bibb lettuce

1 cup arugula microgreens or 1 small bunch (about 1 cup) baby arugula

1 yellow beet, peeled and cut into very thin matchsticks, or shredded in a food processor

½ small bulb fennel, very thinly sliced

4 spears raw asparagus chopped thinly on the diagonal

4 spring onions or 6 scallions chopped into thin rounds

3 tablespoons fruity olive oil, plus more to drizzle when served

1 tablespoons fresh lemon juice, plus more to drizzle when served

Sea salt and freshly ground black pepper

16-20 Shallot Hannahbells

8 long slices (cut on the diagonal) French or Italian bread, rubbed with olive oil, sea salt, and black pepper, and toasted

Preheat oven to 375°F.

Wash and dry Bibb lettuce and arugula well.

In a large bowl, toss together Bibb lettuce, arugula, beets, fennel, and asparagus. In a skillet heat the olive oil to medium, and add onions. Sauté until softened, and just barely browned. Pour warm oil and onions over greens, and toss well. Pour lemon juice over salad, and toss well. Season with salt and pepper.

Meanwhile, place thimble cheeses on a parchment-lined baking sheet, and bake for 3–5 minutes until warm and softened. Alternatively, place in microwave for 30 seconds.

Divide the salad among four plates.

Arrange the warm Hannahbells among the salads, and fluff the salads a bit with your hands, letting the Hannahbells tuck into the nooks of the greens. Add a very light drizzle of olive oil over all, a last squeeze of lemon juice, and sprinkle of sea salt. Add toasts and serve immediately.

SHY BROTHERS FARM

A long gray dairy barn, owned by the Santos family, sits atop Sherman Hill in Westport, Massachusetts. Holsteins and Ayrshires roam in pastures all around, chewing their cud and looking in the distance to the West Branch of the Westport River. Too far to see but close enough to send its breezes and salt-tinged fog, the East Branch of the Westport River juts northward into a pastured and stonewall-laced landscape east of the Santos dairy barn, also known as Shy Brothers Farm. From this windy crest of hill, where the Santos family has been milking their cows for three generations, Main Road runs south quickly. In less than three miles the elevation drops from two thousand feet above sea level to two hundred feet at Westport Point, where those two river branches meet. Just across Westport Harbor is Horseneck Beach State Reservation.

Westport, Massachusetts, is sixty-four square miles in total, and one-fifth of that is water. A town that seems to be nothing but pastureland threaded with saltwater estuaries, Westport was once the dairy farming center of Massachusetts, a bucolic combination of sea breezes and sweet grasses. Cows loved Westport, and proved it with a plentiful flow of high-quality milk. As recently as 2000, there were still fourteen dairy farms trucking milk out of Westport; now there are two.

This is the story of how the Santos family reinvented themselves to become Shy Brothers Farm, a Westport milk-producer turned maker of award-winning cheeses, now with a Whole Foods contract. And, yet, they are still the Santos family—two sets of twin brothers, one set fifty-two years old, the other just fifty—who mostly wants to do what they've been doing since the twins were kids. Norman milks the cows. Arthur feeds them. Kevin runs the machinery, and now Karl, who is famous for fact-keeping, makes the cheese. Barbara Hanley, a friend who was brought in to consult with the brothers on how not to be one more failed Westport dairy farm, helped them make the transition from dairy to cheese. She and Karl traveled to Burgundy, France, in 2006 looking for a cheese style that would suit the Santos dairy.

Hannahbells, named for the boys' mother, is a small thimble-shaped or bell-shaped soft cheese made with fresh Shy Brothers cows' milk and lactic bacteria. In Burgundy they are called buttones de culottes or "trouser buttons." Hannahbells are soft, mellow, and come in shallot, lavender, rosemary, and classic French flavors. Small enough to put four of them, quickly warmed in the oven, on top of a leafy salad for one person's lunch, Hannahbells win the "Dainty doesn't Mean Dull" award for cheeses. These little thimbles may be adorable, but the flavor they deliver is old-world aged, the perfect bite with an aperitif.

Cloumage is a creamy cheese that comes in a tub. It has the texture of baked ricotta, but with the yeast of champagne and acidic tang that makes it a superpower in the kitchen. Cloumage is eaten straight, with almost anything from fresh pears to roasted peppers or simply strewn with fresh chives. Where there is sour cream, cream cheese, ricotta, or crème fraîche, substitute Cloumage, and that dish will always be better.

As the cheese-making flourished, and Barbara Hanley began giving presentations about the farm, people at an event would ask, "Where are these brothers? Can we meet them?" Hanley would confess, "Well, they are shy." And so the dairy has been famously—and honestly—renamed, "Shy Brothers Farm."

Hanley gave me a tour of the cheese-making operation and then took me to see the family farm and the dairy barn, and to meet the cows. She pointed to a small house where Arthur and Norman live next door. I asked how they felt about the exciting new contract with Whole Foods, and about all the excitement buzzing among chefs using the Shy Brothers cheeses. She paused for a second, and then said, "I don't think they even know. All those boys want to do is take care of the cows, the way they have all their lives."

Katie's Cloumage Coffee Cake

Shy Brothers' Cloumage is a soft cultured cheese delicious spooned as is onto roasted pears or baked apples bubbling with brown sugar. Cloumage can bind lobster; it can stuff a pepper, rise in a souffle, even bake into a luxurious coffee cake. Drizzle a dish of Cloumage with local honey, strew with chopped rosemary and serve with slices of toasted baguette. Some Westport chefs say they have yet to find something in the kitchen that Cloumage doesn't improve.

Katie Martin is Karl Santos's cheese-making assistant. A single mother of five, Martin is Shy Brothers Cheese's fiercest defender. (Just try to mention another cheese-maker in the hallowed Cloumage- and Hannahbell-making room!) Martin loves proving the superpowers of Cloumage; the cheese could become famous if only for this outrageously moist and tangy Cloumage Coffee Cake.

SERVES 10

For the filling:

¾ cup sugar

2 teaspoons cinnamon

¾ cup walnuts

For the batter:

16 ounces Cloumage

1 cup sugar

1 cup (2 sticks) butter, softened

2 teaspoons vanilla

2 eggs

1 teaspoon baking soda

1 teaspoon baking powder

½ teaspoon salt

3 cups flour

Preheat oven to 350°F.

Mix sugar and cinnamon together well, then stir in walnuts to distribute evenly without breaking them down. Set aside.

Combine Cloumage, sugar, and butter until smooth. Then add vanilla and eggs and mix.

In a separate bowl, combine baking soda, baking powder, salt, and flour.

Gradually add the flour mixture to the Cloumage mixture to make the cake batter.

Place ⅓ of cake batter in a well-oiled bundt pan and layer with ⅓ of nut mixture. Then repeat until you have three layers. Bake for an hour until done.

Cool on wire racks for 30 minutes before removing from pan. This is delicious both as a breakfast coffee cake or as a dessert with fruit.

CHAPTER TWO

Martha's Vineyard

Legend has it that the mythic Wampanoag giant, Moshup, sleeping along the southern side of Cape Cod, grew irritated with sand in his moccasins, and tossed them at the ocean. One sand-filled moccasin landed south-southwest of Hyannis and is now the island of Martha's Vineyard. The other landed farther to the southeast and became the sandier, less fertile island of Nantucket.

The Atlantic Ocean rolling into the orange clay Aquinnah Cliffs is one of the more spectacular visions in the world, let alone on Martha's Vineyard. It's a view that cannot help but evoke divinity. For the Wampanoag Tribe, the Aquinnah Cliffs are understandably sacred. This area, still rich in fish, berries, and deer, is what the Aquinnah Tribe calls home, and where they pay tribute to their ancestors. Cranberry Day, the second Tuesday in October, is the most important of their many thanksgiving celebrations throughout the year. Wampanoag children are released from school, and only tribe members are allowed to gather at the wild cranberry bogs in Lobsterville to harvest the berries.

Later, friends are invited to the bogs for a large potluck meal, where cranberries are the star. There is drumming and storytelling, and thanks given to the creator for this fruit that has helped the tribe survive for thousands of years.

Along the road to Aquinnah is the pinprick of a fishing village called Menemsha. Small but mighty is the sense of this place. Larsen's and Poole's fish markets line up on the weathered gray dock, where fishing boats tie up to unload or fill their gas tanks. Wander barefoot if you like into the gas station from your beach towel on the white sandy beach, covered with slipper shells, and buy yourself an ice cream. Or get yourself a dozen littlenecks, and maybe a couple of lobster cakes, at Larsen's. Sit on the bleached picnic tables with a glass of white wine and watch the conch catch unload into Poole's. Still hungry? Knot that towel at your hips and stroll twenty yards back to The Menemsha Bite, a diminutive wooden shack with nothing but a take-out window and a fry machine. Order yourself a paper box of fat, steely, screaming-hot fried oysters. With a little Menemsha breeze in your hair, the sweet smell of beach peas in the dune beside you seasoning your oysters, and only the putt-putt of a lobster boat in your ears, experience this different kind of five-star restaurant.

Farm stands are an art form on Martha's Vineyard. One could drive the island all day picking up morning glory muffins, homemade feta cheese, lamb grazed on Chilmark hillsides, meaty Bibb lettuces the size of hubcaps, cranberry apple pies, and bouncing bouquets of field-grown flowers, even locally harvested sea salt. And that's just the beginning. The farming culture is something of a dream here. Not only are farmers celebrities, but some of the farms—such as Allen Sheep Farm and Beetlebung Farm—have been here for more than six generations. Others, like Morning Glory Farm, are working on generation number three. It says something about a place when farmers' children want to stay—or at least return—home to be farmers.

Where there are inspired farms there are beautiful meals. Cooking on Martha's Vineyard begins with its treasured ingredients. A bounty of crops makes every season special, but high summer here looks like the promised land.

"Everything you need to create a beautiful meal is grown locally," says Joan Malkin of Chilmark. That includes coffee from Chilmark Coffees, dairy from Mermaid Farm or The Gray Barns, and local honey that can be found almost everywhere. Martha's Vineyard is truly the land of milk and honey, and bluefish and kale.

Kale is so abundant an impish cult has emerged around its harvest. The leafy green that begins, bridges, and ends each growing season, elicits groans and knowing smiles. Kale is the one green vegetable of which there is always plenty. Kale may be an inside joke on Martha's Vineyard, but good recipes for it keep everyone interested. And now a Martha's Vineyard Kale Festival, probably created with a bit of tongue in cheek, celebrates this favorite cruciferous vegetable in early December: Taste all kinds of new kale recipes or bring your own!

Morning Glory Farm is perhaps the most well-known farm on the island. The glory that is Morning Glory Farm all started in 1975 when Jim and Debbie Athearn began farming on a sandy, infertile eighteen acres that Debbie Athearn's father purchased for seven dollars at auction years before—he purchased the entire thing for seven dollars. Today, Morning Glory Farm employs more people than almost any other private enterprise on the island. It provides local produce, eggs, chickens, beef, and pork, and even a small supply of beech plums to everyone from islanders who have been here their whole lives to movie stars whose Vineyard vacations make newspaper headlines.

The Oak Bluffs Camp Meeting Association, a halo of tiny gingerbread houses circling the large Association Hall in Oak Bluffs, began in 1835 as a weeklong Methodist retreat of sermons and religious revival. Sandy lanes connect the quaint gingerbread houses that grew up from that original arrangement of tents; the Tabernacle Association Hall is the camp's center. Although the Methodist roots have frayed, generations from those original families still return to their

camp cottages each year, where polite rules keep an old-fashioned culture of long, quiet summer days. According to the community cookbook, *A Culinary Tour of the Gingerbread Cottages*, it's a "Victorian city of porches and lace, houseplants and little gardens, chats with the neighbors and passersby, a place to catch up on one's reading and enjoy a glass of iced tea." The recipes they offer are meant for that kind of living, less trendy, often the same recipes they've been serving on their porches for generations, often recipes brought from their lives back across Nantucket Sound, like Camp Meeting Green Bean Casserole. This homemade edition, with honest green beans, sour cream, and fresh bread crumbs, probably launched the ubiquitous version that begins with opening a soup can. Illumination Night in August, when the entire campground is lit with paper lanterns, is a spectacular vision, an event for which many Oak Bluffs residents cook something special to serve from their porches. I recommend Ellie's Fantastic Seafood Chowder, which is honestly named, to be served at your own "porch" event.

Martha's Vineyard Index

Rhubarb Cocktail Malkin

It is hard to find glamour in rhubarb. New Englanders, desperate for spring, tramp across mud-covered fields with sharp knives in pockets, ready to cut stalks from the domes of pan-size leaves at the edge of the yard. They collect the ruby stalks, so happy to have a harvest that isn't a root, that no one cares at first how much sugar it takes to bribe the chopped pieces into being dessert. In the beginning, we're so happy for spring tastes that we don't even make pie; we stop at rhubarb compote, yes with lots of brown sugar, topped with ice cream, cream, or even just yogurt.

But later, as spring days honestly warm and seep into summer, the rhubarb stalks mean more than winter's release. They're appreciated again for the uniqueness and strength of their tang. Come June, we get a little free and easy with our rhubarb; it becomes strawberry rhubarb pie, rhubarb upside down cake, and, in this case, a wonderful spring-on-Martha's Vineyard cocktail: rhubarb getting glamourous.

MAKES APPROXIMATELY 1 CUP

For the rhubarb syrup:

8–10 rhubarb stalks, washed, trimmed, and cut into 1-inch chunks

½–¾ cup sugar

1 teaspoon, or to taste, grated fresh ginger

½ cup water

Place rhubarb in saucepan, add sugar (use more rather than less, as you can always add more if needed) and ginger.

Add water. Cook on medium low for approximately 20 minutes.

When mixture is completely soft and rhubarb pieces have lost all of their shape, remove from burner. Once cool, push mixture through a fine sieve with the back of a wooden spoon or a rubber scraper/spatula to extract as much of the liquid as possible. It should be very syrupy, roughly the consistency of maple syrup. It may be frothy, but that is fine. Taste for sweetness. If you add more sugar, return syrup to low heat long enough to dissolve.

Store in the refrigerator; it should keep a few weeks.

For 1 Cocktail Malkin:

2 ounces rhubarb syrup (page 43)

1–2 tablespoons fresh lime juice

1½ ounces rum

Several ice cubes

Fresh mint or lime slices for garnish

Pour syrup, lime juice, rum, and ice cubes into a shaker and shake well. Pour into desired glass and garnish with fresh mint and/or a lime slice.

Rhubarb and Honey

Rhubarb cooked with honey, particularly a local variety of honey—blueberry, cranberry, or from a hive standing in your neighbor's yard—makes this ultra-simple springtime treat taste like magic from a molecular gastronomist's laboratory. When you think about it, bees are sort of like molecular gastronomists, collecting molecules of this and that from an almost infinitely varied ecology, hauling it back to the lab and working alchemy.

Try not to use the grocery store variety of honey here; the beauty of this simple conserve is what rhubarb does when combined with the hundreds of flavors present in a honey created from your blossoming world.

MAKES 2 CUPS

⅓ cup water

1 cup local honey

1 pound rhubarb, washed, trimmed, and cut into 1-inch chunks

Pinch salt

1 teaspoon vanilla

In a medium saucepan, heat water and honey. Simmer for 5 minutes. Add rhubarb and salt, and cook gently until the rhubarb is tender, about 15 minutes.

When cool, flavor with vanilla.

Serve over fresh, whole-milk yogurt for breakfast, or stir whipped cream or Shy Brother's Cloumage into it; a slice of pound cake wouldn't hurt, either.

Rhubarb Fool

Is it called a "fool" because even a fool can make it? Maybe. But spring rhubarb stewed in honey, folded into custard, and then again into freshly whipped cream, is not foolish. This is a serious dessert. Rhubarb Fool leans on the way cream and custard soothe and befriend the puckery nature of the fruit. Serve it in wine goblets to best show off the pretty pink swirls.

SERVES 6

½ cup honey

3 tablespoons water

1 pound rhubarb, washed, trimmed, and cut into 1-inch chunks

¾ cup milk

2 tablespoons sugar, divided

3 egg yolks

1 teaspoon vanilla

¾ cup heavy cream, whipped

In a large saucepan, combine honey and water. Simmer for 2 minutes to dissolve, then add rhubarb. Cook until fruit is tender, about 15 minutes. Set aside to cool.

In a medium saucepan, combine milk and 1 tablespoon sugar. Heat milk to scald it, but do not let it boil. Set aside.

Whisk together egg yolks and remaining tablespoon sugar. Pour ¼ cup of the warm milk into the eggs and whisk well. Then whisk all back into the milk.

Return pot to the stove, and heat. Stirring constantly, bring milk to a boil then remove from heat. Whisk in vanilla. Cool and set aside.

When ready to serve, whip cream to stiff peaks.

Fold custard into rhubarb. Add whipped cream, and try to swirl it gently through the custard and fruit, not necessarily folding them completely together, but leaving evident lines of fruit and whipped cream. Carefully spoon into wine goblets, and chill until serving.

Blueberry and Butternut Squash Salad with Dried Blueberry Vinaigrette

This dinner salad is a delicious reflection of the high-key colors of a late summer day in Aquinnah. Roasted butternut squash, caramelized red onions, fresh blueberries, and toasted sunflower seeds lay on a bed of local greens beneath the sweet dried blueberry and balsamic vinegar dressing.

With a soup, particularly the Wampanoag Inspired Oyster Chowder, this salad makes a glorious meal.

SERVES 4 FOR DINNER

For the dressing:

1 cup dried wild blueberries

1 cup balsamic vinegar

1 cup oil

½ teaspoon salt

For the salad:

1 butternut squash, or 3 cups peeled and cubed

1 large red onion, cut into wedges

6 tablespoons olive oil, divided

1 teaspoon salt, preferably sea salt

1 teaspoon freshly ground pepper

1 large head Bibb lettuce, washed and torn into pieces

Salt and pepper to taste

Juice from half a lemon, or 1 tablespoon

2 cups fresh blueberries, washed and picked over

1 cup toasted sunflower seeds

To make the dressing:

Place the dried blueberries and vinegar in a pan and bring to a boil. Simmer for 5–10 minutes, or until the mixture is reduced by half.

Cool briefly, and then put it into a blender or food processor with oil and salt. Blend until smooth. This can be done a couple of days ahead and stored in the refrigerator, but it will thicken considerably. To soften, warm briefly in a small saucepan.

To make the salad:

Preheat oven to 400°F. In a large bowl, toss squash and onion wedges with 3 tablespoons olive oil, salt, and pepper. Spread on baking sheet or in roasting pan, and bake until edges are brown and crispy, about 45 minutes. These can be done ahead, and served on the salad at room temperature.

In a large bowl, toss greens with remaining 3 tablespoons olive oil, salt, and pepper. Drizzle lemon juice over all, and toss again. Lay greens on individual plates, or on a large serving platter.

Mound the squash and onions over the greens. Toss the blueberries on top, and sprinkle half the toasted sunflower seeds over that. Pour dressing in desired amount over the salad. Sprinkle remaining sunflower seeds on top.

Wampanoag Inspired Oyster Chowder

Fish essence plumped with spinach and oysters and enriched with cornmeal, this is a beautifully nuanced but rustic fish soup, heavily indebted to the Wampanoag cuisine.

The recipe begins with an ingredient that anyone who cooks should embrace: fish bodies. Broths made from slow cooking bones are not just inexpensive, but are packed with nutrition. Minerals, important amino acids, and gelatin harbor in those bones. Simmering them for hours creates a powerful broth many cultures consider medicinal. Broths made from fish bones are said to fight degenerative joint disease and connective tissue diseases, make hair shiny and skin smooth, but they are also the foundations for some of the world's best ways with things that swim: bouillabaisse, cioppino, even paella and gumbo. This simple but elegant broth—purely American—takes its place on the list of the world's great fish soups.

The most taxing part of this recipe is the fish broth, only because most people aren't comfortable cooking something with eyes. However, the vision of that alabaster fish head lounging in a pot of water with bay leaves, onions, and lemon slices makes you feel as if you've earned the bars of a real cook. One or two fish bodies with seasonings simmer for two hours, and then are strained to make approximately four quarts of broth, sometimes more.

For the flavor and nutrition that fish bodies offer, they are ridiculously inexpensive. A busy fish market is discarding many fish frames a day. If you have access to a fish market like this, or even a grocery store like Whole Foods, ask what's going on with their discarded fish frames. Most fish markets are more than happy to offer them to a customer. It's best to call a day in advance, and forewarn the fishmonger to save one for you from the next day's filleting.

Once the broth is made, this beautiful soup can be assembled in twenty minutes. You will certainly have leftover broth, so be sure to freeze it. With broth in your freezer, this delicious soup—and others in this book— are almost instant.

SERVES 6-8

For the fish bone broth:

5–6 pounds, or 1–2 medium-size fish frames, head to tail, or 1–2 medium fish

1 onion, quartered

1 small lemon, sliced

1 tablespoon peppercorns

1 tablespoon salt

2 or 3 bay leaves

2 quarts water (enough to cover)

For the soup:

6 cups fish bone broth

12 oysters in their shells (or 1 cup jarred fresh oysters) and their liquid

1 cup white wine

1 medium onion, diced

1½ cups diced carrots, about 4–5 whole

6–8 ounces fresh baby spinach leaves (about 4 handfuls)

½ teaspoon red pepper flakes

½ cup cornmeal

Salt to taste

To make the broth:

Place fish frames in large soup pot with onion, lemon, peppercorns, salt, and bay leaves. Cover with water and simmer for 2 hours.

Meanwhile, shuck oysters if necessary, and reserve meat and liquid.

When broth is finished, remove large bones and pieces, and strain broth through a cheesecloth. If you don't have cheesecloth, a kitchen strainer or even a colander works fine, too. Your broth just won't be exactly clear.

To make the soup:

Return 6 cups broth to a clean soup pot, and bring to a simmer. Strain liquid from oysters into broth, reserving oysters for later. Add wine, onion, and carrots. Simmer for 10 minutes, or until carrots are tender. Add spinach and red pepper flakes and simmer for 5 minutes.

With the soup simmering slowly, gradually pour in the cornmeal, stirring gently. Cook for 10 minutes or until soup thickens. Add oysters, and cook for 2 minutes more, or until oysters plump. Serve immediately.

Gladys Widdis's Cranberry Crumble

Tribal elder Gladys Widdis prepares this dish for Cranberry Day, the annual October Wampanaog Festival on Martha's Vineyard that honors their ancestors and the harvest, particularly the cranberry, which sustained the tribe for over twelve thousand years, according to tribal history.

SERVES 6–8

For the filling:

½ cup sugar

¼ cup flour

¼ teaspoon cinnamon

¼ teaspoon powdered ginger

4 cups cranberries, fresh or frozen then thawed

For the topping:

¾ cup brown sugar

½ cup flour

¼ teaspoon cinnamon

¼ teaspoon ginger

¼ cup oatmeal flakes

6 tablespoons butter, cut in pieces

¾ cup chopped pecans

To make the filling:

Preheat oven to 350°F. Butter an 8 x 11-inch glass or ceramic baking dish.

In a large bowl, mix together sugar, flour, spices, and cranberries. Pour into baking dish.

To make the topping:

In the bowl of a food processor blend together the dry ingredients. Add butter, and pulse lightly to cut it into the flour. (Alternately, put all the dry ingredients into a bowl, and cut the butter in with a pasty cutter or 2 forks.)

When mixture is the size of small peas, add pecans. Process or mix a little more, until just blended.

Top the cranberries with the streusel, and bake for 35 minutes or until the crumble is brown on top and bubbling with juice.

Serve warm with vanilla ice cream or whipped cream.

Cherries and Cherries

Sungolds, Camp Joy, Juliet, Sweet 100s—cherry tomatoes are the dripping jewels of July and August on Martha's Vineyard. Cherrystone clams are the gold dug there—in Katama Bay, Tashmoo, Quitsa Pond, and more. Pair these cherries—tomatoes and quahogs—in a quick sauté with a little Portuguese chourico for a bright taste of Martha's Vineyard. Serve it on a toasted Bolos Levedos—either the grocery store variety or homemade—for true Massachusetts coastline authenticity, but a tortilla browned to bubbly and crisp in a skillet is also a great vessel for this sweet and spicy, farm-meets-mudflat dish.

SERVES 4

- 4–6 pounds cherrystone or littleneck clams (There are 5–8 cherrystones per pound; account for 5 per person)
- 1 cup white wine or water
- 1 teaspoon red pepper flakes
- 3 tablespoons olive oil
- 4-inch length of chourico, casing removed and thinly sliced
- 1 pound cherry tomatoes, all different colors if possible, sliced in half
- 1 tablespoon hot sauce, or to taste

Scrub clams under running water, then soak for at least 30 minutes in a bowl of cold, lightly salted water.

In a large skillet, combine wine and pepper flakes, and bring to a simmer. Add clams, cover, and steam over low heat for 5–10 minutes. Remove from heat just as clams open. Overcooking clams will result in them becoming tough and rubbery. Remove meats from shells as they cool, and set aside.

Clean skillet, add olive oil, and heat to medium high. Add chourico, and toss in the pan for 3–5 minutes or until edges become lightly browned. Lower heat to medium low, and add tomatoes. Cook to soften the tomatoes, about 10 minutes. Add clam meats and hot sauce. Heat gently for 3–5 minutes.

Spoon immediately over toasted Bolos Levedos or wheat tortillas.

Martha's Vineyard Gravlax Malkin
with Homemade Horseradish Sauce

Fluke are to Martha's Vineyard what oysters are to Wellfleet, what catfish are to Mississippi, and what salmon are to Norway. This recipe, from Chilmark residents Joan and Jim Malkin, captures this native child in all its freshness. Who says a fresh dill and spice cure is only for salmon? It works beautifully on the Massachusetts coast with this clean, white member of the flounder family. The horseradish crème fraîche is a plush answer to the pine forest flavors of allspice and fresh dill. Serve this on thin rye crackers with an icy gin martini.

SERVES 6–8 AS AN APPETIZER

For the fluke:

2 tablespoons sugar

3 tablespoons kosher salt

2 teaspoons white or black peppercorns

1 teaspoon whole allspice berries

1 large bunch dill

1 pound fluke fillets

For the horseradish sauce:

3 tablespoons freshly grated horseradish

⅓ cup sour cream or crème fraîche

Lemon juice, salt, and pepper to taste

To make the fluke:

Mix sugar, salt, peppercorns, and allspice in a bowl.

On a large piece of plastic wrap, spread half the sugar/salt mixture on an area the size of the laid-out fluke fillets. On top of that, lay half the dill, stalks and all. Then lay fluke fillets. Cover this with remainder of salt/sugar mixture and remainder of the dill.

Wrap plastic around fluke as tightly as possible without damaging the fish. Wrap entire package in a second piece of plastic. Place on a plate with a lip and weigh down with a brick (or similar weight). Refrigerate. The fluke will begin to exude water, which may seep from the plastic, so it's good to have a platter with sides. Check the fish once a day, and pour off too much excess water. Turn the fluke over once or twice during the next day. After 2–3 days, remove fish from plastic wrap. The longer the fish is cured, the dryer and more cured it will taste. Carefully scrape off the dill and sugar/salt mixture, being careful to not damage fish, and making sure to remove all the allspice berries. Pat fish with paper towels to remove excess salt. Slice fluke in 1-inch wide bands, and lay out attractively on a platter. (If not eating immediately, rewrap in plastic and refrigerate.) Drizzle horseradish sauce over the fish. Garnish sides of the platter with lemon wedges and fresh dill.

If you do not have access to fresh horseradish the bottled version can be substituted, but this sauce is too delicious with the fluke to omit it for any reason.

To make the horseradish sauce:

Stir all ingredients together and refrigerate. This yields about ½ cup, and can be made up to 4 hours in advance.

Martha's Vineyard Smoked Bluefish Pâté

August, September, and early October are the months of bluefish season off the coast of Massachusetts. When caught that day and taken straight to a hot grill, slathered in mayonnaise and mustard, bluefish is one of the finest summer meals you can have. The flesh is mild and white, with no sign of oil or fishiness. The mustard and mayonnaise are the perfect balance of acid and sweet for that firm, grilled meat.

The "oily and fishy" complaint most people have with bluefish happens to fillets that sit in a fish market for one or two days. The key to enjoying fresh bluefish is the word "fresh," so catch it yourself or befriend a fisherman.

That said, almost no one ever complains about smoked bluefish, and its best finale, smoked bluefish pâté. This is a classic shoreline summer appetizer, only improved with a chilled glass of rosé and sand between your toes.

MAKES 2 CUPS

8 ounces skinned, smoked bluefish, cut into chunks

2 teaspoons chopped onion

2½ teaspoons anchovy paste

5 ounces cream cheese, at room temperature

8 ounces unsalted butter, at room temperature

Juice of ½ a lemon

2½ teaspoons cognac

½ teaspoon Worcestershire sauce

In a food processor fitted with a steel blade, process all ingredients. Refrigerate, and serve chilled with crackers.

Fluke (or Flounder) Beautiful

With cherry tomatoes dripping from a July vine and the fluke catch heavy, this is the ideal summer dinner on Martha's Vineyard. Shimmering with tomatoes, olives, and capers, this platter of fluke is a dish a painter can love. Fluke or flounder fillets are first breaded and quickly browned in olive oil, strewn with vegetables, and baked in a hot oven. The lively lemon and garlic sauce that will unify all warms on the stove. Pour this sauce over the hot fish, wave some fresh parsley upon the gleaming platter, and you can almost feel the warmth of the sun on Lucy Vincent Beach. Truthfully, even grocery store cherry tomatoes in February will serve, so remember this dish in winter for its doldrums-defeating powers.

SERVES 4–6

½ cup flour

1 tablespoon Old Bay Seasoning

1 tablespoon salt

½ teaspoon pepper

¼ cup olive oil

4 large fluke fillets (or 6–8 small, about 2½ pounds)

2 cups cherry tomatoes, halved

½ cup capers, drained

24 pitted kalamata olives

¼ cup lemon juice

3 tablespoons butter

3 tablespoons chopped garlic

3 tablespoons grated lemon zest

⅓ cup dry white wine

Salt and pepper to taste

2 teaspoons chopped fresh parsley

In a shallow glass baking dish or plate, mix together flour, Old Bay, salt, and pepper.

Heat olive oil in a large skillet.

Rinse fillets, and pat dry. Dredge in flour mixture, and lay in hot oil. Fry quickly, about a minute per side.

Transfer fish immediately to glass or ceramic baking dish, and set aside contents of skillet.

Preheat oven to 400°F. Cover fish evenly with tomato halves, capers, and olives. Sprinkle all with lemon juice. Bake for 10 minutes.

Meanwhile, heat remains of skillet. Add butter, garlic, lemon zest, wine, salt, and pepper. Heat over medium heat, stirring constantly to slightly reduce the sauce, but don't worry too much about that. Just keep it hot while the fish is finishing in the oven.

When fish is ready, remove from oven and pour sauce over all. Sprinkle with chopped parsley.

Broiled Bluefish with Anchovy Vinaigrette

In mid-September, when the bluefish are blitzing off every beach from Lobsterville to Wasque Point, a Martha's Vineyard fisherman needs a good bluefish recipe.

   Bluefish has an affinity for strong flavors. It favors a recipe with ingredients that challenge it, one that stands up to its firm flesh. It loves an Asian-inspired soy treatment, for example. Here, bluefish fillets broil beneath a sauce of anchovy, lemon zest, mustard, and white wine vinegar. More sauce is added when it is served, making a piquant and rich foil for the fish.

SERVES 4

2 pounds bluefish fillets

¼ teaspoon freshly ground black pepper

¼ teaspoon salt

½ teaspoon grated lemon zest

6 anchovy fillets

2 teaspoons Dijon mustard

½ cup chopped fresh flat-leaf parsley

3 teaspoons white wine vinegar

6 tablespoons olive oil

Preheat broiler.

Place fillets, skin side down, on a foil-lined baking sheet

In a small bowl combine pepper, salt, and lemon zest. Set aside ¼ of this mixture for later, and rub the remaining on the fillets.

Place remaining ingredients in a blender along with reserved mixture. Puree until anchovies and parsley are finely minced. Reserve 2 tablespoons of sauce.

Place fillets under broiler, no closer than 6 inches, and broil without turning for 10 minutes.

Not including reserved 2 tablespoons of anchovy sauce, pour remaining over fillets, and broil for 2 more minutes, or until fish flakes easily.

Remove fish from oven, and cover with reserved sauce. Serve immediately.

Scrambled Eggs with Kale

Joan Malkin of Chilmark declares this "very easy for a quick breakfast." I declare it a delicious way to sneak more local kale into a meal.

SERVES 2

2 tablespoons butter

Approximately 1 cup kale, washed and finely chopped, tough stalk removed

½ cup chopped mushrooms (optional)

4 eggs, beaten

2–4 tablespoons grated cheese (Malkin uses what she has in her refrigerator: cheddar, Monterey Jack, mozzarella, Parmesan, or "something far more interesting like aged Gouda")

Salt and pepper

Melt butter in medium skillet. Add kale and cook until it is soft and glistening, about 3 minutes. Chopped mushrooms can be added to the kale when sautéing.

Add eggs, stir lightly to mix, then add grated cheese. Stir only when necessary until you have the desired consistency. Add salt and pepper, and serve.

Kale Pesto with Baked Greek Yogurt

This dish is like a little billboard for all the good things one can find on Middle Road on Martha's Vineyard: beautiful creamy yogurt, fresh eggs, and kale.

Baked yogurt isn't crazy. It has a long history in the Middle East. Top it with a poached egg and kale pesto, and you have a Chilmark kind of farm breakfast—warm, spicy, unctuous, and so homey it's hip. The yogurt boasts a warm, crumby, ricotta-like texture. The pesto is a punch of zest; the egg is the luxury.

This is a small winter meal or a large snack begging to be eaten with fingerless gloves and a scruffy wool cap right before you take the dog out for a walk in Lambert's Cove.

SERVES 2

For the kale pesto:

1 bunch kale (preferably the Toscano variety, but any sort will work), about 8 ounces, tough inner stalk removed

1 garlic clove

⅓ cup shelled pistachios

Juice of 1 small lemon

⅓ cup Pecorino cheese, grated

Red pepper flakes

½ cup olive oil

Sea salt and freshly ground pepper to taste

For the baked yogurt:

4 cups Greek yogurt (whole fat or non-fat)

4 poached eggs

Smoked paprika (optional)

Chili oil (optional)

To make the kale pesto:

Put all ingredients except olive oil and salt and pepper into a food processor and process until mixed. With the processor going, slowly drizzle in olive oil. Add more olive oil if you like it creamier. Add salt and pepper to taste.

To make the baked yogurt:

4 cups Greek yogurt (whole fat or non-fat)

4 poached eggs

Smoked paprika (optional)

Chili oil (optional)

Preheat oven to 350°F. Put 1 cup yogurt each into individual custard cups or ramekins. Bake yogurt approximately 20 minutes, until hot and slightly firm.

Poach eggs according to your favorite recipe. I heat 2 inches of water in a shallow pan, and add a tablespoon of white vinegar. When water is simmering, I crack the egg into a custard cup, then tip the egg into the simmering water, and cook to desired doneness.

To assemble dishes, remove custard cups from oven. Slide one poached egg onto each serving of yogurt. Add a spoonful of kale pesto. Sprinkle with paprika and chili oil if desired. Serve immediately.

Kale Salad
with Miso Dressing and Spiced Pecans

Meals created from farm stand shopping mean kale, the green that is even more healthful than it is available, and I've seen it looking undaunted beneath 3 inches of snow. Therefore, it's smart to have a thick file of kale recipes. This kale salad, with not-so-local avocado, mango, cranberries, and spicy pecans, is a welcome presentation on a Massachusetts winter day when color has fled south; one thing that is definitely local to Massachusetts are long, gray winters. But this salad is also beautiful on a Chilmark deck, in a summer night lit by stars and fireflies. The spiced pecans make this taste as if company is coming; a batch of them in one's cupboard is both handy and dangerous, snackers beware.

The Japanese technique *shio-momi*, "massaging" the kale with your hands to make it more tender, is considered a form of cooking the vegetable, making it easier to enjoy raw. Even the slight bitterness softens.

SERVES 6

For the salad:

6 cups kale, curly leaf or Toscano, tough stems
    removed, and leaves chopped in 1-inch widths

1 red pepper, de-seeded and thinly sliced

1 mango cubed

1 avocado, cubed

¾ cup dried cranberries

½ cup Spiced Pecans (page 59)

½ cup miso dressing, or to taste

For the dressing:

½ cup olive oil

2 teaspoons minced garlic

Juice of 2 lemons (or to taste)

4 dates, pitted

1 tablespoon miso

2 tablespoons tahini

Place kale and ½–1 teaspoon of salt in a large plastic bag or bowl. Toss together, and then actually squeeze the leaves in your hands, rubbing them together, massaging them. Keep massaging until the kale starts to give off a bit of moisture, 1–2 minutes. You'll notice the kale soften noticeably in your hands. Remove to a bowl, and set aside while you make the dressing.

In a small skillet, warm olive oil. Just as it begins to warm, toss in the garlic. Warm the garlic just to bring the flavor out, not to brown it. Remove from heat.

Place all the dressing ingredients, including the oil and garlic, in a blender to combine. Taste for seasoning, and add water to acquire the desired thinness.

Layer kale and remaining salad ingredients on an attractive serving platter or bowl. Either toss with dressing or serve on the side. Some may like a "dollop" of dressing on their jewel-like salad; some may like to toss all, draping the leaves. It isn't quite as beautiful this way, but the flavors all combine nicely. Sprinkle with Spiced Pecans.

Spiced Pecans

YIELDS 1 POUND

1 teaspoon sea salt

½ teaspoon ground cumin

½ teaspoon cayenne pepper

½ teaspoon cinnamon

½ teaspoon powdered ginger

1 pound pecan halves

3 tablespoons unsalted butter

¼ cup packed dark brown sugar

1 tablespoons water

Line a baking sheet with parchment paper, and set aside.

Mix salt, cumin, cayenne, cinnamon, and ginger together in a small bowl and set aside.

Heat a large skillet to medium. Add nuts, and toast, stirring frequently, until they just start to brown, 4–5 minutes.

Add butter and toss to melt. Add spice mixture and stir to combine. Once combined, add sugar and water, stirring until mixture thickens and coats the nuts, approximately 2–3 minutes. Watch the mixture; if there is not enough liquid, add 1 more tablespoon water.

Transfer nuts to prepared sheet pan and separate them with a fork or spatula. Allow nuts to cool completely before transferring to an airtight container for storage. Can be stored up to 3 weeks.

Mermaid Farm Milk Ricotta and Lemon Muffins

Mermaid Farm Milk Ricotta is probably one of the world's most divine foods all on its own, but should you find yourself wanting to make something very special, a batch of lemon muffins is another nice destination for this soft, fresh cheese with notes of a Chilmark Meadow in June.

When you're on the edge of your seat waiting for spring to arrive, for the earth to nudge crocuses and daffodils out of their lightless hibernation, for the air temperature to release you from wool and fleece, make these muffins. Not even spring can resist them. If you must, you can make them with grocery store ricotta cheese.

MAKES 12 MUFFINS

2 cups all-purpose flour

½ teaspoon baking powder

½ teaspoon baking soda

½ teaspoon salt

1 cup granulated sugar

½ cup (1 stick) unsalted butter, room temperature

2 tablespoons grated lemon rind

1 cup whole-milk ricotta cheese

1 egg

1 tablespoon fresh lemon juice

½ teaspoon almond extract

Preheat oven to 350°F. Line 12 muffin tins with paper liners.

In a large bowl combine flour, baking powder, soda, and salt.

Using an electric mixer, beat sugar and butter until light and fluffy. Mix in lemon rind, ricotta, egg, lemon juice, and almond extract. Gradually add dry ingredients, and stir until just combined. Do not overmix.

Spoon batter into muffin tins, and bake for 20 minutes. Cool on wire racks for 5 minutes before serving.

Clarissa Allen's Lamb Shanks

South Road winds down into the Chilmark moors chased by two hundred-year-old stone walls and laughed at by the waves breaking off in the distance as the open Atlantic Ocean rolls into Lucy Vincent Beach. Pastured hills, dotted for centuries with Allen Farm sheep, cradle it all.

The Allen Sheep Farm has been hosting this drama, some of the world's most natural beauty, since the 1760s. For that long Allen Farm sheep have grazed lazily on wind-swept grasses spiced with salty ocean air.

Clarissa Allen, mistress of all this, tends the sheep as her family has for generations. In a sweet building on the property, you can purchase all cuts of this sylvan lamb, pure Chilmark terroir. Here is Clarissa's favorite lamb shank recipe. While it is also delicious with lamb grazed elsewhere, it is special with meat raised on those Chilmark hills.

SERVES 4

4 lamb shanks (about 4 pounds)

3 tablespoons canola oil

Salt and pepper

2 onions, quartered

8 garlic cloves, peeled

2 medium carrots, peeled and cut into 2-inch chunks

2 celery ribs, cut into 2-inch chunks

2 tablespoons chopped fresh rosemary

2 tablespoons chopped fresh parsley

2 bay leaves

2 cups dry red wine

¼ cup tomato paste

1½ cups chicken broth

Zest of 1 orange

Preheat oven to 300°F.

Remove excess fat from lamb. Heat oil in a dutch oven over medium-high heat. Season lamb with salt and pepper. Carefully place the lamb in the hot oil. Brown on all sides, then remove and set aside. Pour out excess fat.

Turn heat down to medium and add onions, garlic cloves, carrots, and celery. Stirring so the vegetables do not brown, cook for about 5 minutes. Add rosemary, parsley, bay leaves, and lamb shanks on top of the vegetables. Add red wine and bring the heat back up to medium-high. Cook for 5 minutes. Add tomato paste and stir to combine thoroughly. Add chicken broth and orange zest.

Cover the dutch oven and place it in the preheated oven. After 2 hours, remove the lid and carefully turn the shanks over. Return to the oven for about 30 minutes more. By removing the lid, you will reduce and thicken the broth a bit. Remove the bay leaves before serving.

Spring Garlic Soup

This recipe celebrates that first garlic pulled from spring soil on Martha's Vineyard. A piping hot garlic broth is whisked into farm fresh eggs to make a light soup, which is poured over buttery croutons then strewn with fresh parsley. Light, bright, and fragrant, the soup defines the perfect early spring meal on the coast of Massachusetts. One stop at Mermaid Farm in Chilmark, and you have the ingredient list. If you cannot find spring garlic, try to find firm, white garlic bulbs with no dried or rotted spots; that indicates the garlic hasn't been rattling in a box all winter.

SERVES 4–6

12 garlic cloves, peeled

6 cups water

¼ cup (½ stick) unsalted butter (divided)

2 cups croutons (sourdough or a crusty baguette)

6 fresh eggs

1 teaspoons salt

1 teaspoon freshly ground black pepper

⅔ cup finely chopped parsley

Place garlic and water in a medium saucepan, and bring to a boil. Cook until garlic is soft, about 15 minutes. Remove garlic cloves, reserving the water. Mash garlic to a smooth paste. This can be done with a fork or in a small food processor.

Return the paste to the water and let it cool.

Pour boiling water into a soup tureen, or into individual bowls, to keep them warm.

Melt 2 tablespoons butter in a medium skillet. Add croutons, and sauté to an even brown, stirring constantly. Empty boiling water from the soup tureen or bowls, and put in the croutons, dividing them evenly if using bowls.

Break eggs into a mixing bowl, and beat to frothy. Add salt and pepper. Slowly add 1 cup of the garlic liquid, beating well as you pour to prevent curdling. Pour egg mixture back into pot of garlic broth, stirring constantly. Add remaining 2 tablespoons of butter, cut into pieces

Reheat the broth, but do not let it boil. Pour the hot broth over the croutons. Sprinkle generously with chopped parsley, and serve.

Morning Glory Farm's Corn and Wild Mushroom Risotto

From the Morning Glory Farm's kitchen, this recipe is one of the more wonderful things to do with the freshest Massachusetts corn. What elevates this dish to the pinnacle of corn dishes is the broth. Do not try to make this risotto unless you make this broth; it's something any cook would consider riches to have on hand.

SERVES 4–6

12 ounces mushrooms, halved or quartered, stems reserved

2 ears corn, kernels removed, cobs reserved

3 tablespoons extra virgin olive oil, divided

1½ teaspoons sea salt, divided

1 tablespoon butter

1 medium onion, finely diced, skin reserved

1 leek, diced with green ends reserved

¼ teaspoon nutmeg

¼ teaspoon black pepper

1 tablespoon sage, finely minced

1 cup Arborio rice

1 quart Corn Broth (recipe follows)

¼ cup grated cheese, Parmesan or substitute a local New England hard grating cheese

Preheat oven to 375°F.

Mix together mushrooms, corn, 2 tablespoons oil, and ½ teaspoon salt. Place on lined baking sheet. Bake 20–22 minutes, until mushrooms are soft, but not dry or crisp, and corn is just beginning to caramelize. The corn will be spotty tan.

While mushrooms and corn are roasting, melt butter and remaining one tablespoon olive oil in saucepan over medium-high heat. Add onion, leek, nutmeg,

remaining 1 teaspoon salt, pepper, and sage. Mix together, stirring occasionally until onions are soft and translucent, 8–10 minutes.

Lower heat to medium-low, stir in rice and mix until coated with oil. Stirring constantly, add broth 1 cup at a time, adding more broth when the rice has absorbed the previous cup. Continue adding broth until all has been absorbed. Fold in mushrooms, corn, and cheese. Serve warm or at room temperature.

To make the corn broth:
Preheat oven 350°F.

On a baking sheet, combine the reserved corncobs, onion skins, and leek greens from the risotto recipe above. Roast for 18–20 minutes, or until they begin to brown.

In a 6-quart saucepan over medium high heat, combine 3 quarts water, roasted trimmings, 1 bay leaf, and any stems and herb ends you have around. Bring to a boil. Reduce heat to medium, and cook for 30 minutes.

Strain, discarding solids. Broth can be kept in the refrigerator for up to two weeks for use in dishes that call for water or canned vegetable broth. It also freezes well in 1 quart plastic tubs, such as yogurt containers.

Camp Meeting Association Green Bean Casserole

Green Bean Casserole, the renowned vehicle for canned onion rings, returns to its purer origins here. This recipe is one of those that was probably carried to this Oak Bluffs summer community years ago, where it remained preserved, unadulterated by "modern" tastes. Remember, this is a community of regulars; the same people have been coming to Oak Bluffs for generations. Women are known for their recipes, and people look forward to seeing the same recipes—enjoying each other's favorite dishes—every year for potlucks and community barbecues.

SERVES 4–6

1½ pounds fresh green beans, woody ends snipped

¼ cup (½ stick) butter

½ cup fresh bread crumbs

2 cloves garlic, minced

2 tablespoons grated lemon zest

1 tablespoon chopped parsley

Salt and pepper to taste

1 cup sour cream

Preheat oven to 350°F.

Steam or simmer the beans until tender. Drain immediately, and toss into a large bowl.

In a small skillet melt the butter. Add bread crumbs, and sauté until nicely browned. Add garlic, lemon zest, parsley, salt, and pepper.

Add crumbs to the beans and toss together. Add sour cream and toss well. Pour all into an 8 x 11-inch baking dish. Bake for 20 minutes.

Ellie's Fantastic Seafood Chowder

This is clearly one of those wonderful summer feast recipes that everyone needs in his or her reper-toire. Put everything in one pot, put the pot in the oven for a good long while, and open the lid to a plentiful chowder that not only feeds a crowd but wows them, too. It's the seasonings here—clove, bay, a tiny pinch of thyme, celery seed, and white wine—that make Ellie's Fantastic Seafood Chow-der a recipe people in this circle of gingerbread cottages must have looked forward to every summer. Don't be fooled by the packaged scalloped potatoes, which I keep in the recipe because they are the one element that screams "meal to be made on vacation!" The flavors balance here with the hand of a skilled chef—Ellie knew what she was doing.

SERVES 8–10

2 pounds of firm, white fish (hake, dogfish, monkfish would be great here, but so would haddock, cod, or halibut)

1 pound medium shrimp

1 pound Nantucket scallops

1 package scalloped potatoes

1 bay leaf

4 cloves

¼ teaspoon thyme

¼ teaspoon celery seed

1 teaspoon salt

1 teaspoon pepper

3 medium onions, sliced

2 garlic cloves, minced

¼ cup (½ stick) butter

½ cup white wine

1 pint cream

2 cups milk

1 quart water

Preheat oven to 325°F.

Combine all ingredients in a large, heavy casserole dish. Bake for 1½ hours covered, or until seafood is cooked and flavors have appropriately melded. This can be left in the oven for longer if you want the flavors to enrich, but do not let it boil.

Illumination Night Apricot Bars

A favorite in the Camp Meeting Association, Doris MacGillvray's Apricot Bar recipe had to be included here.

MAKES 24

¾ cup butter (1½ sticks) at room temperature

1 cup sugar

1 egg

1½ teaspoons vanilla

½ teaspoon salt

2 cups flour

1½ cups shredded coconut

8 ounces apricot preserves

1 cup walnuts, chopped

Preheat oven to 350°F.

Cream butter, sugar, egg, and vanilla until fluffy. Mix in salt, flour, and coconut. Stir well. Reserve ¾ cup for topping, and spread the rest in a greased 9 x 11-inch baking pan.

Spread apricot preserves over mixture. Sprinkle nuts over preserves. Dot reserved ¾ cup batter over top. Bake for 30 minutes, or until batter on top is cooked and slightly browned. Cool slightly, and cut into bars.

Vineyard Pesto

Come July and August, nasturtiums on Martha's Vineyard trail from the edges of every garden, their cheerful yellow and orange faces the unofficial flags of midsummer.

In farmers' markets nasturtium blossoms tumble from packages; farmers often sell colorful baggies-full of just the flowers, which have a fresh herbaceous, peppery flavor. With this blossom bounty, nasturtium pesto begs to be made. The result is a golden paste that colors a bowl of cavatappi beautiful saffron yellow, and has a spicy floral flavor redolent of a Turkish spice market. A bowl of pasta draped in this radiant sauce, a few blossoms tossed on top, may be the most beautiful and provocative dish you will make all summer.

MAKES 1½ CUPS

2 cups nasturtium flowers

½ cup toasted pistachios

Juice of one lemon

4 cloves garlic

1 cup olive oil

¼ cup freshly grated Parmesan cheese

Fresh nasturtium flowers for garnish

Place all the ingredients in a food processor and blend.

To serve over pasta, add ½ cup of pesto to 1 pound of hot cooked pasta, still dripping with some of its water. (The water will help to make the sauce.) Toss very well, draping the pasta, and taste for salt and pepper. Serve in warm bowls. Toss a couple of nasturtium flowers over each bowl. Top with freshly ground black pepper.

Store the pesto in glass or ceramic jars in your refrigerator, but use at room temperature.

Gardener's Delight—
Smoky Eggplant with Fresh Tomatoes and Herbs

There is one person on Martha's Vineyard you want to go on a walk with. You want to go to the farmers' market with her. You want to drive to Menemsha, and watch her choose a piece of bass. A founder of Slow Food Martha's Vineyard, Jan Buhrman knows every shellfish harvester, every worthy fisherman, every farmer, every cheesemaker on the island. And she knows where the heirloom apple trees grow.

Buhrman describes this recipe as "one of those dishes you whip up right out of the garden," a beautiful platter of smoky aromatic vegetables to set down on a cocktail table with slices of toasted pita. A shining centerpiece, this dish calls people to it.

SERVES 8

2 large eggplants cut in half lengthwise

6–8 cloves garlic

⅛ cup + 2 tablespoons olive oil, divided

1 tablespoon Berber Spice*

4–5 heirloom variety tomatoes

6–8 cherry tomatoes

2 tablespoons red wine vinegar

juice of 1 lemon

1 small bunch of parsley, chopped fine

Salt and pepper to taste

*Berber is a hot, spicy Ethiopian spice blend that includes fenugreek, ground ginger, cardamom, clove, cinnamon, and more. If you cannot find Berber, smoked paprika is a nice substitute. It creates an entirely different flavor, but a good one.

Light the grill, allow it to get hot.

Place eggplant, skin side down, on grill.

Wrap garlic in foil with 2 tablespoons olive oil, and grill for 5 minutes. Remove it from grill, but leave it in the foil, as it will continue to cook.

Cook eggplant until the skin is charred all around. Turn as needed. Remove when it is blistered and charred, and the center is soft and clearly cooked. Peel the eggplants when they are cool enough to handle. Remove garlic from foil, and squeeze roasted centers out of each papery cover.

In a bowl, place the flesh of the eggplant and the peeled garlic cloves, and mash with a fork. Add Berber Spice and mix throughout.

Spread eggplant mixture in an attractive shallow bowl or plate. Arrange tomatoes on top of eggplant. Jan uses a variety of cuts: one tomato sliced, one cut into wedges, small cherry tomatoes cut into halves, etc., for variety and interest. Always use the very best tomatoes you can find, hopefully ones still warm off the vine!

In a small bowl or glass measuring cup, mix together remaining olive oil, vinegar, lemon juice, and chopped parsley and sprinkle over the tomatoes and eggplant. Add salt and pepper.

Serve immediately with a pile of toasted pita crisps beside it for dipping.

CHAPTER THREE

Nantucket

A unique alchemy of isolation, independence, ambition, and don't forget the beautiful pearly scallops, all add up to Nantucket today. "A barren sandbank, fertilized with whale-oil only," was how one nineteenth-century visitor described the place, according to Nathanial Philbrook in his book, *Away off Shore.*

Coffin, Starbuck, Folger, Hussey, Macy, the English names that first settled amongst the Native Americans here, still cast long shadows on Nantucket. You'll find them in the names of the streets, in the well-preserved eighteenth- and nineteenth-century homes built by their children and grandchildren. Walking by the gray-shingled homes of Hussey Street, or seeing the twisted branches of an old quince tree in the back garden covered in sparrows on a foggy November morning, one barely needs to daydream to hear Mary Coffin Starbuck's skirts rustling.

Nantucket was not like other "boomtowns," but boom it went when the first whales began to wash up on Nantucket's shores. The first whaling was done on the south side of Nantucket. Watching for whales spouting off shore, jumping in the beached and ready boats when a sighting came, Nantucket's first whaling men practiced this "ashore whaling." This was the origins of

Sconset, the sweet fishing village facing the wide-open Atlantic Ocean that came to be a treasured summer retreat for generations of families. Aunt Lucas's Sconset Chocolate Cake, a recipe written by hand in 1909, is an enormous round of dark chocolatey goodness; slices of it wrapped in parchment paper would have been wonderful nibbled on the beach.

Nantucket was not your typical fishing town of wharves lined with bars to welcome the seamen home. Many a Nantucket whaling captain stepped off his vessel and went to church. The modesty and simplicity demanded of Quakerism stood in stark opposition to the wealth these ships were bringing into the port. The great whaling families recorded the numbers in their ledgers, then went to meeting to pray.

These families thrived. They stayed intact. They lived long lives and had regular access to interesting foods—tamarind, limes, lemons, and coconut. Tamarind, Walnut, and Fresh Ginger Cake, frosted with a lime and confectionary glaze, reflects exactly the kind of dark, fragrant cake that Mary Starbuck may have served for tea. Meals were not dull. An afternoon at the Nantucket Historical Association is a both delightful handwriting assignment (the beauty of handwritten recipes!) and a surprising lesson in what nineteenth-century Nantucketers were eating—elegant coconut cakes, puddings, quince every way, gingerbread, and pickled limes.

Sweet Pickled Lime recipes appear more than once in old Nantucket cookbooks, but also in an old Annisquam cookbook, far to the north on Cape Ann, indicating pickled limes were standard in the eighteenth, nineteenth, even into the twentieth centuries.

Molasses, sugar, clove, and cinnamon with the fresh pucker of lime astounds. It's citrus and pickles, tart and sweet, a kind of fabulous wallop of flavor that was craved mid-winter on Nantucket two hundred years ago the same as we crave it now. The black, molasses-rich Beebe Gingerbread, an authentic recipe that Nantucketers apparently longed for long after Mr. Beebe died, tastes like some wonderful treat you might find in a Brooklyn cafe when you serve it with Sweet Pickled Limes, so startling and yet so perfect is this combination.

On Nantucket the charms of quince were either particularly appreciated or more perfectly preserved. In the town center, Quince Street runs off of Center Street between Hussey Street and Gay. A few town gardens still have mockingbirds calling from knotted old quince trees in the corner of a yard. I'm told old quince trees, relics of English cooks, line the steps of the Wade Cottages in Sconset. Nantucket recipes for quince abound. Quince honey, pickled quince, quince

jam, and quince pudding appear as often as lemon pie, for which there are dozens of recipes.

Quince looks like a large yellow pear wearing a thin coat of velvet. It ripens in the autumn with pears and apples. A quince cannot be eaten raw—it's woody and flavorless—but a bowl of them on a table will perfume your entire home with the scent of honey and jasmine. Cooked, quince transforms into a sweet, claret-colored fruit with spice and character that the best pippin can only envy. Pickled Quince Salad with Blue Cheese and Walnuts is a salad with which to defeat winter. Quince Pudding is like a clafouti, but with that mysterious floral sweetness that only quince can impart. If you find enough quince to make the Quince Honey recipe here (really a quince jam) you will make friends. But you may also learn that Quince Honey is so divinely aromatic on toast that it is difficult to share.

Another Nantucket treasure is the scallop. November through March marks the season for Nantucket Bay Scallops—also called Bay Scallops—which are small, tender, and, sweet. Winter residents of Nantucket and Martha's Vineyard consider this delicious catch just one of many off-season rewards. There is perhaps no other native food so sought after by everyone from the eighth-generation Nantucketer to the Iowan visiting the island for the first time. No one ever tires of Nantucket Bay Scallops; even the most jaded food writer drops his or her pen and picks up a fork when bay scallops are served.

Because the eelgrass in wetlands where these native treasures like to attach has been profoundly compromised, bay scallops are not so abundant anymore. They're hard to find, and they're expensive, but everyone agrees they are worth the hunt and the price. Everyone also agrees that the simplest treatment is the best.

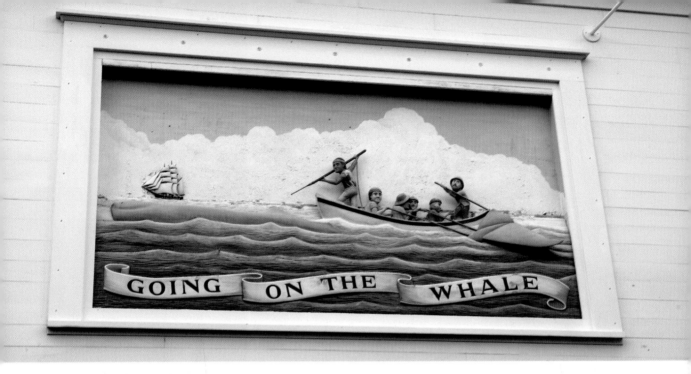

GOING ON THE WHALE

But Nantucket Scallop and Potato Pie must be made just once, at least. This pie has brought a book club to their knees, with normally polite ladies getting mean over the last slice. Yes, Nantucket scallops are beautiful broiled very quickly with a few buttered bread crumbs to protect them, but nothing is ever not wonderful beneath a butter crust and sistered with baby potatoes and cheddar cheese.

April's Daffodil Weekend and early December's Christmas Stroll are weekends that Nantucketers, and those who love this island, plan months, if not years, in advance. Many local Nantucketers flee the island in October, exhausted from a busy summer of shopkeeping or landscaping or doing the work of keeping up a beautiful beach-going destination. Almost everyone, however, returns for The Stroll. Friends who have perhaps worked together all summer but then fled for some peace after the summer craziness, return for Stroll Weekend and greet each other as if they have been away for years. "Are you here for the Stroll?!" they ask, still excited as if this were their first and not their twentieth Christmas season.

Melodic "Noels" ring from carolers through the cold night air. Winter's early-darkened streets are illuminated by dozens of Christmas trees decorated by Nantucket school children. The grand front doors of ship captains' homes are framed in garland and bejeweled in della Robia wreaths. It is hard to stay away this weekend on Nantucket, dangling like a sparkling Christmas ornament itself, "away offshore." A light snow seems to always be blowing in off Nantucket Sound, dusting the cobblestones; it's magic.

If you are lucky enough to have a home on Nantucket, and you have guests arriving for the Christmas Stroll, make wheat berry, cranberry, and apple porridge. If you want to evoke the Starbucks spirits, make some Beebe Gingerbread, spread some toast with Quince Honey, and substitute quince for the apples in the porridge. No Nantucketer, dead or alive, could stay away.

Nantucket Index

Nantucket Wonders

Wonders are a donut with a much better name. Old Nantucket cookbooks include recipes for wonders as often as new cookbooks include recipes for blueberry muffins. In the 17th century, wonders were known to be fried on the isle of Jersey, part of the Channel Islands which lay fourteen miles off the Bay of Mont St. Michel. On the French side they were called *des mervelles* which thus translated on the English side into "wonders." Many early Nantucket settlers came from Devonshire, the closest English coast to the Channel Islands. Certainly Tristram Coffin and his gang carried wonder recipes with them they crossed the Atlantic.

From files in the Nantucket Historical Association, here is a recipe for true Nantucket Wonders. These are the cake-y sort of donut, leavened with baking soda, as opposed to the yeast-raised variation like Raised Donuts "Spring Hill" in the Cape Cod chapter. I've kept this simple recipe as it was written because I like to imagine these exact wonders frying in a kitchen on Hussey St. three hundred years ago.

MAKES ABOUT 20

½ teaspoon baking soda

⅔ cup boiling water

6 tablespoons sugar

3 eggs

2 tablespoons butter, melted and cooled

3 cups flour

6-8 cups vegetable oil for frying

Dissolve baking soda in the boiling water. Let cool slightly.

In a large bowl combine sugar, eggs, butter, and cooled water. Add enough flour to make the dough stiff enough to roll.

In a large cast-iron skillet, dutch oven, or fryer, heat oil to 375°F. The oil should be about at least 4-inches deep. Try to keep the oil at this temperature. (An oil thermometer is critical here.)

Roll dough to ½-inch thick, and cut into rings using a donut cutter or the rim of a large pickle jar for the outer ring, and the lip of a water bottle for the inner ring.

Very carefully drop the dough in the oil and fry until golden, about 2 minutes on each side, depending on the heat of your oil and the thickness of your wonders. Watch carefully that, as the oil gets hotter, the wonders cook very quickly. This takes a bit of dancing between thermometer, burner temperature, and wonder color. When the wonders are done, let cool on paper towels. Roll in cinnamon sugar if desired, but serve these as quickly as possible.

"Beneath Your Eggs" Sconset Fish Pudding

From a batch of handwritten recipes, including the Sconset Chocolate Cake, found in the Nantucket Historical Association, "Sconset Fish Pudding" finishes with the scrawled words "Dream Acres," as if this recipe were prepared in a Sconset cottage by that name. Warm from the oven, with plenty of crusty French bread upon which to spoon it, this fish pudding makes a wonderful casual supper. Slide a poached egg over a scoop of it, add browned potatoes on the side, and you have the ultimate breakfast for a Sconset morning.

SERVES 4 FOR BREAKFAST, 6–8 AS AN APPETIZER

1 pound very fresh haddock or cod, or cod loin if you can find it

2½ cups whole milk

½ cup celery leaves

1 bay leaf

½ teaspoon grated nutmeg

½ teaspoon peppercorns

¼ teaspoon red pepper flakes

½ teaspoon salt

3 tablespoons butter

1½ tablespoons flour

½ cup cream

2 eggs, slightly beaten

2 tablespoons grated onion

¼ cup chopped fresh parsley

Lemon wedges for garnish

Preheat oven to 350°F.

In a wide saucepan, simmer the haddock, milk, celery leaves, bay leaf, nutmeg, peppercorns, red pepper flakes,,and salt together until the fish flakes. Cool.

Process the fish very loosely in food processor.

In a small saucepan, melt the butter. Whisk in the flour, cream, and eggs. Whisk quickly until all is "well scalded," about 1 minute. It doesn't have to thicken. Stir the fish into this mixture. Add onion.

Spread into a buttered 1½-quart baking dish. Lay an old dish towel onto a roasting pan. This keeps the baking dish from slipping. Set the baking dish into the roasting pan. Put the pan in the oven, and then fill the roasting pan with water that goes 1-inch up the sides of the baking dish. Bake the dish, set in the water, for 30 minutes, or until the pudding is set and lightly brown on top. Garnish servings with fresh parsley, and serve with a lemon wedge.

For breakfast or a light dinner, poach four eggs. Divide the fish between 4 plates, and lay the egg over each portion.

Alternatively serve this as an appetizer with crackers. Squeeze lemon over the dish, garnish with parsley, and serve warm or at room temperature.

Christmas Stroll Porridge

Many Nantucketers fill their homes with guests for the Christmas Stroll. This is a wonderful porridge to keep warm in the oven, satisfying early and late risers. There are a few steps that involve beginning the day ahead, but the wheat berries add an irreplaceable texture here. It's worth a little fuss for a special occasion. For an especially Nantucket breakfast, substitute fresh quince for the apples. Roxbury Russet apples, the oldest variety in North America, or a couple picked from a favorite tree—maybe one growing wild in Sconset—would be good, too.

SERVES 6

1 cup wheat berries

2 cups cranberries, washed and chopped

1 cup sugar

1 cup honey

4 cups skim milk

2 teaspoons cinnamon

2 apples, peeled, cored, and chopped

Zest from 1 lemon

Pinch of salt

1 egg

2 egg whites

1 teaspoon vanilla

Soak wheat berries in water overnight. In a separate bowl mix cranberries, sugar, and honey. Allow to sit overnight, also.

Drain wheat berries, and put them in a saucepan with 4 cups water. Simmer for 30 minutes and drain. Add milk and cinnamon to the berries, and cook for another 30 minutes. Stir in the cranberries, apples, and lemon zest.

Preheat oven to 325°F.

In a separate bowl, whisk together salt, egg, egg whites, and vanilla. Take a spoonful of the wheat berry mixture, and stir it quickly into the eggs. Then turn the eggs back into the whole wheat berry mixture, and combine well.

Pour porridge into a deep, buttered, 2-quart casserole. Bake for 35 minutes.

Serve warm with a pour of cream.

1874 Nantucket Corn Pudding

Corn pudding—Quaker versions, native versions, even Barbara Bush's version—abound in New England cookbooks; this recipe, from the 1874 Nantucket compilation of recipes, says, "Discard the others!" The crackers magically provide both the weightlessness and body that doesn't interfere with the milk and eggs trying to be custard. Adapted to modern methods, the recipe becomes a dish that challenges the laws of gravity and flavor. It's like corn on the cob in a cloud. Shyly placed on the page in an old recipe collection beneath "Bread Omelet," this is the Cinderella of corn puddings.

SERVES 8–10

12 ears fresh corn, kernels removed, or 6 cups frozen organic corn

2 cups loosely crushed oyster crackers (not too fine)

4 tablespoons sugar

1 teaspoon salt

Black pepper to taste

4 cups whole milk

5 eggs, lightly beaten

Preheat oven to 350°F. Butter a 2-quart glass baking dish.

With a food processor, pulse the corn many times to achieve a mixture of half-ground and half-whole corn kernels. Pour into a large bowl.

Stir in remaining ingredients, and mix together well. Pour into a prepared dish. Bake for 30 minutes or until a fork inserted in the center comes out clean. Serve warm or room temperature.

Chilled Fresh Corn and Coconut Soup

Native fresh corn, coconut milk, lime, and fresh basil as a chilled soup makes an ethereal summer meal packed in a thermos for a remote picnic on Tom Nevers Beach or served in a sherry glass to start an elegant Edgertown dinner. Organic frozen corn could be substituted, and is often better than fresh corn that has been trucked hundreds of miles, but a Nantucketer should head to Bartlett Farm in early August for the first native corn and beefy leaves of local basil. The other ingredients here recall once again those South Seas whaling trips, when Nantucket pantries were well stocked in coconuts and limes.

SERVES 4

3 cups fresh corn kernels, plus ½ cup for garnish

1 (14-ounce) can light coconut milk

½ habañero pepper (optional)

2½ cups water

Salt and pepper

1 tablespoon olive oil

Juice from 3 limes, plus more for garnish

½ cup chopped fresh basil

In a medium saucepan put corn, coconut milk, habañero (if desired), and water to a boil. Reduce heat, and simmer until corn is tender, about 20 minutes.

With an emulsion blender or a stand blender, puree soup. If you want your soup velvety, with no texture from the corn, press through a sieve, discarding solids. It's still very good without this process, particularly if you blend it well. Season with salt and pepper.

Toss the corn for the garnish in olive oil, salt, and pepper, and roast in a 450°F oven for 10 minutes, or until toasted brown. Set aside.

Chill soup at least 3 hours. Stir in lime juice. If you're not packing this in a thermos, garnish each serving with a tablespoon roasted corn kernels, basil, and a squeeze of lime.

Sweet Pickled Limes

A school yard staple in nineteenth-century Massachusetts, pickled limes were the source of May's tears in Louisa May Alcott's *Little Women*. Young girls traded pickled limes for valuables in those years, but the limes, amazingly sold in candy shops as treats, had presumably already been declared contraband by the teacher, such was a pickled lime's ability to distract a student. May was caught, and her limes thrown out the window.

Chop these sweet pickled limes in ¼-inch chunks and sprinkle them on top of 1630 Salem Chicken for a bowl of the Salem China Trade; it's just as delicious and surprising today. Or just squeeze the sweetened citrus over a simple baked chicken. The lime adds a wallop of flavor to many mid-winter New England ingredients. The best way to have a Sweet Pickled Lime is beside Beebe Gingerbread, a fusion dessert right off a 1785 Nantucket table, still exotically delicious.

MAKES 1 DOZEN LIMES

12 limes

1½ cups vinegar

¼ cup water

1 tablespoon molasses

2 ¼ cups sugar

8–10 whole cloves

1 stick cinnamon

Place limes in a heavy saucepan and cover with cold water. Bring to a boil, and simmer until tender, about 10 minutes.

Pour off water, cover with boiling water this time, and simmer again until very tender, about 10 more minutes. Drain in a colander and allow to cool.

To make the syrup, put vinegar, water, molasses, sugar, cloves, and cinnamon in a heavy saucepan over medium heat. When sugar dissolves, simmer for 5 more minutes, or until the mixture thickens slightly. Allow to cool.

When cool, put limes in jars and pour cooled syrup over them. Store in refrigerator. Limes will keep for up to 3 weeks.

Beebe Gingerbread

The notes for Beebe Gingerbread in the *Nantucket Cookbook: One Hundred Recipes Collected from Nantucket Housewives Past and Present*, published by The Inquirer and Mirror Press, Nantucket, MA, 1874, promise with more irony than remorse that this recipe is as close as it gets to the beloved Beebe Gingerbread produced by Nathan Beebe, a popular Nantucket baker in the eighteenth century.

The compiler is assured that this is the veritable recipe of the famous Nantucket baker Beebe. "The few people now left who have ever eaten it tell us regretfully that there was a secret about it that he never imparted; but may it not be that the missing ingredient was the splendid appetite of childhood?"

Feel free to include that special ingredient in the recipe below, but even without it, this molasses-healthy gingerbread is ready to restart the memory making. So many gingerbreads taste like too much flour, too much powdery ginger, too much baking soda, or all three. Some are upgraded with candied ginger, which seems like a gummy interruption in the cake. This interpretation of the Beebe Gingerbread produces a seamless taste of velvety molasses nuanced with spice. It's moist, not cakey. It's the gingerbread to carry into modern times.

I'm sorry to even mention them in the same sentence, but I promise that one or the other—Caramel Ice Cream or Sweet Pickled Limes—are both delicious with Beebe Gingerbread. You choose.

MAKES ONE 9-INCH SQUARE PAN

½ cup (1 stick) butter

1¼ cups molasses

½ cup milk

3 teaspoons ginger

1 teaspoon baking soda

2 cups flour

Preheat oven to 350°F. Grease a 9-inch square metal pan.

Cream the butter. Pour in the molasses and beat until it is completely integrated, and the mixture is a fluffy, pale brown mixture, about 5 minutes. Scrape the bowl occasionally to make sure butter isn't sticking to bottom.

Gradually pour in milk, and mix in. Add ginger and baking soda. Then mix in flour ½ cup at a time, mixing to incorporate each addition.

Pour into prepared pan, and bake for 40 minutes or until a fork inserted comes out clean.

Aunt Lucas's Chocolate Cake, Sconset, July 22, 1909

In 1894 on the eastern-most tip of Nantucket, in Sconset, where the first whaling boats shipped off the beach, aiming at whales that were simply breaching off-shore, John Grout asked Levi Coffin if he could lease land that had been the old Bloomingdale Farm. Coffin said yes, and Grout laid out a golf course. In 1900, The Casino, a building in which a new class of summer residents could play cards, dance, and watch a live performance of real Broadway actors, was constructed beside the golf course. Outside the Casino there were tennis courts. Life was good in Sconset in July of 1909 when someone copied down this recipe for chocolate cake.

Penned in loose cursive handwriting, the recipe is simply labeled, "Aunt Lucas's Chocolate Cake, Sconset, July 22, 1909." A magnificent cake in traditional taste, not molten, not gooey, no promises of orgasm or death, this is a beach-going American picnic cake, a lovely wedge that will leave tender crumbs in your lap. Leave out the frosting because frosting doesn't go to the beach. This is the cake to remember what chocolate cake was like before it became popular as an under-done, flourless pudding. Moist, tender, definitely chocolatey, this makes a grand presentation, certainly something that must have impressed the new American aristocracy who had discovered the beaches of Sconset by 1909. This cake must have sat triumphantly on a stand in Aunt Lucas's Sconset kitchen, before hungry nieces and nephews ran off with their slices.

SERVES 12

½ pound good quality dark chocolate or
 baking chocolate

1 cup (2 sticks) butter

2½ cups sugar

2½ cups flour, sifted

2 teaspoons baking soda ("in some milk")

1 cup buttermilk

5 egg yolks

4 egg whites

Preheat oven to 325°F. Grease and flour a 10-inch bundt pan.

In a double boiler melt together chocolate and butter. Allow to cool.

In a large mixing bowl stir together sugar and flour.

In a 2 cup glass measuring cup mix together soda and buttermilk. Add egg yolks and mix well.

Beat egg whites to soft peaks.

Alternately, in 3 additions, add chocolate mixture and buttermilk to dry ingredients, stirring well after each addition. Fold in egg whites. Pour into pan, and bake for 45 minutes. Watch the cake carefully; you may need to cover it with aluminum foil if the top begins to brown too quickly.

Cool cake on wire racks. Remove from pan when it is completely cool.

Aunt Lucas offers no serving tips, but I hope she would approve of the center filled with **brandied whipped cream:** Whip 1 cup of heavy cream to soft peaks. Add 2 tablespoons sifted confectionary sugar and 2 tablespoons brandy.

MOBY DICK'S NANTUCKET CHAPTER

Nantucket! Take out your map and look at it. See what a real corner of the world it occupies; how it stands there, away off shore, more lonely than the Eddystone lighthouse. Look at it — a mere hillock, and elbow of sand; all beach, without a background. There is more sand there than you would use in twenty years as a substitute for blotting paper. Some gamesome wights will tell you that they have to plant weeds there, they don't grow naturally; that they import Canada thistles; that they have to send beyond seas for a spile to stop a leak in an oil cask; that pieces of wood in Nantucket are carried about like bits of the true cross in Rome; that people there plant toadstools before their houses, to get under the shade in summer time; that one blade of grass makes an oasis, three blades in a day's walk a prairie; that they wear quicksand shoes, something like Laplander snow-shoes; that they are so shut up, belted about, every way inclosed, surrounded, and made an utter island of by the ocean, that to the very chairs and tables small clams will sometimes be found adhering as to the backs of sea turtles. But these extravaganzas only show that Nantucket is no Illinois.

–Moby Dick, chapter 14

Tamarind, Walnut, and Fresh Ginger Cake

"Casks of pickled limes, of cocoanuts, of Cape Horn nuts, as English walnuts were called, and Castile nuts, now known as Brazil nuts. And small kegs of lime juice and of tamarinds, both of which made refreshing drinks for warm days." This is how Mary Starbuck (1856–1938) described the South Seas prizes her father, Captain Charles Starbuck, presented to his children on Nantucket after a voyage on his ship *Islander* "from beyond Cape Horn," according to an essay by Ben Simon for the Nantucket Historical Association. Imagine a nineteenth-century Nantucket pantry stocked this way. For almost two centuries the South Sea Islands were more familiar to Nantucketers than Boston.

If that list were a cake, it would be this one. Tamarind, Walnut, and Fresh Ginger Cake is even more delicious than it is interesting, a moist, date-sweet, gingery cake, with a citrusy mystery from the tamarind. It is lighter and more tender than either fruit cake or even gingerbread, with almost caramel notes. The lime icing glaze is a sharply sweet crackling counter to the date and spice in the cake.

MAKES A HIGH 1-LAYER, 8-INCH CAKE

½ cup chopped dates

⅓ cup tamarind paste

1¼ cups water

1 cup (2 sticks), plus 2 tablespoons unsalted butter, cut into chunks

2 tablespoons freshly grated ginger

⅔ cup dark brown sugar

2 large eggs, lightly beaten

2½ cups all-purpose flour

2 teaspoons baking soda

½ teaspoon salt

8 ounces walnuts, roughly chopped

1½ cups confectionary sugar

Juice from 2–3 limes

Preheat oven to 350°F.

Spray an 8-inch cake pan with cooking spray. Line it with a round of parchment paper, and spray the paper.

Put dates, tamarind paste, and water in a pan over medium-high heat. Boil for 1 minute. Remove from heat, add butter and set aside for 10 minutes, stirring occasionally to encourage butter to melt.

Stir in ginger and brown sugar. Add eggs, and beat until smooth.

In a separate bowl, whisk together flour, baking soda, and salt. Add this to the batter, and beat until smooth. Stir in the walnuts.

Spoon the cake mix into the prepared pan, and bake for about 1 hour, or until a skewer poked into the center comes out clean. Remove and leave to cool.

When cake is cooled, remove from pan, and turn onto a cake plate. Remove parchment from the bottom.

To make the icing, put the confectionary sugar through a sifter or strainer to remove lumps. Add the lime juice and whisk until smooth. Spread on slightly warm cake, so that it dribbles down the sides.

Old Boyfriend Pie or Nantucket Scallop and Potato Pie

This is a savory pie to make on a clear, cold winter day with sea smoke rising off the harbor. It is a combination of tastes everyone loves—pastry, cheese, potatoes, cream, and tender scallops. I have seen this pie bring a book club to their knees.

Old Boyfriend Pie is memorable on its own merit, but the name might help keep the recipe from becoming lost to dinners made just once. Offered to me by a former boyfriend, even my husband warmly refers to this as "Old Boyfriend Pie." It may be the most requested meal in my house.

The opalescent Nantucket scallops are precious, and most people beg to treat them in a kitchen with reverence and simplicity, but there isn't much that suffers beneath a buttery piecrust. Cuddling with newly dug winter potatoes, cheddar cheese, and thyme, this may be the happiest a Nantucket scallop could ever be. But purists may feel this is too much apparel for a Nantucket scallop; meaty sea scallops are delicious here, too.

SERVES 8

For the filling:

About 8 small (1-inch) round potatoes

2 large onions, chopped

1 tablespoon olive oil

2 teaspoons dried thyme

A good pinch of red pepper flakes

Salt and pepper

1½ pounds bay scallops; sea scallops can also be used

1½ cups grated cheddar cheese

½ cup cream or milk

1 double crust pie dough (page 91)

For the 1 double-crust pie dough:

2 cups flour

Dash salt

¾ cup (1½ sticks) unsalted butter, cut into pieces

5–6 tablespoons ice water

To make the filling:

Keep potatoes whole, but parboil them in lightly salted water.

Sauté onions in olive oil until clear with the thyme, red pepper flakes, salt, and pepper.

Add parboiled potatoes to the pan, and toss all together.

Roll out the bottom pie dough, and line a 9-inch pie pan with it.

Put the potatoes and onions into the bottom piecrust. Take the scallops and press them into the nooks in the potatoes, pressing all down. Sprinkle the cheese over the top. Pour the milk or cream over all.

Place the other piecrust on top and cut attractive slits to release the steam.

Bake at 350°F for about 45 minutes, or until crust is browned. Allow to sit for at least 20 minutes before cutting, as there is a lot of delicious sauce that runs out otherwise.

To make the pie dough:

Put flour, salt, and butter in a food processor and pulse until it is like meal.

Add 5 tablespoons of ice water and pulse again, fairly aggressively. If it doesn't come nicely into a ball, add the last tablespoon of water. Chill for at least an hour, and roll out.

Nantucket Scallop Chowder with Homemade Oyster Crackers

Unadulterated. That's how most consumers of the beloved Nantucket Bay Scallop want their pearly mollusks. This chowder comes close. Fresh organic milk (local milk would be ideal) is warmed to piping hot. The scallops are seared at a high temperature very quickly, just to declare their browned nuttiness. The scallops are then laid directly into each serving bowl, and doused in steaming hot milk. A teaspoon of herb butter slips in to deliver brightness, and a homemade cracker is floated across. Just adulterated enough.

SERVES 4

For the herbed butter:

2 tablespoons softened unsalted butter

½ cup chopped fresh parsley

2 teaspoons red pepper flakes

1 teaspoon finely chopped lemon peel

2 teaspoons sea salt

For the chowder:

1 quart organic whole milk

1 pound Nantucket bay scallops (or sea scallops)

2 teaspoons butter

2 teaspoons grape seed oil, or other oil with a high smoke point

Salt and pepper to taste

Homemade Oyster Crackers (recipe follows)

To make the herbed butter:

Put butter, parsley, red pepper flakes, lemon peel, and sea salt in a small food processor, or mash well by hand, until thoroughly blended into a paste.

Divide butter into 4 portions, and, with wet hands, roll each portion into a ball. Chill well.

To make the chowder:

Heat milk in a saucepan to piping hot, then reduce the temperature to low while you prepare the scallops. You can keep a lid askew on the pot, but do not cover it completely or condensation will cool the milk. Warm 4 bowls in the oven.

Remove the small side muscle from the scallops, rinse with cold water and thoroughly pat dry.

In a skillet large enough to hold all the scallops, or 2 medium skillets, over high heat, combine butter and oil.

Season the scallops with salt and pepper. Once the oil and butter begin to smoke, gently add the scallops, making sure they are not touching each other. Sear for 2 minutes, and then turn the scallops. Let cook for 1 more minute, depending on the size of the scallops. They should be just turning opaque, but the second side does not have to brown.

With the well-browned side up, remove scallops to the 4 bowls, dividing them evenly.

Check that the milk is hot, and pour it gently around the scallops. Drop an herb butter ball into each soup, and float a homemade oyster cracker. Serve immediately.

Homemade Oyster Crackers

MAKES 15 2-INCH CRACKERS

2 cups flour

1 tablespoon baking powder

1 teaspoon sea salt

½ cup (1 stick) chilled unsalted butter, cut in pieces

½ cup whole milk

Coarse salt for garnish

Preheat oven to 350°F. Line a baking sheet with parchment paper.

In a food processor, blend together the flour, baking powder, and sea salt. Add butter and blend to crumbly. Add milk, and blend until the dough forms a ball.

Roll out dough to just barely ½ inch thick. Cut into 2-inch circles, or shape of choice. Sprinkle generously with coarse salt. Bake until golden brown, about 20 minutes.

Simple Broiled Nantucket Scallops

Almost everyone agrees that these winter pearls require the lightest of touches. This recipe—a few fresh bread crumbs, a little butter, some parsley and lemon—is just enough.

SERVES 4 AS AN ENTREE, 6 AS AN APPETIZER

1½ pounds bay scallops

1 cup milk

1½ cups fresh bread crumbs

Salt and freshly ground pepper to taste

¼ cup (½ stick) plus 2 tablespoons,
    melted and divided

Juice from ½ lemon

½ cup chopped parsley

Lemon wedges

Carefully rinse scallops, and pat very dry with paper towels.

Set up 1 shallow bowl with the milk and 1 shallow dish for the bread crumbs.

Dip the scallops in the milk, and roll them in the bread crumbs.

Arrange breaded scallops on a jelly roll pan or shallow clay casserole dish. The pan should have sides, and allow the scallops to be in one layer.

Sprinkle scallops with salt and pepper to taste, and drizzle with ¼ cup melted butter.

Broil 4–5 inches from the heating unit for 5–7 minutes, or until the bread crumbs are golden brown. Do not overcook.

Remove from oven. Arrange on a platter or on individual plates. Drizzle with 2 tablespoons melted butter and squeeze lemon over all. Garnish with chopped parsley and lemon wedges.

Scalloped Scallops

Here is another very basic, if not classic, way to prepare scallops. Almost every cookbook from New Bedford to Newburyport includes a variation of this in the shellfish chapter, and for good reason. With thick, buttery crumbs and hot, sweet scallops—easily baked in a casserole—the recipe is an almost flawless assignment, acceptable preparation for both the delicate Nantucket scallop or the beefy sea scallop. It can be made for family or guests, with no last-minute policing of bread crumbs browning beneath the broiler. This particular edition was found hand-typed on a loose piece of paper in the Nantucket Historical Society.

SERVES 4

1 pound scallops

1½ cups crumbled unsalted saltines

¾ cup (1½ sticks) butter, melted

1 cup whole milk or half and half

½ teaspoon salt

Freshly ground pepper to taste

4 lemon wedges to garnish

½ cup chopped parsley to garnish

Preheat oven to 350°F. Butter well an 8 x 11-inch ceramic or glass baking dish.

Carefully rinse scallops, and remove the tough piece of muscle on the side.

Sprinkle ⅓ of the crumbs on the bottom of the dish. Top with half the scallops.

Sprinkle second ⅓ of the crumbs on top of the scallops. Put second half of scallops on top of that. Top with last of crumbs.

Pour melted butter over the whole dish. Pour in milk. Sprinkle all with salt and pepper.

Bake for 25–30 minutes, or until the dish is golden brown and bubbling hot.

Serve immediately with lemon and parsley.

Quince Honey

The ancient Greeks layered cooked quinces with honey in clay vessels for a year; the result was a treasured condiment, actually the nascence of marmalade. This recipe, found in the Nantucket Historical Association, proves the Greeks' recipe has staying power. It is luxuriously perfumed. Toast becomes dessert buttered with quince honey. My favorite way to have this is with fresh ricotta cheese, perhaps from Mermaid Farm on Martha's Vineyard, for breakfast.

MAKES 2 CUPS

3 large quinces, about 1½ pounds, peeled and
   cored, peels and cores reserved

Lemon juice

1 cup water

6 cups sugar

Put the quince flesh through a food processor fitted with a steel shredding blade, or grate by hand. Put all the quince shreds into a bowl, and toss with lemon juice to prevent discoloring.

In a large saucepan simmer the peels and cores in the water for 30 minutes to color the water. Strain the solids out.

Return the water to the saucepan, and add sugar. Cook until all the sugar is dissolved. Add the quinces, and cook for 15–20 minutes. Turn into sterilized glass jars, and cool. Jars will keep indefinitely in the refrigerator. If storing on the shelf, process as for jams.

When cool, this preserve is the consistency of honey.

Quince, Apple, and Cranberry Jelly

Pure Nantucket in a jelly jar, that's what this recipe is. Quinces, apples, and cranberries combine to make a clear jelly more floral than French perfume, as pink as a Nantucket rose.

Quinces have magical properties, as the eighteenth-century Nantucketers who transported the fruit trees here from England could attest. The original source of all marmalade, quinces are the pectin Superman of the botanical world; their natural gelling properties have been exploited since the ancient Greeks left an urn of sliced quinces unopened for a year, and discovered a beautiful, thick, magically "jellied" confection. Quince peels and cores included in the cooking make the finished result a delicate blushing pink. Set a jar of this aromatic jelly in your windowsill and imagine a hedge of Nantucket roses.

FILLS APPROXIMATELY 8–12 8-OUNCE JELLY JARS

3 pounds quinces, or about 6 quinces, cut in quarters, NOT cored

4 pounds apples, or about 8 apples, cored and quartered

1 pint cranberries, washed well

About 8 cups sugar (The amount will depend on how much juice you get from your fruit; see instructions)

Place all the fruit in a large stockpot. Just barely cover with cold water. Simmer until all the fruit is very soft, 1–1½ hours. (The quinces will take a while.)

Put softened fruit in a suspended jelly bag, or create a cheesecloth bag, so that, tied to a cupboard handle or a doorknob, the fruit drips over night into a large pot, collecting all the beautiful, rose-colored juices. You can also lay a cheesecloth across a colander, and strain the juices that way.

When all the juice is out, and the fruit is mostly dry, measure the amount of juice you have. You will later add ¾ cup sugar to every 1 cup juice.

In the meantime, pour strained juice into a clean pot, and bring to a simmer. Cook for 20 minutes, occasionally skimming off scum that rises to the top.

After 20 minutes, add sugar gradually. Continue to boil until the jelly coats a spoon thickly, or until a candy thermometer inserted reads 220°F.

Pour into sterilized jelly jars. If storing on the shelf process as for jams. Jelly will keep indefinitely in the refrigerator as is.

NANTUCKET QUINCE

According to Alan Davidson in *The Oxford Companion to Food*, the first quince fell from a branch somewhere in the Caucacus. This chunk of land where Europe ends and Asia begins is considered to be one of thirty-four biodiversity hotspots on Earth. A few thousand years later, after traveling to Crete, Spain, Portugal, and England, a quince fell from a tree on Nantucket, maybe in Sconset.

A few treasured quince trees still stand on Nantucket. If you are lucky enough to know a quince tree there, or anywhere, pick some. Even gather "drops," just wash them well. Don't be afraid if you think the fruit is too gnarly and crooked; sometimes the old, untended varieties, once cut up, make the sweetest, thickest jams.

If you have no quince tree, but are curious, the produce section of many grocery stores often stock a small section of quince in the autumn. If not, ask the produce manager to order them; September through even late November quince are easily sourced in the United States. Asian markets will also stock quince.

Maybe the best solution of all is to plant your own tree. Quince trees grow to no more than eight feet, and boast fragrant pale-pink blossoms in the spring, an iconic vision with narcissus and grape hyacinths ruffling around its narrow trunk. Quince are the ideal "small garden" fruit tree. In the autumn, cooked quince rival the best apple in the kitchen, but, if nothing else, a simple bowl of whole quince in a bowl on your counter will perfume your room enough for you to always be grateful for that little tree.

"Trees of Antiquity," a supplier of heirloom fruit trees, are a good source for quince trees.

Pickled Quince Salad with Blue Cheese and Walnuts

Before the nineteenth century, from Gloucester to Westport, quinces appear in old cookbooks more frequently than apples. These pickled quinces are beautiful and versatile; serve them on their own beside chicken or meats. In this salad, they make spice-trade memories tossed with blue cheese and walnuts on Bibb lettuce.

Again, the floral quince perfume is unique, but quinces also have the amenable quality of preserving the flavors around them and remaining firm when poached.

SERVES 4

For the syrup:

1¾ cups water

1½ cups sugar

12 black peppercorns

2 bay leaves

6 strips orange peel

1 cup red wine

3–4 medium quinces, about 2 pounds

Lemon juice

For the salad dressing:

¼ cup sherry vinegar

¼ cup reserved quince syrup, strained and bay
    leaves removed

2 teaspoons coarse ground mustard

½ cup olive oil

Salt and pepper to taste

For the salad:

3 cups large leafy Bibb lettuce

4 ounces soft blue cheese, or Shy Brothers
    Lavender Bud Hannahbells Thimble Cheese

½ cup chopped walnuts, lightly toasted

To make the syrup:

Preheat oven to 300°F.

In a medium dutch oven or lidded saucepan put water, sugar, peppercorns, bay leaves, orange peel, and red wine, and simmer just until sugar dissolves. Set aside.

Peel quinces, reserving all peels. Brush quince flesh with lemon to prevent browning. Cut quinces into quarters, and remove the core from each section. Reserve the cores, too; peels and cores contribute a beautiful color.

Put cores and peels into syrup, and simmer on top of the stove for 15 minutes. Strain out cores and peels, and add quartered fruit to syrup. Cover the pan, and bake for 2 hours. The quince should be tender and a beautiful rosy pink. Cool in syrup. Pickled quince (in syrup) can be stored in sterilized jars in the refrigerator for up to 6 weeks.

To make the salad dressing:

Stir together vinegar, quince syrup, mustard, olive oil, salt, and pepper.

To make the salad:

Toss the lettuce in 2 tablespoons of dressing, or to taste. Divide the leaves among 4 plates. Arrange quinces upon the lettuces. Add cheese, and toss walnuts over all.

Nantucket Quince Pudding

Chopped quince folded into a custard and baked, this velvety pudding is another way to understand quince. You will learn that its perfume is not an apple or a pear but a floral essence of its own. This pudding has the soft, light character of a zabaione, which makes an ethereal cover for the warm chopped fruit.

SERVES 6

6 medium quinces

¼ cup lemon juice

1½ cups sugar, divided

5 egg yolks

1 cup cream

3 egg whites, beaten stiff

Preheat oven to 350°F.

Wash quinces and peel. Cut in quarters, remove seeds, and chop. Toss in lemon juice to prevent from browning.

Put chopped quince in a medium saucepan with ½ cup sugar. Bring to a simmer and cook for 5 minutes, or until tender, but be careful not to overcook; you want the fruit to still have "tooth." Allow to cool.

In a mixer, beat egg yolks. Add remaining sugar and cream. When well blended, fold in stiffly beaten egg whites. Then fold in the quince.

Pour into a shallow 1.5 quart buttered dish (clay or glass) and bake for 25 minutes, or until firm and lightly browned on top.

CHAPTER FOUR

Cape Cod

Drive through the sweeping arch of either the Sagamore Bridge or Bourne Bridge, and set your feet on the sandy soil of Cape Cod, where thickets of beach plums and bayberry still grow, where cranberries first went from wild to domesticated, where the herring run still lures young Wampanoag boys with fishing poles.

Each town is a little different and a little the same. In Sagamore, a strong Italian community still takes scissors to tender dandelion greens for that first taste of spring salad. In Sandwich, the wheel of the Dexter Grist Mill turns while behind it swans paddle with dull interest through the glassy surface of Shawme Pond. The spire of the Christopher Wren Church points to the heavens across the street; time stands still.

Down Route 6A in East Sandwich, the row of gas burners in the cornflower-blue Greenbriar kitchen fill the room with the sweet clove fragrance of simmering Piccalilli, or maybe Miss Blake's Spiced Pear Jam. In the autumn the mincemeat preparation will begin; at one time there was a long waiting list for a treasured jar of Miss Blake's mincemeat. Her home and commercial jam kitchen are museums and a nature center now, but Mizue, once Miss Blake's assistant, is still aproned in the sun-filled kitchen creating the best Greenbriar preserves and pickles.

West Barnstable is a Finnish community settled in the late nineteenth century. Able, athletic men who loved a day of brush clearing or ditch-digging, the Finns were warmly welcomed into the nascent cranberry business, which in 1890 needed acres of land cleared and dug for more commercial growing.

The West Barnstable Finns brought their affection for fruits and berries to Cape Cod, where local blueberries and cranberries made them very happy. Jewel-like fruit soups find their way to Finnish tables in West Barnstable all year round. They are served as a light lunch, a first course, or as dessert. They are served warm and cold. They are served alone for a light, refreshing, and healthful dish, and they are served by the tablespoon luxuriantly over a bowl of rice pudding.

Ojala Farms is closed now, but many Cape Codders fondly remember the tiny wood-framed building with two sunny windows facing Route 6A and the white-washed simple interior. They remember the homemade pies, the chicken pies, the Finnish spice bread, the cucumber salad, and the fruit soup. A treasured restaurant run by a West Barnstable Finnish family, Ojala Farms offered beautiful home-cooking Finnish–Cape Cod style.

Martha Ojala came to West Barnstable from Finland when she was ten years old. Initially Martha and her family simply sold chicken, eggs, and vegetables off their West Barnstable farm. Wealthy families in Hyannis would send their chauffeur over to shop for produce. Alice Sorvo, Martha's daughter, remembers many a chauffeur sitting in the kitchen shelling lima beans, because the household had requested he return without pods.

Martha began the restaurant in the 1950s, serving lunch and dinner in the early years. Martha's son Arne said that in the evening the gravel space for cars in front filled with Cadillacs from Osterville and Hyannis, the best review a restaurant can receive long before Yelp.

While Martha prepared Massachusetts classics such as lobster bisque and clam chowder, Finnish simplicity was the main event in the dining room, which boasted six tables and a fireplace. (Martha had died in 1999, at almost one hundred years old). Finnish scalloped potatoes were served everyday at Ojala Farms, as were cabbage rolls filled with ground beef. On every plate was always a cranberry, orange, and apple conserve, a Finnish fruit preserve interpreted with Cape Cod ingredients.

Martha would spend the mornings in the farm's bakeshop and arrived at the tiny restaurant down the hill on the property just before lunch,

ready to start cooking. Her daughter would have already turned the sign on the door to "open." Alice tells the story of a man from Sandwich named Mr. Leonard who came for lunch every day and sat at the window. If he arrived early, before Martha. Alice would ask him if he would like her to begin his lunch for him. He would always answer politely, "No, thank you, I'll wait for the atmosphere."

In Mashpee, a wooded land laced with salt water estuaries and fresh water ponds, the Wampanoag Tribe struggles with its modern identity, but Earl Mills, Chief of the Mashpee Wampanoags, still cherishes the Cape's natural bounty. Mills has been making beautiful meals out of the Cape's wealth of herring, mussels, venison, cranberries, and so much more long before "local" was a trend. He grew up seeing wild ducks on a pond in the morning, or eels darkening the bay, and then later that day seeing those ingredients in a family dinner that smelled so good the kids begged to be served. If anyone understands the honest Cape Cod terroir, it is Earl Mills, Chief Flying Eagle.

Chief Flying Eagle, Mills's Native American name, was also owner of one of Cape Cod's most popular restaurants, The Flume, in which Mills created his treasured family recipes. Open for twenty-seven years, The Flume closed its doors in 2004. Customers once drove great distances for Flume meals, compelled by their devotion to dishes like The Flume Indian Pudding, prepared slowly in a double boiler to a warm, silken custard. To many, there has never been another Indian Pudding. Flume patrons were equally devoted to Mills's corn chowder, his succotash, and his venison stew. Mills's recipes are part native and part elegant Cape Cod cooking, prepared with profound reverence for the ingredients, along with good sense: Don't be afraid

to add a little sugar to a dish with fresh corn. Always start a muscular cut of meat like venison in a cold pan, or the heat will cause the muscles to seize up and toughen.

In Chatham, at the elbow of the Cape's crooked arm, young commercial fishermen and -women have started a small revolution, and the world is paying attention. Fishing sustainable species with sustainable methods older than pilgrims—hooks and lines—the Cape Cod Commercial Fisherman's Alliance is putting skate and dogfish in fish markets and teaching us to love the white, delicate meat on these not-so-familiar species.

In Provincetown, the party is happening. The artists of the Provincetown Fine Arts Workshop and the gay community happily whoop it up all summer; the streets of Provincetown on an August day groan with visitors. The restaurants and shops, more Greenwich Village than end of the world (which Provincetown can feel like on a winter afternoon) seem to be always just managing a high-tide of guests. Through it all, one trips over shards of the Portuguese community who came here a hundred years ago to go fishing. Almost everyone in Provincetown still toasts sweet Portuguese Sweet Bread for breakfast; almost every restaurant serves a Portuguese Kale Soup.

Of course, Falmouth, Hyannis, Barnstable, Dennis, Yarmouth, Truro, and Wellfleet are all pieces of the Cape Cod map. Each town is distinct, and yet they all share sandy beaches, some rippling with beach grass–tufted dunes. They share cranberry bogs and high-bush blueberries. They share shellfish and fishing; each of these towns still has at least a few commercial boats parked at a dock. In Sandwich they unload along the Cape Cod Canal; in West Barnstable they shelter in the harbor. In Provincetown, one can see their tangled rigging from the nightclubs lining Main Street.

Cape Cod Index

Edward Gorey's Eggnog Muffins

Edward Gorey, the author and illustrator of cryptic Edwardian cartoons that celebrate obscure vocabulary words and Gothic if not marginal humor, died in 2000. He never missed a performance of the New York City Ballet. If he wasn't wearing fur coats and high-top sneakers, he was drawing men stealthily approaching Victorian carriages wearing fur coats and high-top sneakers. He loved bats and cats. He attended Harvard, and roomed there with the poet Frank O'Hara. Upon graduation Gorey began a poetry club with two of America's great poets, Donald Hall and John Ashbery. He was a genius, an obdurate idiosyncratic, and lived with many cats in Yarmouth, on Cape Cod.

To find Edward Gorey's Eggnog Muffin recipe is, for the large cult that has risen up around this gentle man with almost unidentifiable tastes (along with George Balanchine and Balthus, Edward Gorey unashamedly enjoyed the television series *Petticoat Junction* and *Cheers*) an emotional goldmine. "E" is for eggnog, which makes muffins mellifluous.

MAKES 24 SMALL OR 12 LARGE MUFFINS

2 cups flour

⅔ cups sugar

1 tablespoon baking powder

½ teaspoon salt

¾ cup eggnog

½ cup rum

5 tablespoons butter, melted

1 egg, beaten

½ teaspoon nutmeg

Preheat oven to 400°F. Grease muffin tins or line with paper liners.

In a large bowl, combine flour, sugar, baking powder, and salt.

Stir in eggnog, rum, butter, egg, and nutmeg.

Spoon into muffin tins. Bake for 20 minutes, or until a tester inserted comes out clean.

Raised Donuts "Spring Hill"

Turn onto Spring Hill Road in East Sandwich and you turn into another century. For stretches, Spring Hill Road tunnels through shady privet and lilac thickets; the town seems to have forgotten to widen it for more than passing carriages. Spring Hill Road weaves along the eastern side of Spring Hill Creek, past modest cranberry bogs and silver-shingled cottages where yards flare with buttery yellow daffodils every spring.

Maybe it's the salt air off the tidal marsh meeting the cool air rising from the actual spring for which the road is named, but old Cape Cod seems to "spring" eternal here.

Who could not want to make Raised Donuts "Spring Hill," a recipe discovered in an old Cape Cod cookbook, circa 1930?

Heaven, when you get there, may smell like fresh donuts, spiced with cinnamon and nutmeg, cooling in a warm Spring Hill breeze.

MAKES ABOUT 24 DONUTS

1¼ cups milk, scalded

1 teaspoon salt

1 cup sugar

2 tablespoons butter, melted

1 package yeast

¼ cup warm water

1½ cups, plus 2 cups flour, divided

1 egg

¼ teaspoon nutmeg

½ teaspoon cinnamon

About 2 quarts of oil for frying

Mix together milk, salt, sugar, and butter.

In a small bowl, proof yeast in warm water for 10 minutes.

Add yeast to milk with 1½ cups flour. Beat well, and let rise for an hour.

Add the egg, spices, and remaining 2 cups flour, and beat well. Let rise again for an hour.

Push down, and roll dough out to a ½-inch thickness. Cut with a donut-shaped cutter, and spread shapes out on a board to rise for 1 more hour. (If you don't have a donut-shaped cutter, use a pickle jar for the large hole, and a water bottle top for the inner smaller circle.)

Heat a cast-iron dutch oven or fryer with 2 inches of vegetable oil to between 360°F and 375°F.

Fry donuts, turning once, for about 1 minute per side, until golden. You will have to carefully watch the temperature of the oil (a thermometer is important here) and the color of the donuts as they fry. The oil will cool when the batter is added, so you will have to raise the temperature. But don't let it get too hot or the donuts will burn without cooking through. It's a dance! Drain donuts on paper towels. Enjoy warm.

Spiced Buttermilk

From a collection of old Sandwich recipes, this drink recipe offers something like a vintage smoothie, borrowing from the Finnish spice box. Serve it in the morning with a Spring Hill Raised Donut or a Nantucket Wonder. Add a jigger of rum in the evening and serve it with an Aquinnah Salad.

SERVES 2–4

4 cups fresh buttermilk

½ teaspoon vanilla

½ teaspoon allspice

2 tablespoons honey

¼ teaspoon ground cinnamon

½ teaspoon ground cardamom

2 ice cubes

Grated fresh nutmeg

In a blender, mix all ingredients except nutmeg together until frothy. Serve immediately with grated nutmeg on top.

SANDWICH GRISTMILL

Millers—the men who ran gristmills—were a grumpy bunch, so say the tour guides at The Dexter Grist Mill in Sandwich, Massachusetts, where organic corn is ground between three-hundred-year-old machinery, and scooped into cotton bags.

Housewives two hundred years ago would have been embarrassed to have this coarse, irregular grind on their shelves, but, living in a homogenized, pasteurized, uniform century in which things always pour freely and evenly, it's easy to appreciate this character-heavy stuff that results when cracking corn between two seven-hundred-pound stones turned by a wheel powered by the rushing waters of Shawme Pond.

Millers were grumpy, as mentioned, and women weren't allowed at mills. The pretty colonial home across the street from the Dexter Grist Mill was a tavern in 1693, the reasonable antidote to the long, hot walk to the mill, but a culture not welcome to wives and daughters.

The whole thing about grinding corn is that is has to be dry—really, really dry—or else those seven-hundred-pound wheels get all stuck with yucky, sticky mushed corn kernels. It's not like taking apart a Cuisinart, although a seventeenth-century gristmill has almost as many moving parts. Imagine a hot September day, those stones turning, all that friction, all that dry corn, and everything starts warming up. The expression "keep your nose to the grindstone" is about paying attention to a spark, or combustible moment, because in one turned nose your gristmill might be nothing more than a memory memorialized in some painter's landscape. Wood and corn can easily be one big lit match. Porous millstones, by the way, eased the fear of fires in the eighteenth century, as they helped to dissipate the heat produced during grinding.

Dried corn, sealed in nature's perfect time capsule, the kernel, can survive free of mold or decay indefinitely—so long as it's not cracked or damaged. Think of Peruvian mummies curled in their tombs clutching woven bags that hold symbolically precious kernels of corn. Corn has no gluten, so partnered with yeast it's never chartered any great gastronomical territory. It does best when heat makes it pop or toast.

This local cornmeal—still filled with natural oils, so it needs to be refrigerated or frozen for long-keeping—should be polenta. Fresh, crumbling with corn integrity, this cornmeal—cooked in salted water and stirred occasionally for an hour—rivals anything from a bag in Northern Italy. If you drive to Sandwich, it's available at the mill itself, the Hoxie House, and various other town venues.

Ojala Farms Fruit Soup

Fruits and berries are a critical part of Finnish cuisine, and appear in both savory and sweet forms. Fruit soup in Finland is considered both a true soup, to be served either warm or cold as a light meal, or as a dessert. For the latter, it is served by itself or over rice pudding. It is pretty much heavenly when both rice pudding and fruit soup are warm, but it's also delicious when both are cool. I cannot choose. You could also lay a couple of tablespoons of Fruit Soup over a piece of toasted pound cake. Ojala Farms Fruit Soup is quite thick, much more like compote than soup. Keeping a jar in your refrigerator is like keeping a pot of gold.

SERVES 8

¾ cup dried apricots

¾ cup dried whole pitted prunes

¼ cup golden raisins

¼ cup currants

1 slice orange

6½ cups water

2 cardamom pods, crushed with the side of a knife

1 cinnamon stick

2 teaspoons lemon juice

1 tablespoon finely diced crystallized ginger (optional)

1 apple, peeled, cored, and cut into thin slices

2 tablespoons cornstarch

In a 3-quart pan, combine apricots, prunes, raisins, currants, orange, 6 cups water, cardamom pods, cinnamon, and lemon juice. Cover and bring to a boil. Remove from heat, and let sit for a ½ hour. Add ginger if using and apples; turn heat to medium, and simmer for 15 minutes. Stir occasionally to make sure fruit doesn't stick to bottom of pan. Add extra water if necessary.

Strain the fruit through a strainer to reserve the juice. Pour juice back in saucepan, and set aside the fruit.

Mix cornstarch with ½ cup cold water, and add to juice. Bring mixture to a simmer, and cook for 10–15 minutes, stirring occasionally.

Add fruit back to juice, and heat a little longer, but do not let it return to a boil.

Pour soup into a large bowl, and remove cinnamon stick. Chill well.

Serve alone, or over yogurt or rice pudding for breakfast, a light lunch, or dessert.

Kesakeitto

(Finnish Summer Soup)

This Finnish Summer Soup would have been served at many West Barnstable kitchen tables. A bouquet of jewel-like vegetables, this soup would make a beautiful dish for an Easter brunch.

Look for a variety of the best vegetables you can find. Be creative. Jerusalem artichokes chopped into thin rounds, celeriac in a tiny dice, broccoli cut into tiny florets, almost anything works. Keep only the tiny baby potatoes whole. The chopping and dicing takes a bit of time, but remember you only need about a ½ cup of each vegetable. It goes quicker than you would expect.

All the vegetables are cooked in boiling, salted water, beginning with the vegetables that take take the longest (perhaps the potatoes, use your judgment).

Half the deliciousness of this soup is the milk broth; look for a local dairy for the freshest milk.

SERVES 6–8

1 tablespoon sugar

2 tablespoons flour

2 teaspoons kosher salt, plus 1 tablespoon for the vegetables

4 cups organic whole milk, preferably local

8 cups of tiny, fresh vegetables (broccoli, green beans, cauliflower, new potatoes, zucchini, carrot, onion, asparagus tips, kohlrabi, beets, turnips, fennel, radishes, and especially peas)

½ pound hot-smoked salmon

Small radishes, thinly sliced

Fresh peas, or the tiny peas from inside 4–5 snap peas

Fresh dill, chopped

Fresh pepper, use white pepper if you want to retain the whiteness of the milk

In a large saucepan, stir together the sugar, flour and salt. Slowly at first, stirring to blend, add the milk. Whisk until mixture is smooth. Gently heat the milk, whisking it occasionally to keep the flour from cooking on the bottom of the pan. Do not let it boil.

In a separate large pot, bring 6 cups salted water to a boil.

Meanwhile, prep the vegetables. Peel potatoes, carrots, beets, and turnips to keep them tender. Cut all into roughly equivalent size. Chop green beans, zucchini, kohlrabi, turnips and beets into a tiny dice. Break cauliflower and broccoli into tiny florets.

When the water boils, drop in the vegetables that will take the longest to cook (potatoes, carrots, turnips, parsnips, etc.). Cook for 1–2 minutes, and then add the lighter vegetables (radishes, peas, broccoli, etc.). Remove the vegetables with a slotted spoon or sieve, and distribute them evenly into heated bowls. Pour the hot milk over the vegetables but not to cover. Allow vegetables to rise attractively in a mound out of the milk.

Crumble the smoked salmon over the top, and garnish with radish, peas, and dill. Dust pepper over all, and serve immediately.

West Barnstable Finnish Blueberry Soup

This blueberry soup works beautifully with frozen wild blueberries. Try it warm; try it cold; try it with a dollop of yogurt, or try it with whipped cream. Definitely make a batch of rice pudding and try blueberry soup warm on top. The words "soup" and "pudding" are much too humble for this very refined combination of textures and flavors.

SERVES 4 AS SOUP, OR 6 IF SERVED OVER RICE PUDDING

2 cups water

2 cups blueberries

3 tablespoons sugar

¼ teaspoon mace

1 stick cinnamon

½ teaspoon salt

3 tablespoons arrowroot (or cornstarch)

3 tablespoons cold water

¼ cup port

yogurt or whipped cream

Bring water to a boil in a saucepan and add blueberries, sugar, mace, cinnamon, and salt.

Add arrowroot (or cornstarch) to cold water, and mix into a smooth paste.

When the berries have cooked about 10 minutes, slowly stir the arrowroot mixture into the boiling soup. Cook 2 minutes more, or until thick. Add port. Remove the cinnamon stick.

Serve warm as is, or chilled, with a dollop of yogurt or whipped cream on top. Again, this is also delicious served over warm rice pudding.

Joululimppu

(Swedish Limpa Bread)

Every morning before dawn, Martha E. Ojala arose to bake the Ojala Farms bread—nisu, oatmeal, and joululimppu. Even though it was a Christmas bread, guests begged year-round for the fragrant rye loaf spiced with fennel and anise.

Nothing sounds better in the dark snowy days before Christmas on Cape Cod than a warm, dark loaf fresh from the oven, filling the kitchen with the smells of anise and caraway. Joululimppu has a molasses glaze that makes it distinctively shiny and particularly beautiful. But you don't have to wait for Christmas; you can be like Martha and make it all year-round.

MAKES 2 LOAVES

1 teaspoon ground fennel

1 tablespoon caraway seeds

¾ teaspoon powdered anise seeds

½ cup dark unsulfured molasses

4 cups rye flour

2 teaspoons salt

1 package active dry yeast

¼ cup, plus 1 tablespoon warm water, divided

4–5 cups white flour

1 tablespoon molasses

In a medium saucepan, bring 3½ cups water to a boil. Add spices and simmer 5 minutes to infuse water.

In a large mixing bowl, mix 1½ cups of the boiling water with the molasses and 1 cup rye flour. Beat well. Let stand for 30 minutes.

Then add another 1 cup rye flour and another 1½ cups boiling water, and beat well. Let stand again, for 1 hour this time.

Add remaining ½ cup boiling water, and beat well. Cool until mixture is lukewarm.

Stir in the salt. Dissolve the yeast in ¼ cup warm water, and add to the flour mixture. Slowly add the remaining 2 cups rye flour, and the white flour, beating well after each addition. When the dough is stiff, let it rest in the bowl for 15 minutes.

Turn onto a floured board and knead until smooth. Place in a lightly buttered bowl. Turn the dough over to butter the top of it. Cover with a cloth towel, and let rise in a warm place until doubled in bulk, 1–3 hours.

Turn out again onto a lightly floured board. Divide the dough in half and shape each portion into a ball, rolling it to a peak on one side. It should be shaped like a huge Hershey's Kiss. Place each loaf, flat side down, on a greased baking sheet. With your thumb, punch the peak down into the loaf as far as possible. Let rise again until not quite doubled.

Preheat oven to 375°F. Bake loaves for 45–50 minutes, or until the loaves sound hollow when tapped.

While the dough is baking, mix the molasses and 1 tablespoon warm water together to form a glaze. Pour over loaves when cooked and still hot. Let cool on wire racks.

Earl Mills's Succotash

There is poetry in the fact that a Wampanoag chief offers us the best modern interpretation of succotash, certainly a variation on the corn-and-vegetable Wampanoag stew called sobaheg. The natives are still teaching us how best to prepare American dishes, no matter how many miles the recipe has seen.

Mills uses corn from the cob, briefly adding the cobs themselves into the mix for flavor, but he promises that Del Monte canned niblets are delicious, too. (He firmly recommends Del Monte.)

SERVES 6

4 stalks celery, chopped fine

1 medium onion, minced

3 tablespoons butter

3–4 cups chicken broth (or water)

2 cups frozen lima beans

3–4 cups corn (fresh or canned)

Salt and pepper to taste

In a large saucepan, sauté the celery and onion in 3 tablespoons butter. Add the cobs (if you have them) to the sautéed celery and onions.

Add chicken stock or water to the saucepan, and let simmer for 5 minutes. Add lima beans, and let simmer until beans are tender. If using fresh corn from the cob, add it with the lima beans. If using canned corn, add just before the lima beans are done. (You may want to add a pinch of sugar if using canned corn.)

Remove cobs before serving. Add salt and pepper to taste. Serve warm or at room temperature, but this is best made no more than 1 hour before serving.

Earl Mills's Venison Stew

Earl Mills insists that no Cape Cod recipe collection could be serious without venison. Well into the last century, so rich was the game life on the peninsula that hunting was as Cape Cod an activity as clamming and fishing. Many Wampanoag and Cape Codders survived hard times, grateful not just for the salt cod soaking in their sink but for a freezer full of deer meat, either their own shot or that of a generous neighbor. This is Mills's classic venison stew.

SERVES 4-6

4 pounds venison stew meat, cut into 1–2-inch chunks

1 cup red wine

Freshly ground black pepper

2 bay leaves, divided

2 cups chopped onions

2 tablespoons olive oil, divided

2 teaspoons salt

6 cups beef stock

2 cups julienned carrots

2 cups parsnips or turnips

1½ cups diced celery

4 medium potatoes (about 1 pound) peeled and cut into ¾-inch chunks

2 tablespoons Worcestershire Sauce or good quality soy sauce

1 tablespoon red wine vinegar

Chopped fresh parsley

Marinate venison by putting it in a bowl or heavy-duty plastic bag with the red wine, ground pepper, and 1 bay leaf. Marinate for 2–24 hours. When ready to prepare the stew, remove the meat and reserve the marinade.

Using a large stockpot, sauté onions in 1 tablespoon olive oil until brown. Remove onions from pan, and let pan cool.

When the pan is cold, add the remaining tablespoon of olive oil and as much venison to not crowd the pan. Heat the pan to medium high. (Mills says that a tough meat like venison should always be started in a cold pan, discouraging the meat from contracting and thus toughening even more when suddenly introduced to heat.) This can also be done in 2 pans. Brown the meat on all sides.

When the meat is browned, return it all to the large stock pot, along with the reserved marinade and the second bay leaf. Return onions to the pan with the salt and beef stock. Simmer uncovered for 1 hour.

Add carrots, parsnips or turnips, celery, and potatoes, and simmer uncovered for another hour. The vegetables should all be cooked, and some may be beginning to fall apart. Stir in the Worcestershire Sauce or soy and the red wine vinegar. Simmer 5 more minutes. Serve in warm bowls garnished with parsley. Broa, Portuguese Cornbread, would be delicious with Earl Mills's Venison Stew.

EARL MILLS, CHIEF FLYING EAGLE

The many facets of Wampanoag Chief Flying Eagle, Earl H. Mills Sr., sparkle like sun off the flashing Mashpee herring run in April.

One side of Mills, now eighty-five, is the simple kid who grew up in the town of Mashpee on Cape Cod at a time when mayflowers in the woods signaled spring's start, and meant money in kids' pockets when they sold the small fragrant bouquets for fifteen cents by the side of the road. He talks about this in both his cookbook, *The Cape Cod Wampanoag Cookbook*, and in his memoir, *Son of Mashpee: Reflections of Chief Flying Eagle, a Wampanoag.*

It was a time when a morning in the streams and ponds meant trout, smallmouth bass, yellow perch, and pickerel for dinner. Cape Cod herring were corned or marinated; its roe was sautéed in bacon fat and served with parslied potatoes and creamed corn. (Today only the Wampanoag are allowed to fish for herring.) Mills's father knew it was time to smoke the herring by the arrival of the sweet fern in the woods.

Scallop season came in the fall with cranberry picking; young Mills's hands would be cut and bleeding after an afternoon of shucking the day's harvest with friends, although camaraderie and ceviche sampling came with that shucking. "The Scallop Man" passed by every night during the season to collect that day's harvest, a ten-bushel non-commercial limit. Mills says that in those days—even when hand harvesting—almost everyone got his or her limit.

"From the time we were eight or nine years old, my brother Elwood and I led fishing and hunting expeditions. Like our father, grandfather, and uncles before us, we prepared the boats, baited the hooks, rowed for the better part of the day, and cleaned the fish for the men who hired us as Indian guides. Our father taught us how to fly cast as well as to use a rod and reel, the clamming rake, and the eel spear. He taught us how to carry a gun safely and how to clean it. He taught us how to use an ax and a bucksaw and showed us the proper way to clean and cook game. He taught us skills exactly the way his own father had taught him."

The Cape Cod woods were flush with quail, partridge, rabbit, and deer.

There's the Cape Cod boy, and there is Mills, the high school star athlete, who went into the army after finishing high school, and from there went to Arnold College to play football and run track. He was later athletic director at Falmouth High.

In the army, Mills first honestly connected with his Wampanoag heritage. One night at Fort Dix, a group of soldiers was sitting around, and a young Iroquois from New York got up and started a tribal dance. A Chippewa from Montana joined him. It was that moment, far from Mashpee, that Mills first recognized his Indian background as something to be celebrated. When he returned to Mashpee fifteen months later, he went directly to the tribal leaders, and said, "Teach me."

In 1956, in the Old Indian Church at Mashpee, Reverend C.C. Wilson and Supreme Sachem Ousa Mequin—Yellow Feather—declared Mills "Chief Flying Eagle." "You receive the name—Flying Eagle— and, as such, you are in charge of all council meetings held by the Indians of Mashpee, Massachusetts, and none is above you in any office."

While respect for the land that nurtured his people, for his ancestors, and for the generations of family that lovingly surround him grace almost everything he does, Chief Flying Eagle is no grave

Indian. Possessing a meltingly lovely tenor, Mills slides in and out of show tunes when he cooks—"Shoefly Pie and Apple Pandowdy!—Makes your heart light and your tummy rowdy!"

Dance moves are necessary to explain exactly why lobster salad (with a little extra lemon) on a toasted hot dog bun express culinary perfection. (Cool sweet lobster; the acidity of lemon; warm crispiness of the outside of the roll; the soft, sweet inside of roll.) Dance moves—and the guy can dance—are just another verb in Mills's vocabulary.

"My name as a kid was Path Finder," Mills said, after a flurry of hip shimmies. "I never felt like I was a Flying Eagle," he admitted, those eyes sparkling like waters running with jumping herring.

In 1972 he opened his own restaurant, The Flume, "near the herring run" in Mashpee. From 1972 until 2004, The Flume was considered the best place to taste beautifully prepared, honest Cape Cod foods. Mills learned to cook from his parents, who made feathery fish cakes and a fish stew as complex and flavorful as a *soupe de poisson*. He also learned while working in the best Cape Cod kitchens: The Coonomesset Inn, Wimpy's, and The Pompenesset Inn. Far ahead of its time really, The Flume combined the best of traditional restaurant dining with supreme respect for local ingredients. Herring was on the menu, served with cucumbers.

Cooking for Mills is love, art, and heritage. "My ancestors are with me as I prepare or enjoy favorite foods. I never make fish cakes and beans without feeling my father is back in the kitchen with me."

Mills explains the fine points of breading shellfish: Never use anything finely ground with clams or oysters; a finely ground meal like flour will absorb too much liquid and turn quickly to mush, not giving the shellfish the delicious "crunch." Unsalted saltines are oysters' ideal breading.

Hold shucked clams in your hands, in a shallow bowl of a little water and the clam liquid. Gently feel for broken shells, cupping your hands in the liquid beneath the clams. Lift the clams, again with your hands, gently out of the liquid and into the breading.

"As you want to get the breading on, you want to get it right off again!" As soon as the clams land in the breading lift them out and shake them a bit to get any excess breading off. That would be the "too moist" breading that will again make the crust too mushy.

Baked or broiled scallops need only a dusting of bread crumbs on top because they will take a shorter time to cook. Oysters and clams need a thicker cover of bread crumbs, basically to protect them from the heat in the time it takes to cook them.

The "milk," the white liquid that bay scallops release when heated, has lots of flavor, and needs to be saved. Broiling the scallops is tricky, because that "milk" just runs right out.

Mills understands more about what grows, swims, and moves on Cape Cod than most naturalists. There isn't much that subdues that sparkle in Mills's eye; mention of the current Wampanoag issues is one.

"My tribe is my family; I deal only with my family now. Those people (current Wampanoag leaders) don't understand who we are or what we represent."

And yet, in *Son of Mashpee*, Chief Flying Eagle makes the plea, "In spite of the pain we had had to endure in the past, the Wampanoags ought to participate in shaping the future of this town, so that coming generations will inherit Mashpee with deep imprints of our heritage, our culture and our vision."

Mills also told me this: "I don't know anyone who has had as wonderful a life as I have."

Earl Mills's Indian Pudding

Almost everyone who dined at Earl Mills's restaurant, The Flume, in Mashpee left declaring the warm, creamy Indian Pudding the best ever. I was lucky enough to have lunch with Mills in Mashpee, and he shared his secrets: a tablespoon each of grapenuts cereal and tapioca, and an hour of stirring. The hour of stirring is worth this ethereal edition of the classic Massachusetts dessert; if you can find one, have a teenager do it. This Indian Pudding is as homespun as polenta but as suave as flan, ideal with vanilla ice cream melting into it.

Herman Melville in Moby Dick referred to "the invisible police officer of the Fates," a nice way to describe the events that made Earl Mills not only an admired restaurant owner and chef, but a revered Wampanoag Indian chief.

SERVES 6–8

4 cups milk

⅓ cup cornmeal

½ cup molasses

2 eggs

3 tablespoons brown sugar

1 tablespoon grape nuts

1 tablespoon tapioca

1 teaspoon salt

1½ tablespoons butter

1 teaspoon ground ginger

1 teaspoon vanilla

Combine all ingredients in a double boiler, and whip over simmering water.

Continue to cook over a low flame for an additional 1–1½ hours, whipping occasionally, until the pudding starts to thicken. Once it starts to thicken, remove the whip and allow the pudding to thicken naturally and form a skin or crust on top.

Serve warm with vanilla ice cream or whipped cream.

If serving later, refrigerate. Warm in a microwave or double boiler, adding more milk if necessary.

Salt Codfish Hash and Eggs

Cookbook author Harriet Adams, in the 1930s in Provincetown, felt she had to apologize for the simplicity of Cape Cod recipes. "We don't have exotic ingredients or beguiling methods," she lamented. She worried that Cape Cod recipes were not glamorous enough to invite someone to try one for the first time; and yet, she declared, using Cape Cod Salt Codfish Hash as an example, if you have ever tried these simple recipes with just a few plain ingredients (and salt cod sounds, on paper, like plain ingredient number one), you will want them again and again and again. It is the tasting of these pure combinations, done well, that makes a small club of people honestly crave a dish so Cape Cod as Salt Codfish Hash and Eggs. Harriet and I invite you to join the club.

This hash also makes a wonderful light summer dinner by omitting the bacon and eggs, and serving it with the vibrant Farm Stand Salsa tumbling on top of it.

SERVES 4 FOR A HEARTY BREAKFAST OR DINNER

1½ pounds salt codfish

¼ pound pancetta, diced in ¼-inch cubes

8 slices bacon

4 cups mashed potatoes

1 medium onion, grated

Freshly ground black pepper

8 poached eggs

Parsley for garnish

Soak the codfish for 24-36 hours, changing the water several times a day. In the last 6 hours, remove fish from water and soak it in milk.

When you're ready to prepare the dish, drain the codfish, cut it in 2-inch chunks, and put in a medium pot with cold water to cover. Bring to a boil and simmer for 10–12 minutes, or until the fish flakes easily. Drain, and set aside.

In a large skillet, fry the pancetta until light brown.

Remove from pan and set aside.

Wipe the pan clean, and add the bacon; cook until crispy. Set aside. Pour out half the bacon drippings from the skillet.

In a mixing bowl combine potatoes, flaked codfish, pancetta, onion, and black pepper.

Heat the skillet with the remaining bacon grease, and put the mixture in, shaping it into a large cake, about 1½ inches thick. Fry for 10–15 minutes, until the cake is well browned on the bottom. You can try to turn over the whole thing, or else divide it into four wedges, and flip each individually, returning to a complete disk. Brown the other side well.

Divide whole cake into eighths, and serve with bacon and poached or fried eggs. Garnish with chopped parsley.

Farm Stand Salsa

YIELDS 3 CUPS

2 cups halved cherry tomatoes, preferably a variety of colors

1 cup chopped parsley

½ cup diced onion

½ lemon, peel on, diced to ¼ inch

Freshly ground black pepper

Combine all ingredients in a small bowl at least 30 minutes before using. Let sit at room temperature to meld the flavors. Or make a day in advance and keep covered in the refrigerator.

Codfish Scrapple

Scrapple—the cornmeal, pork, and sage charcuterie that defines breakfast in the Pennsylvania Dutch countryside—has been re-outfitted in Massachusetts clothing by savvy Cape Codders. Here we introduce Codfish Scrapple.

The Pennsylvania Dutch version of scrapple is pork parts ground with spices and cornmeal; it is chilled to solid, sliced, fried, and served with fried, scrambled, or poached eggs—and maybe fried tomatoes. Main Line mothers to Maryland millionaires consider it the best way to begin a day.

And they are kind of right. The savory taste of fried cornmeal and spices complements a fresh egg like polenta does grilled sausages. Speaking of polenta, if the idea of scrapple scares you, imagine this as polenta con baccala. The Italian dish *baccala all vicentina* is not far from Codfish Scrapple. As is *baccala mantecato*—grilled polenta with dried cod mousse. Cornmeal and salt cod make sense. Even if you don't trust rural American country dishes, you should always trust Italy.

The velvety texture and richness of salted cod combined with that cornmeal and spice challenge the best fish cakes. These would also be delicious as a light meal served with Hingham Baked Tomatoes, a coastal Massachusetts dinner with so much character and basic good cooking that it rivals the best of Italy's *cucina povera*. But it would also be delicious smothered in sautéed shiitake mushrooms, spring fiddleheads, and a squeeze of lemon for a spring feast. Then again, I've served it with Finnish Beet Salad; the bronze scrapple beside the ruby-pink beets is a stunning, if not wonderful, taste combination (a small plate of these would be a wonderful first course).

MAKES ONE 9 x 5-INCH LOAF

1 pound salt cod

Milk for soaking

1 cup cornmeal

1 cup cold water

3 cups boiling water

1 onion, minced

½ teaspoon dry mustard

1 teaspoon poultry seasoning (dried sage, thyme, marjoram, rosemary, nutmeg, and black pepper)

1½ teaspoon salt

¼ teaspoon pepper

Rice flour or all-purpose flour for coating

1 tablespoon butter

2 tablespoons rice bran or grape seed oil for frying

Soak cod for 24–36 hours in cold water, refreshing the water several times a day. In the last six hours, remove the cod from the water and soak it in milk.

When ready to prepare the dish, put cod in a large saucepan covered with fresh cold water, and bring to a boil. Simmer for 10–12 minutes. Drain, and pull apart into flakes.

In a separate large saucepan, mix together cornmeal with cold water. Slowly pour in boiling water, bring to a boil, and simmer for 15 minutes, stirring frequently.

Add cod, onion, mustard, seasoning, salt, and pepper to the cornmeal, and blend together.

Pour into an oiled 9 x 5-inch bread pan, and chill until solid, 6 hours or longer.

To serve, remove scrapple from pan. WIth a serrated knife, cut into ½-inch slices. The loaf may be crumbly, but it is forgiving. If slices begin to fall apart, press them back together, and toss quickly into flour. This will hold the slices together better. (If your slices look more like "cakes" in the end, that is okay.) As mentioned, dip lightly in flour. Heat a skillet to medium high, and add butter and oil. Fry scrapple slices until toasted brown on both sides.

Serve warm beside eggs for breakfast, or as discussed above. For a very simple but beautiful appetizer, cover two slices in a quick sauté of red onion, colorful cherry tomatoes, and fresh parsley.

Fried Cod Squares with
Whipped Potato, Garlic, and Olive Oil Dressing

Discovered between the pages of a Provincetown cookbook, this Mediterranean-born recipe deserves a place on the coast of Massachusetts, with its long history of cod fisheries.

Greek skordalia, a garlic potato sauce bound with velvety olive oil, floats like a cloud upon a golden square of fried Massachusetts (or Icelandic or Norwegian, if that's what's available) cod. The combination of warm, crispy fried cod and garlicky whipped potatoes makes magic. Serve these right from the frying pan with guests standing in your kitchen, chilled wine very close.

SERVES 4 AS AN ENTREE, 6 AS AN APPETIZER

3 medium Yukon Gold potatoes, peeled and cut into 1-inch cubes (2 cups mashed)

1 tablespoon, plus 1 cup olive oil, divided

6 cloves garlic, minced

3 tablespoons lemon juice, divided

Salt

Freshly ground black pepper

1½ pounds fresh cod

Grape seed or safflower oil for frying

1 cup rice flour, approximately

Chopped parsley for garnish

Lemon wedges

Cook potatoes in salted water until very tender.

In a small sauté pan, warm 1 tablespoon olive oil. Add garlic, and soften very gently, but do not brown. This keeps the garlic in the dish from being too overwhelming. Set aside.

Drain potatoes, and mash with a fork. You want 2 cups mashed potatoes. Pour in remaining 1 cup olive oil, beating the potatoes at the same time. This could be done by hand or in a mixer. Mix in 2 tablespoons lemon juice and the garlic in oil, and taste for salt and pepper. Beat or whip until mixture

resembles a light mayonnaise, about 5 minutes. You can't do this too long. Set aside.

Meanwhile, rinse cod, and pat dry. Cut into strips approximately 3 inches long and 2 inches wide.

Heat a large skillet to medium high. Add grape seed oil to ½-inch deep, and heat to barely smoking.

Preheat oven to 300°F. Set wire baking racks on cookie sheets.

Put rice flour into a shallow bowl or glass baking dish. Roll fish pieces in flour, and put into the hot oil. Cook 3–4 minutes or until golden brown on each side. Remove to racks and keep warm in the oven until all the fish is cooked.

To serve, place a heavy dollop of garlic-potato sauce over each piece of warm cod. Sprinkle with the last tablespoon of lemon juice. If serving on a platter or dinner plates garnish with chopped parsley and lemon wedges.

Provincetown Sopa do Espirito Santo
(Soup of the Holy Ghost)

The French have pot-au-feu, the Italians have ragu alla bolognese, both the quintessence of soul-nourishing family cuisine.

It is difficult to imagine an honest American dinner that has the thorough dining pleasure of these European dishes while remaining a family meal. This may be it.

Kale soup probably arrived hundreds of years ago with Portuguese immigrants, but it has been on coastal Massachusetts soil so long that even the primmest cookbooks include it. Discovered in the bowsprit room of the Provincetown Library, this particular recipe lands in the Cape Cod chapter, but every town on the Massachusetts coastline—New Bedford, Gloucester, even Hingham—declares some version of kale soup its own.

This version is what the Portuguese call Sopa Do Espirito Santo, or Soup of the Holy Ghost. A homey, substantial soup, it is traditionally served at Portuguese and Azorean Holy Ghost Festivals, but it's basically a special occasion soup in Portuguese homes.

It is light and yet substantial with layers of flavor, yet time is the only taxing ingredient. (Time, not process; the soup is left almost completely alone to simmer for three-and-a-half hours.) The kale remains a healthy green, the potatoes crumble at the touch of a fork, and the chorizo gives the spicy heat that banishes New England's inclination towards bland. The cabbage and meats, which have shyly sweetened the broth, melt away in the final bowl. The whole compilation shines in gold and green like an N. C. Wyeth painting. American cuisine so often reflects the best of what traveled here, and stayed to become our own. Serve this thoroughly American, soul-full soup to European friends, and they will smile with recognition.

SERVES 10–12

1 large onion, sliced

1 beef shin bone

1 pound stew beef, cubed

1 pound chuck steak, left in one piece

½ pound chourico, sliced into ¼-inch rounds

1 pound fresh kale, washed and chopped

4 potatoes, quartered

½ medium cabbage, cut into thirds

1 (16-ounce) can "Stewart's" shell beans or "horticultural beans"

Salt and pepper to taste

In a large soup pot, add onion, shin bone, beef, and chuck steak. Cover with water (about 2 quarts), and simmer for 1 hour.

Add the chourico, and simmer for another 30 minutes, adding more water if the level gets low.

Add kale, potatoes, cabbage, beans, salt, and pepper. Simmer for 2 more hours.

The meat should have fallen into beautiful tender chunks. If some seem too large to serve, take them out and put on a warm platter for people to take as they like. Otherwise, serve the soup in warm bowls.

SALT COD

Call it baccala, bacalhau, kala, or just salt cod, dried cod, stockfish. Cut into pieces after that required soaking, rolled in rice flour and fried, salt cod becomes a golden, pillowy, crispy gift from the sea. Those who say salt cod is an entirely different being from its fresh cousin are correct; salt cod is salt cod, a sweet chunk of firm white fish still wearing some ocean. Fresh cod is more fragile, with a little less body. In France, Italy, and Spain, there is no word for fresh cod. While they adore salt cod, and have hundreds of traditional dishes made with it—Brandade du Morue, Baccala alla Trevigiana, Bacalao con Pimientos y Cebolla—these countries simply have no interest in the fresh stuff. That says everything about what Americans who love fish but don't prepare salt cod are missing.

In a small Provincetown cookbook dated 1941, the author, Harriet Adams, wrote this:

A booklet I have just read – a very modern booklet – says that to freshen salt fish you should lay it in a kettle of cold water, bring it almost to a boil, drain, refill with water, rebring almost to a boil. All in all, performing the process four separate times.

The idea, I presume is to persuade your salt fish to imitate the flavor of a fresh one. Well, a fresh fish certainly has its virtue. But, if we want a fresh fish, it isn't too difficult to get one. Remember, a salt fish has a virtue all its own. If we don't take steps, they will soon be topping it with Fudge Sauce.

Let us not give our salt fish velveteen breeches, an Eton collar or an Oxford accent. But, gentle ladies, let us not be too primitive. A salt fish really needs freshening. Some of its salt must really be removed. And by the length of time that you soak or boil it you are able to control the amount that you remove . . . But whatever you do to it be sure that you keep the essence, the salt-fish-ness of the fish. Be sure you save the gamey and yet invigorating whiff of that old billy goat – the sea.

When purchasing salt cod, make sure to pick out a piece with a thick, white center. Stay away from pieces that are mostly tail. Also, although the little wooden box is charming, it's also the easiest way to disguise poor quality salt cod. Like purchasing a piece of fresh fish, you want to be able to inspect your dried cod. It should be kind of beautiful—large, thick, and meaty. "Boneless and skinless" salt cod is the easiest to work with.

I keep a couple of bags of thick salt cod fillets in my refrigerator. On a week that I think I may be preparing salt cod, Monday morning I rinse the cod under cold water, and then put it in a bowl of fresh cold water to cover. I leave it, and go on with my week, but refresh the water a couple of times a day as I go by.

By Wednesday or Thursday, I think, hmm. . . salt cod hash would be a quick and easy dinner tonight. Maybe I consider a dandelion salad if it's spring. That night, I drain the cod, and poach it for ten minutes in milk to gently cook and add some sweetness. It's then ready to become that very quick hash, or scrapple, or fish cakes.

Doctors are beginning to understand that cured and fermented old-world foods had a nutritional value that modern, processed diets neglect. The bacteria created in the fermentation process—and every culture fermented something—may have been an important partner in fighting disease. Perhaps some modern disease processes can be traced to the fact that today's dinner mostly omits cured and fermented foods. Call salt cod health food; its time has come again.

Cumin and Saffron Clam Chowder

This "chowder" has fresh littlenecks and chunks of steak fish studding a light cumin- and saffron-scented tomato broth. It has not a drop of milk or cream, and not a potato in sight; call it "the other chowder." This is quick to prepare and adaptable; use whatever fish you like, or leave fish out all together and go right for clams. The clams offer a wonderful brininess to the chowder, but it would be delicious with fish alone if clams weren't an option. See? Be a Cape Cod fisherman and adapt. The chourico makes it all a little bit Portuguese. Use boxed fish stock and you quickly have a delicious family meal; use homemade fish stock, and you have dinner for a king, or a discerning Provincetown fisherman.

SERVES 6

About 36 cherrystones or little neck clams, scrubbed well

1 teaspoon salt

2 tablespoons butter

1 medium onion, chopped

2 cloves garlic, minced

Chourico, about 5-inch length, sliced thinly

2 fresh tomatoes, diced

½ cup chopped fresh parsley

1 quart clam broth or fish stock

½ teaspoon saffron

½ teaspoon ground cumin

1 cup dry white wine

1½ pounds any firm fish, cut into 2-inch chunks (Swordfish, dogfish, or monkfish are all great options, but this is very flexible, and the fish optional)

Olive oil

Hot sauce

Fresh cilantro and lemon zest to garnish

Rinse clams under running water until, when put in a bowl and covered in water, the water is clear from sand. Leave clams in the bowl covered with water to which a teaspoon of salt is added. This will clear out any more sand.

In a large stockpot or wide sauté pan, the one from which you will serve the chowder, melt butter over medium heat. Add onions, garlic, and chourico, and cook until onion is soft.

Add tomatoes and parsley, and cook 2 minutes. Add fish stock, saffron, cumin, and wine. Lower the heat, and simmer for 10 minutes.

Add fish if you are using it, and let cook for 3–4 minutes, then add the clams in their shells. Cover the pot, and simmer until all the clams have opened, remembering that the smallest clams take the longest to open. After about 10 minutes, remove and discard any clams that will still not open. Unopened clams may or may not be "bad," but it is not worth the risk.

Serve chowder in hot bowls, placing clams all around. Drizzle liberally with olive oil, dot with hot sauce to your taste, and sprinkle with cilantro and fresh lemon zest if desired.

Provincetown Haddock Almandine Meurniere

According to cookbook author Howard Mitcham (1917–1996), Provincetown was once a city where a fisherman brought his trash fish into a bar and handed it to the wife of the Portuguese owner. She took the fish into the kitchen and returned with a steaming skillet of monkfish, squid, clams, and linguica, which everyone ate for free. But you had to be polite, no greed was allowed. Only the beer cost something.

Once upon a time, on the waterfront in Provincetown, whole mackerel were cooked on a clean shovel in a coal or wood-burning stove, and the mackerel was declared best served in early summer with gooseberries.

Mitcham says that "fried codfish jawbones were eaten like fried chicken legs, and many thought the codfish bones tasted better."

Clambakes were done in galvanized trash cans on top of the stove. Fish were cooked on the scalding pipe of the ship's engine, or cloaked in spinach, butter, bread crumbs, and a jigger of absinthe. This was Provincetown cuisine; fish were everywhere, and people were cooking them on any surface that got hot.

In his now-out-of-print cookbook, *The Provincetown Seafood Cookbook*, Mitcham—artist, fisherman, and chef—declared Haddock Almondine Meurniere the most popular dish ever in that town. In every Provincetown restaurant he worked in, the Haddock Almondine Meurniere sold out. The highest praise, Mitcham admitted, was when the fishermen ordered it, too.

"And, brother, when you sell a piece of fish to a Provincetown fisherman, you have got it made; when they dine out in restaurants they usually eat T-bone steaks."

SERVES 6

6¾–pound haddock fillets

Milk

Flour

1 cup (2 sticks) butter

Juice of 2 lemons

¼ pound sliced natural almonds

4 fresh mushrooms, sliced thinly

Dip haddock fillets in milk, then dredge them in flour, shaking off the surplus.

Melt butter to foamy in a large skillet, and place the fish in it (skin side up if there is skin on it). Cook slowly until brown, 7–10 minutes, and then flip the fish over. Cook the other side the same way, being very gentle with the heat.

Remove the fish and place on warm serving plates.

Add lemon juice, almonds, and mushrooms to the butter in the pan. Raise the heat to medium high, and stir, scraping bottom and sides of pan to release any browned crumbs. Cook until the almonds become golden brown, about 7 minutes. Pour this sauce over the fish, and serve immediately.

Monkfish, dogfish, and (more or less) skate, are fished in abundance off the coast of Massachusetts. Each in its own way is a great fish to cook with. These are white, mild fish with character that welcomes strong treatments. Monkfish loves to be roasted. Delicate skate comes in a tender wing that classically loves a caper and lemon bath, but here it's served on a bed of roasted cauliflower cloaked with an indulgent bacon vinaigrette. Wrap chunks of firm white dogfish in pancetta, lay them on a Brussels sprout slaw, and everyone is happy. That said, I cannot promise that you will be able to find any of these fish in a fish market. Fishing is complicated business. Because of the way fishing works these days, it is very unlikely that a fish swimming off the coast of Massachusetts will actually be sold in Massachusetts. There are small fishing boats and organizations like the Cape Cod Fisherman's Alliance and Community Supported Fisheries working hard to counter this movement, and I encourage you to look for organizations like these near you. Nonetheless, with a little advance work or asking your fishmonger a couple of days ahead, you could probably have any of these fish, particularly the more familiar monkfish. While they may be more difficult to find in a market, monkfish, skate, and dogfish are so common to Massachusetts waters it's important to have a few great recipes for them.

Pan-Roasted Skate Wing
with Caramelized Cauliflower, Toby Hill

The French love skate. Many chefs love skate. The Cape Cod Commercial Fisherman's Alliance loves skate. It is one of this small boat operation's most cherished fisheries. While there are some issues with overfishing (skate grow slowly and have low reproduction rates, so stocks need to be treated delicately), skate are a superb coast of Massachusetts fish.

The Cape Cod Commercial Fisherman's Alliance provided this recipe from celebrated Cape Cod Chef Toby Hill; it's a magnificent way to begin loving this fish-with-wings, and proves just how happy skate is with strong flavors like cauliflower and bacon.

Skate fillets are the wings of the "ray." They are wide, flat fillets made of connected strands of clean, white meat. These strands make this a delicate tasting fish, but also just a little tricky to turn over in a pan, so use a wide spatula and be patient. Hill's recipe lays this breaded fillet over a bed of caramelized cauliflower, and dresses it with a bacon vinaigrette. You will want to put this bacon dressing on everything, so make more than you need here!

SERVES 4-6

1½ tablespoons canola oil

1 head cauliflower, cut into small florets

4 slices applewood bacon, roughly chopped

1 onion, chopped

½ tablespoon Dijon mustard

¼ cup white balsamic vinegar

¼ cup olive oil

2 pounds skate fillets

1 cup panko crumbs, ground fine

Salt and freshly ground black pepper to taste

Heat canola oil in a sauté pan to medium heat. Add cauliflower, and cook until caramelized, tossing regularly, about 15 minutes. Set aside.

Heat a separate pan to medium. Add bacon, onion, mustard, vinegar, olive oil, and cook until onions caramelize and bacon crisps, about 15 minutes. Allow this to cool slightly, then pulse to a paste in a food processor. Set aside.

Dredge the skate wings in bread crumbs.

Heat remaining canola oil in a large skillet to medium high, add skate fillets, and fry until golden brown on both sides, 2–3 minutes per side.

Divide cauliflower among the plates. Top with skate, and drizzle with bacon vinaigrette. Serve immediately.

DOGFISH

Dogfish are one of the important species that the Cape Cod Fisherman's Alliance is catching, and encouraging us to make for dinner.

Dogfish, *Squalus acanthias*, are Marine Stewardship Council Certified, meaning the fishery meets the three overarching principles that the Marine Stewardship Council requires for it to be declared a healthy fishery. Along with "31 more detailed criteria," some specific to each fishery, these are the "general" qualifications according to the MSC website:

Principle 1: Sustainable fish stocks
> Fishing activity must be at a level sustainable for the fish population. Any certified fishery must operate so that fishing can continue indefinitely and not overexploit the resources.

Principle 2: Minimizing environmental impact
> Fishing operations should be managed to maintain the structure, productivity, function, and diversity of the ecosystem on which the fishery depends.

Principle 3: Effective management
> The fishery must meet all local, national, and international laws and must have a management system in place to respond to changing circumstances and maintain sustainability.

Dogfish are sharks, which means, among other things, they are cartilaginous—only a spine of cartilage runs down their center, no bones. Because they have no ribcage, out of water a dogfish would collapse beneath its own weight. Dogfish are bottom-dwellers, and the longest lived in the shark family; some dogfish live to be centenarians.

Dogfish are delicious—firm flesh, abalone-white, mild to sweet tasting, there is almost no fish recipe to which dogfish don't kindly adapt. The meat sisters beautifully with caramelized onions and silken red peppers in a fish fajita; its mild taste and pearly meat are a happy counter to any slowly braised vegetables, tomato-rich puttanesca, or a spicy cilantro- and cumin- laced taco. Dogfish, in fact, given its name, is like the cheerful yellow lab of fish, happy to go along with just about anything you do to it.

Many agree that dogfish make the best fish-and-chips.

"The meat is white as snow, very lean, and firmer even than halibut. And, eaten cold the next day, tastes astonishingly like cold fried chicken," says cookbook author Hank Shaw.

Most of Europe and Asia, the major dogfish markets, think so, too. For years the traditional English fish-and-chips was always made with dogfish.

Dogfish had a great market in Europe, got overfished, got protected, and now it's back, trying to be the new darling. And it should be the new darling—there's lots of it, and it tastes good. Many say that dogfish are the key to the survival of the small fishing boats in Massachusetts.

The greatest dogfish irony is that this star of the fish-and-chips plate, with its weighty local landings and Marine Stewardship Council badge, is almost impossible to find in retail markets. Cape Codders are learning to embrace it, particularly Cape Cod chefs. Here are some excellent recipes for dogfish; start asking your fishmonger where it is!

Pancetta-Wrapped Dogfish
with Brussels Sprout Slaw, Toby Hill

Europe loves dogfish. It's great availability (in the oceans, not necessarily in American fish markets) and its white, mild flesh, with almost no bone, has made it the ideal protein in fish-and-chips for years. Here, chef Toby Hill wraps dogfish chunks in pancetta and lays them on a brussels sprout slaw, an autumn anthem of a recipe. If you cannot find dogfish, this fall-forward recipe adapts easily to monkfish, chunks of cod loin, or even large sea scallops.

SERVES 4

For the slaw:

18 brussels sprouts, shredded

1 carrot, grated

3 tablespoons mayonnaise

2 tablespoons apple cider vinegar

1 tablespoon finely chopped parsley

Salt and freshly ground black pepper to taste

For the dogfish:

Canola oil

1 pound dogfish fillets, cut into 12 chunks

12 (4-inch-long) strips pancetta or bacon Salt and freshly ground pepper to taste

In a mixing bowl, combine all the ingredients for the slaw, and mix together. Chill for at least 2 hours.

When ready to prepare, heat a large skillet with ¾ inch oil to 350°F.

Wrap each chunk of dogfish with a slice of pancetta, and secure with toothpicks.

Fry the dogfish in the oil until pancetta is golden brown and crispy, about 1 minute.

Arrange slaw on 4 plates, and lay 3 dogfish chunks on top of each mound of slaw. Serve immediately.

Spicy Cornmeal Fried Dogfish

To make this Spicy Cornmeal Fried Dogfish is to learn exactly why dogfish has become the eminent fish in fish-and-chips. White, fluffy, tightly grained fish steaming within a crunchy coating, this is the fried fish worth its weight in a little frying oil. Dogfish behaves so perfectly (it's not watery, it remains whole, its flavor is a pillow upon which the spice in the batter rests) within this hot, crunchy cover, it is certainly the king of fried fish. If you succeed in finding dogfish, make this recipe immediately, if only to understand what Brits have known for years. Wouldn't it be great to steal back our dogfish, and begin a whole new industry of Massachusetts fish-and-chips shacks?

SERVES 4

2 pounds dogfish fillets

Salt

4 cups vegetable oil for frying

2 cups plus 1 cup all-purpose flour, divided

1 teaspoon garlic powder

½ teaspoon Old Bay Seasoning

Freshly ground black pepper

2 bottles beer, your choice of brands

¼ cup cornmeal

Salt the fish and set aside at room temperature. In a dutch oven or electric fryer, using a cooking thermometer, heat oil to 350°F. Preheat your oven to warm. Prepare a cookie sheet with a wire rack on top, and set aside.

In a large bowl mix 2 cups flour, seasonings, and beer together, stirring all the while. Cookbook author Hank Shaw describes the texture you want as "the consistency of house paint or melted ice cream." Let the batter rest for 20 minutes.

Meanwhile, in a medium bowl mix together the remaining 1 cup flour and cornmeal.

When the batter is ready and the oil hot, dredge the fish in the batter and let the excess drip off for a second or two. Then roll the dredged fish into the dry flour-cornmeal mixture.

Lay each piece gently into the hot oil. Allow the end of the fish to fry for a second or so in the oil before letting the whole piece drop into the oil. This helps prevent the fish from sticking to the bottom of the pot. Dislodge any pieces that stick to the bottom with a long fork.

Fry in batches until golden brown, 5–8 minutes. Remove each to the rack on the cookie sheet, and keep the cookie sheet in the warm oven until all the fish is prepared. Serve immediately with ice cold beer.

Greenbriar Cranberry Conserve

This conserve is as delicious served with meats as it is with toast and tea. Miss Blake always began with the juiciest, most flavorful produce, and strictly only what was in season. Apply this Greenbriar rule to your preserves and more than half the deliciousness battle is won.

MAKES ABOUT 4 CUPS

1 quart cranberries

1 orange, peeled, seeded, and chopped

⅓ cup chopped raisins

1 cup chopped walnuts

4½ cups sugar

Finely chop the cranberries fine. This should not be done in a food processor, as they will become too mushy.

Put all the ingredients into a kettle, and cook very slowly to keep from burning. Let simmer until mixture thickens. Pour into sterilized jars. The conserve will keep indefinitely in the refrigerator, but, for shelf storage, you can process by canning using your favorite method.

Spiced Pear Jam

Miss Blake traveled twice to Europe on a steamship, almost the only time she ever took away from running Greenbriar Jam Kitchen. But her sense of humor, her warmth, her judgment, and her excellent taste all reflected a worldliness one wouldn't expect in a small, bright kitchen in Sandwich, with red geraniums bursting in the window. Try Spiced Pear Jam in a grilled cheddar cheese sandwich for a very worldly lunch.

MAKES APPROXIMATELY 3 PINTS

1 orange, seeded and chopped

1 lemon, seeded and chopped

1 pineapple, cored and chopped into ½-inch pieces

3 pounds ripe Anjou pears, cored and chopped into ½-inch chunks

4 cups sugar

1 teaspoon cinnamon

½ teaspoon ground cloves

1-inch piece of fresh ginger, peeled and chopped into fine dice

In a large pan cook orange, lemon, and pineapple until tender. Add pears, sugar, spices, and ginger. Simmer for 30 minutes, stirring occasionally, or until sugar is dissolved and jam is very thick.

Pour into sterilized jars, and seal. Store in the refrigerator, or process by canning using your favorite method if storing on the shelf.

GREENBRIAR

Off the back of a two-hundred-year-old Cape Cod home in East Sandwich, Massachusetts, sagging beneath wisteria and trumpet vine, extended a long commercial kitchen, added at the turn of the century when Ida Putnam began selling her jams to the public. Down the center of the kitchen stretched two rows of Glenwood gas burners, ten stoves long. Against the walls ran copper counters where the hot jam was ladled into jars, and the jars wiped and labeled before being stacked into a wooden cart and rolled into the bead-boarded sunroom at the front of the house. There, visitors selected from jams, pickles, and the thick, shining preserves cooked in trays in the sun, to which brandy and kirsch was often added because Ida Putnam in 1903 knew how to improve upon perfection. The entire kitchen was cornflower blue and white, except for four leggy red geraniums in the window facing the driveway.

Built before electricity, the Greenbriar Jam Kitchen was naturally illuminated by a row of skylights over the stoves. The sensible planners then knew the long room would naturally be too dark in the center away from the wall's windows to see into the simmering pots of fruit and sugar. Every cooking utensil, of which there was only what was minimally necessary, had its own hook sited on the wall at exactly the place it was needed. The spoons had been stirring beach plum jam for seventy years by the time I worked here as a teenager for a summer job. They were worn down to half their size by then, and conformed perfectly to the bottoms of the pots.

To the left of the door, a lidded bin opened to two large barrels of sugar, the only other jam ingredient besides the unblemished, perfectly ripened produce. Okay, there were a few spices around for pickles. The room's pristine beauty coolly advised one not to set a purse or newspaper down anywhere. Any architect would be proud to have created a room as naturally bright and cheerful as the Greenbriar Jam Kitchen even on the gloomiest Cape Cod day. Add the scent of blueberry jam simmering on a burner and you have a peak moment for civilization.

Martha Blake (always "Miss Blake") purchased the business from Ida Putnam sometime near 1930 and changed nothing—not one blue and white enamel pot. Mizue Murphy, a beautiful Japanese woman, was Miss Blake's only full-time employee. I was the summer help. Mizue, the mother of a middle-school daughter then, had met her American husband when he was in service in Japan.

Even on the hottest summer days a breeze ran through the screened doors and windows of the kitchen from the Spring Hill Creek, an Eden for birdlife, beyond the back door. The three of us would sit in the summery blue back room picking through the fruit that would later be jam. We sat on stools around a large table covered in a tumble of perfect peaches or cartons of strawberries dripping in juices. We would talk about Mizue's girlhood in Japan, or how moody her daughter had been that day, or Miss Blake's two trips to Europe on a steamship, the only vacations she ever took away from her East Sandwich business. Or we'd laugh about the fat, fearless resident woodchuck. Miss Blake and Mizue both had sharp, sensitive wits. Miss Blake's shoulders shook with laughter at a good story, and there was often girlish mirth in her gray eyes, but she and Mizue were both shy. My job was to talk to the four or five visitors we had each day, people who somehow had heard about these secretly perfect preserves, and found their way down the tiger lily–lined road to the Greenbriar kitchen. Miss Blake lived in the rest of the Cape house, but I would take the customers to the room with the glowing shellacked shelves so they could make their jam and pickle choices. I made the small-talk that Miss Blake dreaded. But, as I led the guests to the front room, I would sense them looking longingly back at the sparkling blue and white kitchen sweet with simmering fruits, Miss Blake and Mizue moving quickly about. That's where the visitors really wanted to go.

Miss Blake shipped many of her jars. The Mellon family bought all their jams, jellies, and pickles from Greenbriar. There was a man in Paris who sent a bottle of Kirschwasser to Miss Blake each year, and she would send him back a box of sun-cooked cherries in kirsch.

The sun-cooking system was a wooden shelf, maybe five feet long, that extended off the back room of the kitchen. Glass windows covered the shelf outside. From inside, one passed the pans of slightly cooked fruit through small doors opened to the shelf and rolled them out beneath the glass. The jams, cooked over four days in the greenhouse-like arrangement, ended in a sweet, thick, regal preserve, rare with sunshine and time.

From every batch of jam or piccalilli there was always a small bit left that would not completely fill a jar. These remnants were sent to a large set of shelving in the back room, which gradually filled up as the year went on. In early November, long after I had returned to school, Miss Blake would empty all the jars—everything from last bits of bread and butter pickles to a few sun-cooked cherries—together into a large pot, and produce a mincemeat so treasured there was a waiting list for it.

Fully aware what a cultural treasure Greenbriar was, Miss Blake confessed over peach-peeling that she worried what would happen to the kitchen when she could no longer run it. When she finally retired, Greenbriar became preserved as a museum within the Thornton Burgess Wildlife Center. Springhill Creek flows slowly by the dock in the back, blue herons hanging above it, as if nothing has ever changed.

Classic Whole Cranberry Sauce and Classic Cranberry Jelly

No Cape Cod food discussion is complete without the basic recipes for whole cranberry sauce and cranberry jelly, foundations of Thanksgiving dinner, and millions of pounds of cranberries' fate. This is also useful if you're making Cape Cod Pork Chops or Braised Duck with Cranberry Sauce.

MAKES 4 CUPS WHOLE CRANBERRY SAUCE OR 2 CUPS JELLY

2 cups sugar

2 cups water

4 cups cranberries

To make cranberry sauce:

In a heavy saucepan combine sugar and water and stir to dissolve. Bring to a simmer, and add the cranberries. Cook on medium heat until cranberries begin to break their skins, 6–8 minutes. Remove from heat and cool.

To make jelly:

Prepare recipe above, but do not allow mixture to cool. Remove berries from heat, and strain liquid into a second saucepan. Bring that liquid to a boil, and simmer for 10–12 minutes, or until a small amount poured onto a chilled plate "sets," or stands up like a firm bead.

Pour into sterilized glass jars. Store in the refrigerator, or process by your favorite canning method if storing on the shelf.

Fresh Cranberry and Orange Relish

A gem of a recipe that Cape Codders have been serving for generations, this refreshing relish blends raw cranberries and oranges, and macerates them in sugar. The result is a fruity, light alternative to, or pairing with, traditional cooked cranberry sauce, and fabulous in a whole new way on a turkey sandwich. But this recipe is old news on Cape Cod, where it's been a Thanksgiving tradition for years.

One word of advice: Almost all Cape Codders, and probably your grandmother, own an old-fashioned meat grinder that attaches to a table. Fitted with a coarse blade, it's the best way to prepare this relish. Alternative methods are chopping by hand, which works but might be tedious, or using a food processor, where the danger is over-processing to mush. If you use the food processor, pulse lightly, and stir mixture in between pulses.

MAKES 4 CUPS

4 cups cranberries

2 oranges, quartered and seeded, but not peeled

1½ cups sugar

Toss cranberries and orange quarters together in a bowl to distribute evenly. Pull all through the coarse blade of a meat grinder.

Stir in the sugar and mix well. Serve chilled with turkey or pork.

Cape Cod Pork Chops

Pork loves fruit; it's broad shoulders of mild flavor welcome jammy sweetness. On Cape Cod pork and cranberries have had a long courtship.

As the Wampanoag were introducing the pilgrims to the plump, tart merits of native cranberries—the natives called it sassamenesh—the pilgrims, who were woefully bad fishermen, longed for meat. Cows and sheep wouldn't cross the Atlantic for a few years; nor did they reproduce quickly enough to be a regular source of protein. But pigs did well in the New World. They arrived early from England, and had two litters a year.

Therefore, not only are pork and berries classically delicious together, but they share a long history in the colonies. These two should be officially entered in the culinary ledgers as "married."

SERVES 4

4 (1-inch thick) pork chops with bone

Salt and pepper

1 tablespoon olive oil

¼ cup (½ stick) butter, melted

¾ cup celery

½ cup onion

3 tablespoons parsley

1 cup bread crumbs (previously toasted in butter to a light brown)

3 cups Classic Whole Cranberry Sauce (page 148, or use canned whole cranberry sauce), divided

½–¾ cup port (to taste)

Rind of 1 orange

1 teaspoon red pepper flakes

½ teaspoon cinnamon

Cut pockets into pork chops through to the bone. Salt and pepper chops well on both sides.

In a heavy skillet, heat olive oil to medium high. Add pork chops, and brown well on one side. Remove from heat and set aside.

In the same skillet, melt butter and add celery, onion, and parsley. Cook for 5–7 minutes, or until the vegetables soften and begin to brown. Add bread crumbs, and 1 cup cranberry sauce.

Preheat oven to 350°F.

Stuff pork chops well with the cranberry mixture, making them look overstuffed.

Lay chops in a ceramic or glass baking dish so that they fit snugly. If there is leftover stuffing put it around the chops.

Meanwhile, in a small bowl mix together the remaining 2 cups cranberry sauce, port, orange peel, red pepper flakes, and cinnamon.

Spoon this mixture over the chops, letting it run down around them. Sprinkle tops with a pinch of salt and a generous grind of pepper. Bake for 40–45 minutes or until the meat is browned on top and tender. Avoid over-cooking. Baste occasionally with cranberry mixture.

Serve hot with buttered green beans for an honest Cape Cod dinner.

Cranberry, Date, and Ginger Chutney

Two gifts come from this chutney: the ginger-spiced cloud that fills your kitchen when it's simmering and the pleasure it evokes when you give it as a gift. This makes a lot; give it away and you will have very good friends. But keep a jar for your own roast chicken dinners. Even better, make cream cheese and cranberry chutney tea sandwiches on thinly sliced Portuguese Sweet Bread.

MAKES 4 PINTS

4 cans whole cranberry sauce

1 cup pitted dates

1 cup currants

1 cup slivered almonds

1 cup cider vinegar

2 tablespoons chopped candied ginger

1 teaspoon ground allspice

1 cup packed dark brown sugar

In a large stainless steel soup pot combine all ingredients. Bring slowly to a boil, stirring constantly. Simmer uncovered for 30 minutes, or until sugars are all dissolved and the chutney is very thick.

Pour into sterilized jars. Chutney can also be stored indefinitely in the refrigerator, but process for canning if you are storing on the shelf.

Eastham Turnip Oven Fries

Eastham Turnip legend claims that Ray Brackett first knew what he was doing with soil and turnips on outer Cape Cod, and then passed his heirloom seeds on to Art Nickerson. Those seeds have been coddled for over one hundred years. Eastham Turnips are famous among those who know. Mr. Nickerson shipped Eastham Turnips as far away as Florida; Colonial Williamsburg once requested two bushels of Eastham Turnips for a special dinner.

Eastham Turnips are small and sweet with purple tops, and have a signature green band in between the white body and the purple top. If they don't have that band, they're not Eastham Turnips, or so I am told.

Some believe the Eastham Turnip is related to the Macomber Turnip from Westport, Massachusetts. Some believe the Eastham Turnip is a rutabaga/turnip cross. Old-time Cape citizen Charlie Horton believes the Eastham Turnip arrived centuries ago from Scotland, and is the Scottish version of a turnip called a "neep."

Mr. Nickerson has passed, but he left the heirloom turnip so popular that it has its own festival at which the Eastham Turnip is celebrated every which way. I offer a recipe here that may inspire more people to choose turnips for dinner more often—Eastham Turnip Oven Fries, which have become more popular in my home than regular fries.

SERVES 4–6

3 pounds turnips, peeled and cut into french fry–
    size sticks (about ⅓- x 4-inch)

1 tablespoon grape seed or olive oil

¾ cup grated Parmesan cheese

1 teaspoon garlic salt

2 teaspoons paprika

Freshly ground black pepper

Preheat oven to 425°F. Line baking sheet with lightly greased aluminum foil.

Place turnip sticks into a large bowl with oil. Toss to coat. Place Parmesan cheese, garlic salt, paprika, and pepper in a resealable plastic bag, and shake to mix. Place oiled turnips into the bag, and shake until evenly coated with the spices. Spread out on the prepared baking sheet.

Bake until outside is crispy and inside is tender, about 20 minutes. Serve immediately.

Award-winning Eastham Turnip Pie

In an unofficial survey, mashed turnips served very hot with butter, salt, and pepper, even luxuriously sprinkled with crisp bacon or pancetta, is Eastham's favorite recipe. But the Eastham Turnip Festival invites all kinds of turnip creativity. People submit both adventurous and tame turnip recipes, and children carve turnips into Sesame Street Characters. The festival is usually the first weekend in November, time for the first crop of Eastham Turnips to be harvested.

Geoffrey Antoine has won at least twice, once with this Turnip Pie (imagine pumpkin pie made with mashed turnips) and once with his Turnip Crème Brûlée.

SERVES 8

3 eggs, slightly beaten

½ cup sugar

½ cup brown sugar

½ teaspoon kosher or sea salt

1 teaspoon cinnamon

¼ teaspoon ginger

¼ teaspoon nutmeg

¼ teaspoon ground cloves

2 cups well-cooked, mashed turnip

1 cup heavy cream

1 9-inch deep-dish piecrust

Whipped cream

Preheat oven to 450°F.

Line pie plate with piecrust, set aside.

In a large bowl or in a blender, combine eggs, sugars, salt, and spices. Beat well. Blend in turnip, add cream, and mix well (it will look soupy). Pour into piecrust.

Bake for 10 minutes; then reduce oven temperature to 350°F and continue baking 40–45 minutes. Pie is done when a knife inserted into the center comes out clean. Serve at room temperature or cold, topped with whipped cream.

Sagamore Dandelion Salad

John Carafoli grew up in Sagamore on Cape Cod, the dot of a village at the foot of the Sagamore Bridge. One glance at the radio dial as you drive off the bridge and you've missed it.

A church, Louis' Market, the Pierpoint Glass Factory, and a cluster of simple gray-shingled homes add up to Sagamore today. For all its anonymity, the small village of Sagamore has impacted the Cape Cod peninsula more than any other town. This is the village the Italians called home when they arrived in the nineteenth century to dig the Cape Cod Canal. They brought their cuisine and they dug the ditch that connected Buzzards Bay to Cape Cod Bay, something English settlers had been imagining since 1627. Recipe boxes all over Cape Cod hold Italian meals born in Sagamore. There was so much good to be learned from what Italians do with tomatoes, herbs, and vegetables. By the middle of the twentieth century, ships were passing through the canal and lasagna was becoming a household word.

John Carafoli experienced first-hand the wonderful kitchens in this neighborhood. He grew up to be a food stylist and cookbook author, documenting the unique culinary treasures tucked away in Sagamore. Carafoli remembers springtime in Sagamore, when the ladies would be out in their yards with knives, cutting at the first tender dandelion leaves, grateful for that first "spring tonic." Those greens appeared on the table as the simplest of salads, a culinary depiction of early Cape Cod spring.

SERVES 4-5

4 tablespoons fruity olive oil

1½ tablespoons red wine vinegar

1 teaspoon sea salt

1 teaspoon (or to taste) freshly ground black pepper

1 pound dandelion greens (about 3 cups), washed and dried with tough stems removed

2 hardboiled eggs, chopped

In a large salad bowl, the one in which you will serve the salad, whisk together olive oil, vinegar, salt, and pepper. Whisk well until it appears emulsified.

Add greens and toss well to coat the leaves. Add eggs, and toss again. Serve immediately.

Fish Balls and Parsley Sauce

Mixed gently with riced potato, fresh Cape haddock becomes a lightly scented base for small appetizer-size croquettes. Stand the crispy round croquettes on a platter pooled with lemon, garlic, and parsley sauce, and they look like the stone walls along a West Barnstable field in the springtime. Be prepared to have the first batch go very quickly.

SERVES 10 – 12 AS AN APPETIZER

For the poached fish:

2½ cups milk, whole or skim

1 bay leaf

1 dried hot chili, or ½ teaspoon red pepper flakes

Salt and pepper to taste

1½ pounds haddock or cod

For the fish balls:

2 large baking potatoes, peeled and cut into 1-inch cubes

2 eggs

3 tablespoons milk from the poached fish

2 tablespoons grated onion

3 tablespoons grated Parmesan cheese

2 tablespoons lemon juice

Salt and pepper to taste

1 cup grape seed, rice bran or any oil with a high smoking point

½ cup skim milk for dipping

½ cup rice flour for dipping

Parsley Sauce

Grated lemon rind and red pepper flakes to garnish

To make the poached fish:

In a wide saucepan, put milk and seasonings. Bring to a simmer and add fish. Simmer 10 minutes, or until the fish flakes easily. Remove from heat and allow fish to cool slightly in the milk.

When just cool, remove fish, but reserve the milk. Process the fish for 3 seconds in a food processor, just enough to break it down uniformly. Be careful not to make a paste.

To make the balls:

Put the potatoes into salted water. Bring to a boil and cook for 10 minutes or until the potatoes are soft through. Drain and put into medium bowl.

Add processed fish, eggs, milk from cooking broth, onion, cheese, lemon juice, salt, and pepper. Fluff all gently with a fork until mixed well.

In a large sauté pan, add oil, and heat to just before smoking point.. With a small ice-cream scoop or a tablespoon, make 1-inch balls with the fish-potato mixture. Dip into milk, and then rice flour, and set in the hot oil. Allow a side to brown, and then turn carefully. At first it will seem as if they will only cook on sides, but as a side cooks all of the ball will brown nicely. Adjust heat of oil to keep from burning or cooking too slowly. Add more oil to pan if it gets too low. Remove balls to paper towels, drain, and keep warm in a 300°F oven.

To serve, spread Parsley Sauce (below) over a platter. Set fish balls on sauce. Sprinkle lightly with finely grated lemon rind and red pepper flakes if desired.

Parsley Sauce

YIELDS ¾ CUP

1 cup parsley leaves

3 cloves garlic, minced

3 tablespoons lemon juice

½ cup olive oil

Salt and pepper

In a small bowl, whisk together all the ingredients. The sauce can be served like this, with small bits of parsley and garlic evident, or pureed well in a food processor for a smoother sauce.

LINE-CAUGHT OR NOT?

You're scanning the restaurant menu; your eyes find the fish choices. Suddenly the air gets misty; the music swells, and you feel better about the entire world because this restaurant is serving line-caught cod. You think, Fish stocks are coming back! The family farm is saved! Peace stands a chance! All because this restaurant is serving line-caught cod.

In fact you have no idea what line-caught cod is. You vaguely believe that eating this fish excuses those bottles you didn't recycle last week, but you don't know much more than that. You believe this fish will taste better than, well, than what? What other kinds of fishing are there? Do you even know? Maybe you've heard of "dragging," and there must be some reason why this restaurant isn't advertising freshly dragged cod, but you don't really know that either.

Here are some terms: "Line-caught" fish is better known in the fishing industry as "hook fish." A more dated but still accurate term for it is "tub-trawlers." That's because one very long piece of fishing line is intermittently hooked, and each hook is baited by hand. The entire extension of line is coiled and stored in a tub on the boat until it is let out to sink to the ocean floor. Cod are bottom feeders, also known as ground fish, so the lines fall to the bottom of the ocean and lie in one spot for the fish to come along and eat the bait, and get hooked. The lines are hauled back up to the boat after a change of tide, or whatever measure of time the boat uses, and the fish are hand-removed from each hook.

"Gillnet fishing" is another way to catch fish. In gillnet fishing a big net is dropped to the bottom of the ocean, and left there, static, in one spot. Fish swim into it, get stuck, (they can swim in but not back out because their gills catch, thus the name). The boat later hauls the whole thing up with whatever is inside. The controlling factor here is the size of the holes in the net; bigger holes will only contain the bigger fish; the smaller will be able to swim away.

A third fishing practice is "dragging," in which a net is dragged actively behind a boat. A sweeping gesture, this is the "gotcha!" school of fishing as opposed to the static "heeere fishy, fishy, come-and-get-my-bait" kind of fishing. Obviously, the size of the holes in the net in this case, too, can protect against hauling up too much young catch.

Another term to pay attention to here is "day-boat fishing," which is simply a boat that goes fishing, using any of the above methods, and returns the same day. The key phrase here is "same day," which can translate into being on a plate in New York twenty-four hours later.

The one cornerstone in the fishing industry is freshness. How long was it on that line before it was hauled up? How long was it in a boat before it got back to shore? This is where day-boat fishing comes in to save the day. Some day-boat fishermen trawl, some drag, some hook, but they're all back in a day. Get it? Maybe this doesn't help the confused diners, but a line-caught cod is probably excellent quality, but not definitively. Freshness is what's definitive.

Clam Pie

A sink full of freshly dug quahogs was once a regular sight in Cape Cod kitchens. Cape Cod house-wives and fisherman were regularly challenged to find the most delicious end to a bushel of clams; eating that many on the half-shell just wasn't practical.

Today, a sink full of clams is a rare and expensive treasure; most of us would get out the lemon and begin shucking. But clams and quahogs were as regular as chicken dinner on Cape Cod at one time. And when you have to find a place to put that abundance, between two layers of pastry almost always works.

Cape Cod—and Martha's Vineyard and Nantucket—cookbooks are riddled with clam pie recipes. Today, it may seem like an unnecessary indulgence. But this is such a wonderful old coastal tradition it's worth trying at least once. Its Cape Cod honesty makes it a great Thanksgiving side dish, or cut it in small slices for a luxurious appetizer.

I omitted the bottom crust to this pie, emphasizing all the good crispiness around the clams, and no soggy bottom.

SERVES 4-6 FOR DINNER, 8 AS AN APPETIZER

2 cups minced clams (quahogs or soft-shell clams or a mix of both), preferably fresh

¾ cup crumbled unsalted saltines

1 beaten egg

1 cup milk

¼ cup liquid from the clams

2–3 drops Tabasco, or more to taste

Salt and pepper

2 tablespoons butter

Pastry to cover an 8-inch pie (See Nantucket Scallop and Potato Pie, page 90)

Preheat oven to 350°F. Butter an 8-inch pie pan, including the top edge where the pastry will touch.

In a large bowl, combine well all the ingredients except the butter. Pour mixture into the pie pan and dot with butter.

Cover with pastry, and crimp the edge decorative-ly. Cut slits in the top for the pie to release steam. Bake for 1 hour or until pastry is golden brown.

South of Boston Quahog Chowder

Remember, Quahog Chowder is not Clam Chowder. Clam Chowder is made with soft-shell clams, *Mya arenaria*, the bivalves about 2 inches long with soft, breakable shells, also known as steamers. These are most famous in Rowley, Essex, and Ipswich, Massachusetts, where they are usually dipped in evaporated milk and corn flour, and fried. There, Laurie Lufkin, whose family has raked Essex clams for generations, makes an award-winning traditional clam chowder.

Quahog Chowder is not that. It is made with quahogs, the hard-shell *Venus mercenaria* that include littlenecks, cherrystones, and sea clams. The meats are plump, briny, and sometimes a little tough. That's why the best way to include them in chowder is to shuck them first, and then chop them. Steaming them open just invites more toughness. It's also why restaurant quahog chowder usually fails. A chowder that sits around on a heated burner or steam table is a chowder with tough, ropey quahogs.

There are more rules to making a quahog chowder: Never, ever, ever let it cool with the lid on—the condensation will spoil everything. In fact, the cooling pot of chowder should not even sit directly on a counter, but should be on a rack, cooling the way a loaf of bread cools, with air circulating all around it. If you don't have a rack, stick a wooden spoon beneath the pot, so air flows below.

That said, there are many who believe that quahogs, with their briny, spritely taste of the sea, are the only way to make a chowder. Their liquor offers exactly the right ocean-ness; the meats, if freshly shucked, give just enough resistance to quietly say "there is a mudflat close-by that I call home."

SERVES 6

¼ pound salt pork, cut in small cubes

3 medium onions, chopped

2 large potatoes, diced

1½ quarts chopped quahog meats

2 cups quahog liquor

2 tablespoons flour

1 quart plus 2 tablespoons milk, divided

1 pint evaporated milk

Salt (if necessary) and freshly ground pepper to taste

Fry salt pork in a large stockpot, adding water as necessary to keep it from scorching. When pork is nicely browned, add the onions. Cook until soft, again adding water if it gets too dry; this will depend upon how much fat is in the salt pork.

Add potatoes, and enough water to cover. Simmer until potatoes are cooked through, about 15 minutes.

Add quahogs and quahog liquor. Dissolve flour in 2 tablespoons milk, and add it to the pot, stirring well. Cook for about 10 minutes. This is the quahog base.

When ready to serve, add milk and evaporated milk and heat through, but do not boil! Add salt to taste (it will already have a lot of natural salt) and freshly ground black pepper. Serve in large bowls with oyster crackers, available in the cracker section of the grocery store, or use Laurie Lufkin's Homemade Crackers.

QUAHOGS

Don't call a quahog a clam. On Cape Cod, and other parts of coastal Massachusetts, a clam is *Mya arenaria*, the soft-shelled variety whose happiest end is a deep fryer, then brimming golden and crispy out of a cardboard box. The flats of Rowley, Essex, and Ipswich, Massachusetts are most famous for these guys.

Quahogs are *Venus mercenaria*, an entirely different genus and species. A quahog is a hard-shell clam. Cape Codders pronounce it "ko-hog." The Webster dictionary pronounces it "kwo-hog" or "kwa-hog." Jeremiah Digges, a salty Cape Cod writer circa 1937, responded to this perennial dichotomy, "Quahogs were meant to be eaten—not pronounced."

Quahogs come in three sizes; the smallest are littlenecks, about two inches in diameter. Cherrystones are one size up the chart, about three inches in diameter. Both are delicious steamed open with garlic, lemon, parsley, and cilantro, as in Clams Bulhao, but they are also some of the world's best things to eat raw in their salty brine, with at most a squeeze of lemon and a dot of hot sauce.

"Chowder Clams" and "Sea Clams" are the next size up, and they are huge, seven inches or more. Sea clams are best with a bit of cooking, as in stuffed, or in Clam Pie, or chopped for fritters. Sea clams love the toss and tumble of the surf and shifting sands; they live in moving water, not in the wide flats scenically (but laboriously!) raked by locals. When you buy canned clams, you are always buying sea clams, although to use canned clams excludes the characteristic brightness of this shellfish, so just don't.

"Clams are for happy people," Howard Mitcham, author of the *Provincetown Seafood Cookbook*, declared.

Blueberry Grunt

Named for the sounds the dumplings make as they bake, Blueberry Grunt is perhaps the truest of Cape Cod desserts, and the most heavenly. Warm stewed blueberries and light biscuity dumplings served with a pour of cream, or the very classic New England Nutmeg Sauce, this is almost an inside-out berry shortcake. And, I repeat, it's served warm.

Blueberry Grunt dates back to colonists cooking over an open fire. A pot of wild blueberries would be stewing in the fireplace, and upon that a colonist would plop biscuit dough. They put a lid on the pot, and sat back to enjoy the country music, the hissing and popping of stewing blueberries and dumplings.

Blueberry Grunt has remained an honestly coastal dessert. Although some seem to have traveled to a few kitchens in Nova Scotia, Blueberry Grunt recipes are almost only found in local Cape Cod cookbooks. Neither Harold McGee in his *On Food and Cooking: The Science and Lore of the Kitchen* or *The Oxford English Dictionary* include a mention of "grunts." James Beard, not one to miss a good dessert, includes a Blueberry Grunt recipe, but his is more of a biscuit-topped cobbler baked in the oven. He got the name right, but missed the music.

There is much to adore in Blueberry Grunt, from the fun of making it, to saying it, to the wonderful end result. Pour New England Nutmeg Sauce over it for authenticity. But, there is also a covert pleasure knowing you are enjoying a dessert secreted away in Cape Cod recipe boxes.

SERVES 4

For the blueberries:

4 cups fresh blueberries

Grated rind and juice from 1 lemon

½ teaspoon cinnamon

¼ teaspoon nutmeg

¼ teaspoons ground cloves

¾ cup brown sugar

¼ cup water

¼ teaspoon salt

For the dumpling batter:

1½ cups all-purpose flour

2 tablespoons sugar

2 teaspoons baking powder

½ teaspoon salt

3 tablespoons unsalted butter, chilled and cut into ½-inch chunks

¾ cup milk (or more if the batter is not moist enough to "drop" in dumpling-like clumps from a spoon)

To make the blueberries:

Combine all ingredients in a heavy 2-quart saucepan. Bring to a boil and simmer for 10–15 minutes, or until the blueberries are slightly "stewed."

To make the dumplings:

In a medium bowl, stir together dry ingredients. Cut in butter with a pastry cutter or a fork until the mixture looks like fine meal. Add milk and stir just so the dough comes together as a sticky mass.

Drop tablespoons of batter close together over the simmering blueberries in the saucepan. Cook uncovered over medium low for 15–20 minutes, or until dumplings are firm and a tester inserted comes out clean. This can be made ahead, but do not leave the cover on or the condensation will dampen the biscuits. Reheat in original pot, with the dry lid returned.

Serve dumplings in bowls with blueberries poured over them. Top with vanilla ice cream, fresh cream, or hot New England Nutmeg Sauce (below).

New England Nutmeg Sauce

YIELDS 2 CUPS

1 cup sugar

1 tablespoon flour

1 cup boiling water

1 tablespoon butter

1 teaspoon fresh nutmeg

In a small saucepan, mix together sugar and flour. Add boiling water and cook, stirring constantly, until sauce bubbles and thickens slightly, 5–7 minutes.

Add butter and simmer gently for 5 minutes. Remove from heat, and stir in nutmeg.

Serve hot over Blueberry Grunt.

Strawberry Jam Cake

Yet another Cape Cod treasure that seems to have slipped quietly to the back of the recipe box behind everything from Apple Cheesecake to Zucchini Gelato, Strawberry Jam Cake was once a standard favorite in Cape Cod cottages. Don't misread the name—this is no cloying cake sticky with jam. It's a spice cake made bold with strong coffee, gently sweetened with good quality preserves. I've heard that blackberry jam works, too. The combination of spice, coffee, and strawberries is a what's-old-is-new-again taste. Fill this with Strawberries and Whipped Cream (below) for a spectacular birthday cake.

MAKES 1 TWO-LAYER CAKE

1 cup (2 sticks) butter

½ cup sugar

1 cup strawberry or blackberry jam

½ cup strong coffee

1 teaspoon cinnamon

¼ teaspoon ground clove

3 eggs, separated

1 teaspoon baking soda

4 tablespoons sour cream

2½ cups flour

Preheat oven to 350°F. Grease and flour 2 8-inch round cake pans.

In a mixer, cream together butter and sugar until light and yellow. Add jam, coffee, and spices. Beat egg yolks and blend into mixture.

Dissolve soda in the sour cream. To the butter and sugar mixture, add sour cream and flour alternately, beating well after each addition.

Beat egg whites until stiff but not dry. Fold into cake batter.

Pour into pans, and bake for 45–55 minutes. Let cool in pans for 10 minutes, and then remove and cool completely on wire racks.

Fill with Strawberries and Whipped Cream. Dust top with powdered sugar.

Strawberries and Whipped Cream

YIELDS 8 CUPS

1 quart strawberries, washed, hulled, and cut in half

2 tablespoons sugar

2 tablespoons sherry

½ pint whipping cream

¼ cup sifted powdered sugar

Sprinkle strawberries with sugar and sherry and let stand for 15 minutes.

Whip cream to very stiff peaks. Fold in powdered sugar. Stir strawberries with sugar and sherry, and fold them into the whipped cream.

Green Tomato Mincemeat

This mincemeat recipe has beautiful flavor, uses up those green tomatoes, and is made without meat. The fresh orange and lemon give it a lovely high note. Mincemeat like this is extremely versatile, beginning with how wonderful it would be in a sandwich with good cheddar cheese.

MAKES ABOUT 15 PINTS

4 quarts green tomatoes (chopped and drained of extra liquid)

4 quarts cored and chopped apples

3 pounds sugar

½ cup vinegar

1 tablespoon salt

1 tablespoon ground clove

1 tablespoon cinnamon

1 tablespoon allspice

1 teaspoon nutmeg

1 pound raisins

1 pound candied citron (optional)

1 orange, peeled, sectioned, and chopped

2 finely chopped lemons, peel included

In a large stockpot, combine all ingredients. Cover, and simmer on very low heat for 3 hours.

Pour mincemeat into 15 sterilized pint jars. Process in a hot water bath the way you would preserves.

Save-all Mincemeat

Another meatless mincemeat, this one celebrates the "kitchen sink" method that Miss Blake used at Greenbriar. Discovered in an old Dennis cookbook, this recipe uses lots of apples, raisins, a cup of preserves, spices, and ½ cup of strong coffee. It all simmers slowly for 2 hours, reducing considerably. The apples became almost candied along with the raisins, but the coffee gives this mincemeat a gutsy taste that is simply gorgeous on pound cake or over a dish of salted caramel ice cream. Of course, to describe a mincemeat recipe as gutsy is already stating the obvious, but the coffee and preserves are the game changer here. This is bold and candied mincemeat, almost best as a wonderful topping for everything from a scone to a chicken breast.

MAKES ABOUT 1 PINT

4 cups chopped apple

½ cup seeded and chopped raisins

1 cup preserves or jelly

1 cup brown sugar

1 teaspoon salt

½ teaspoon cinnamon

½ teaspoon allspice

½ teaspoon nutmeg

½ cup strong coffee

¼ cup vinegar

In a large saucepan mix all ingredients together thoroughly. Cook slowly for 1½–2 hours.

Pour into sterilized jars.

Again, this is wonderful as a fall and winter dessert topping over a cake or ice cream, but it also makes an interesting pie. To bake the pie, use 2 cups mincemeat to 2 cups chopped apples. Bake between two crusts in a 9-inch pie pan at 450°F for 10 minutes. Reduce the oven temperature to 350°F and cook for 35 minutes more.

CHAPTER FIVE

Plymouth, Duxbury, Scituate

This chunk of Massachusetts ground is still shuddering with the landing of the Mayflower. In Plymouth every year on December 22, the oldest gentlemen's club in the country, along with the descendants of the Mayflower, shoot canons and make an enormous batch of "Forefather's Day Succotash," honoring the men and women of the Mayflower who stepped ashore in December, 1621.

That succotash recipe descends from the Wampanoag stew called sobaheg, a delicious pot of fresh local vegetables and turkey or venison, thickened with ground sunflower seeds. Probably served at that first Thanksgiving, sobaheg is still prepared every day over an open fire by Wampanoag tribe members in the Native American camp at Plimoth Plantation. They also make cornmeal and blueberry dumplings, because the Wampanoag like the way the cornmeal crumbles and thickens the sauce.

After their first few winters in Plymouth, the passengers of the Mayflower began to disperse along the coast, incorporating towns as they went and naming them for family properties they left behind in England. In all these towns an Englishness prevails, from the colonial architecture to recipes like Hog's Back Son of a Seacook (actually a nice baked fish, potato, and tomato dish) or Miss Rowe's Old Timey Cake (two hundred years old) or Apple Pandowdy, all recipes that grace local cookbooks. In later years, as Bostonians found these towns excellent sites for summer homes, and eventually year-round communities, the local cookbooks reflected the fact that these families lived well and traveled. There are a surprisingly many recipes for things lyonnaise, but the adjective seems to indicate nothing except a longer list of ingredients, or sometimes crème fraîche. There is proof here that honest Massachusetts recipes made with good, local ingredients are superior to the Italian imports such as Mrs. Bates's Vegetable Casserole from Rome, a layered tomato, Parmesan cheese, and mozzarella concoction that cannot begin to compare to the haunting simplicity of Hingham Baked Tomatoes, layers of tomatoes, sliced baguette, and a little brown sugar luxuriously baked for hours and hours. Mrs. Bates's recipe did not make it into this book.

But, there are many wonderful recipes in cookbooks from this area, recipes that not only fit in well with the good, simple, local food movement, but that also make the pilgrims' landing feel like yesterday. Stuffed Buttercups is one of those dishes. Buttercup squashes are filled with ground turkey and fresh corn, then roasted. The browned, splintering squashes are cut and served in wedges, garnished with toasted spicy pumpkin seeds and homemade cranberry sauce. This is a delicious dish full of wonderful local flavors, particularly when the squash is sweet and firm, and is thus scooped out along with the stew.

The Wampanoags probably taught the colonists to use pumpkins and squash as cooking vessels. A custard baked in a pumpkin, a regular colonist recipe, was certainly the origin of pumpkin pie. This wonderful tradition has unfortunately been reduced to a holiday gimmick, but baking stews inside a sweet-fleshed local squash, like buttercup or kabocha, makes a seriously flavorful dish.

Plymouth to Boston, the coastline changes between stretches of some of the state's most lovely sandy beaches to torturously carved saltwater estuaries; the former has been famous for offering refuge to crews of ships run aground on Minot's Ledge or Cohasset Rocks; the latter is renowned for shellfish.

For two centuries residents of Scituate accommodated shipwrecked passengers and crews that waded up Egypt or Minot beaches. (Egypt was thus named because this far northern point of Scituate was much more fertile than the rest of the town. As men would pass by the general store on their way to pick corn in North

Scituate, the owner, an early relative of S. S. Pierce, would ask kiddingly, "You men going to Egypt for corn?")

An excerpt from the Scituate Historical Society describes how shipwrecks became both entertainment and an industry for the people of Scituate:

> It was a common occurrence to see from one hundred to five hundred vessels of all shapes and sizes in the harbor. After a heavy storm, five or six would be ashore. Our house was always full of sailors and passengers from these vessels after a storm. The government would award us for saving lives with either a medal or $10.00 in gold. We probably collected over $700 rather than the 70 medals as the money was more appreciated at the time.

It had been earlier determined, but never remedied, that a lighthouse meant to alert ships of the dangers of Minot's Ledge and Cohasset Rocks, was actually being mistaken by the ships as the Boston Light; ships were therefore navigating wrongly, and turned straight into these treacherous ledges. The heavy casualties piled up, keeping nineteenth-century life in Scituate both lively and lucrative.

The First Parish Church cookbook describes Duxbury, after its shipping heyday of the nineteenth century and a little excitement when the first Atlantic cable connected the town to France, as a beautiful but drowsy town. But now there are oysters, and Island Creek Oyster Company has recently placed Duxbury on the world map, at least for the $1 oyster and I.P.A. crowd.

Duxbury oysters are now stars of the restaurant chalkboards. All those bars serving craft beers in Brooklyn are also highlighting Duxbury oysters. The Island Creek Oyster Bar in Boston is a bit of a temple for the young hipsters with surfboards sticking out the back of their trucks.

One third of Duxbury is water, with shellfish beds famous since the Wampanoags. Mussels and quahogs are also part of these mudflat riches. It is certainly the town in which to make Zarzuela, a wonderful shellfish stew that could be considered a Massachusetts Jubilee: oysters, littlenecks, soft-shell clams, mussels, lobster, squid, and shrimp are gently steamed together in a tomato, brandy, and saffron broth, and topped with almond and parsley crumbs. It is the Massachusetts coastline in all its glory. It's a stew that probably resembles something the Wampanoag created over hot coals on a beach, and yet the brandy and saffron reveal the European arrival. This is everything about the Massachusetts coast—the shellfish, the fish, and the history. As the recipe says, "Begin with Duxbury oysters . . ."

There are many recipes for oysters here, because if you love oysters you're just looking for an excuse. If you are one of those people, the Duxbury Sunday Morning Oyster Omelet is a must. The broiled Oyster Melt—broiled oysters and cheddar cheese eaten right out of a muffin tin with warm, crusty French bread—is a homey treat to put together on a Friday night, to be eaten at your kitchen counter with a glass of something dry and sparkling. Chicken Smothered in Oysters is a straight Duxbury dining room recipe that is as delicious and elegant today as it was in 1930 when Duxbury ladies shared the recipe.

At Island Creek they insist that raw is the way to go, and there are rules, starting with no cocktail sauce, which was apparently invented in Ohio as a means of masking rotten oysters (although that would indeed require strong stuff). Tabasco is okay, so is lemon. A sharp mignonette sauce calls out that wonderful steel in an oyster.

Raw oysters are the newest "what's old is new again." Who knows? Maybe stuffed pumpkins are next.

Plymouth, Duxbury, Scituate Index

Cornmeal and Wild Blueberry Dumplings

The Wampanoag at Plimouth Plantation serve these with sobaheg. The cornmeal and blueberries soak up the stew, contributing sweetness and that lovely crumbly dimension. Earl Mills says that traditionally the Wampanoag served cornmeal dumplings with herring, as the toothsome crumb of the dumplings somehow kept people from choking on the tiny herring bones.

MAKES 12 DUMPLINGS

2 quarts water

½ cup stone-ground grits or cornmeal

½ cup flour

¼ cup dried blueberries

½ teaspoon sugar

½ teaspoon salt

Hot water

Bring water to a gentle simmer.

Combine the next five ingredients together in a large bowl, mixing well.

Once mixed, slowly add a spoonful at a time of hot water. When mix is thick enough to hold together, shape it into 2-inch rounds, 1⅓–2 ounces a piece.

Drop carefully into the water. Push gently if they stick to the bottom.

When the dumplings rise to the surface they are done, about 40 minutes. With a slotted spoon remove them to a platter and keep warm until ready to serve.

Turkey Sobaheg

Sobaheg translates to "stew" in Wampanoag. At Plimouth Plantation a version of sobaheg with venison, turkey, or just vegetables is cooked over the fire in the Wampanoag camp almost every day. But pretend you didn't know that. This stew has all the wonderful qualities—freshness, wholesomeness, warming nutritive goodness—of chicken soup, only better. It's lighter and brighter. It tastes more "just harvested," less "stewed," although time is an ingredient for it, too.

There is something truly American in its character, something very "amber waves of grain" about this dish; maybe it's the cornmeal that cooks with it. With all native ingredients, sobaheg is an honest American meal, a revelatory substitute for those nights you want homemade chicken soup. Symbolically, this would be a lovely first course for a Thanksgiving dinner.

SERVES 6–8

1¼ cups dry beans (white, red, brown or spotted kidney-shaped beans)

1 cup stone-ground grits or stone-ground corn-meal

2 pounds turkey (about ½ a small breast; turkey legs, venison, or chicken may be substituted)

½ cup finely chopped onion

1 tablespoon minced garlic

3 quarts cold water

½ pound green beans, trimmed and cut into 1-inch lengths

½ small–medium winter squash, trimmed and chopped into ½-inch cubes

2 teaspoons salt

Freshly ground black pepper to taste

½ cup raw sunflower seed meats, made into a coarse flour in a food processor

Toasted sunflower seeds

Coarse sea salt

Lime

Chopped cilantro

Hot sauce

In a pot combine beans, grits, turkey (or other meat), onions, garlic, and water. Bring to a simmer over medium heat, turn down to a very low simmer, and cook for about 2 hours. The only problem with this stew is that the cornmeal tends to stick to the bottom. Scrape the bottom often to prevent a scorched pot.

When dried beans are tender but not mushy, remove meat from pot. Remove any skin and bones, break into pieces, and add back to soup.

Add green beans, squash, salt, and pepper, and simmer very gently until tender, about 20 minutes.

Add sunflower flour, stirring until thoroughly blended. The soup will thicken considerably at this point.

Garnish with toasted sunflower seeds, a good dusting of coarse sea salt, and freshly ground pepper. It's not "native," but fresh lime, chopped cilantro, and a red pepper sauce like Pimenta Moida are also delicious on top of the finished soup.

Stuffed Buttercups

What may seem like a gimmicky way to serve beef stew at a dinner party was in fact a sensible and obvious early American cooking method. Pumpkins and squash were pots and pans to the colonists. It was easy to fill a hollowed pumpkin with meats and vegetables, or sometimes eggs, milk, and seasonings, and slowly bake all together. Certainly, pumpkin pie began here.

Choose either buttercup or kabocha squash, which are very similar. Both are smaller than pumpkins but large enough to fill well. Their flesh is very sweet but with a firm, dry, texture, like chestnuts.

The recipe here includes ground turkey, fresh corn, and mashed potatoes; consider creating your own squash-filled dinner with Thanksgiving leftovers. Another great combination would be crumbled cornbread, sausage, and sautéed apples. And imagine the fun of transporting your whole stuffed squashes to a potluck!

But the main story here is how wholly delicious this is. The squash are small enough to cut the cooked whole into wedges, serving each person a wedge of squash piled with filling. Whether you prepare pumpkin or buttercup squash, the spicy pumpkin seeds garnish is a must, as is Colonists' Baked Cranberry Sauce.

SERVES 6

2 medium buttercup or kabocha squash, about 5 pounds each

½ cup toasted squash seeds

2 teaspoons, plus 2 tablespoons oil, divided

½ teaspoon smoked paprika

1 teaspoon cinnamon

1 teaspoon coarse salt

2 tablespoons butter

1 cup chopped onion

¾ cup chopped red pepper

1 cup chopped celery

2 tablespoons minced garlic

3 tablespoons dried sage

¼ teaspoon cayenne

1 pound ground turkey (or beef)

3 medium potatoes, cooked and mashed (about 1 pound, 2 cups mashed)

¾ cup chicken broth

2 cups freshly grated corn

Chopped fresh cilantro or parsley

Cut off the top of the squashes and save them for lids. Scoop out the seeds and strings, making the inside of the squash clean. Reserve the seeds for toasting. Sprinkle inside of the squash with salt and pepper. If you can, do this 1 day ahead and let the squash sit upside down to let the moisture extracted by the salt drain out of it. But, doing this 1 hour in advance is okay.

Preheat oven to 350°F. Rinse seeds under cold water to clean completely, pat dry on paper towels. Toss in a bowl with 2 teaspoons olive oil, smoked paprika, cinnamon, and coarse salt. Spread on baking sheet, and roast until toasted brown, 12–15 minutes. Set aside.

Reduce oven to 300°F.

Heat butter and remaining 2 tablespoons oil, and cook onion, red pepper, and celery for 12–14 minutes, or until very softened and glazed. Add garlic, sage, salt, pepper, and cayenne, and cook for 3 minutes more.

Add ground turkey to the vegetables, and cook until turkey loses its pinkness, about 10 minutes. Push and stir the mixture as it cooks to break up the turkey evenly. Let cool slightly before proceeding, about 5 minutes or until turkey is no longer steaming.

Place potatoes in a pot of salted water and boil until very soft. Drain and mash with a fork. Add chicken broth while mashing until potatoes are soft and fluffy. Season lightly with salt and pepper.

In a large bowl, gently mix together the turkey mixture, mashed potatoes, and corn.

Fill the 2 squashes with the turkey mixture, and place the lid on top. Set the squash on foil brushed with oil spread on a baking sheet. Bake for 2 hours, or until the whole squash looks "roasted." They will look a little browned, and may begin to split. If they do, just wrap aluminum foil around them to bind together. Remove from oven and let cool for about 15 minutes before serving.

To serve, cut the entire squash into wedges, serving each person a wedge of squash piled with the filling. Serve in heated bowls and garnish with toasted pumpkin seeds and fresh cilantro. Colonist's Baked Cranberry Sauce is a wonderful accompaniment.

Reheat slowly, but serve hot.

Colonists' Baked Cranberry Sauce

This is another recipe that not only dates back to the colonists, but also remains a worthy, if not particularly great, way to make cranberry sauce. Slow baking invites a more sumptuous taste to the berries, particularly if you add that splash of port.

MAKES 3 CUPS

4 cups cranberries

1 cup sugar

1 cup seedless raisins

1 cup boiling water

½ teaspoon cinnamon

¼ teaspoon ground clove

¼ cup port (optional)

Preheat oven to 350°F.

In a roasting dish, baking pan, or dutch oven, combine all ingredients, except port. Cover with aluminum foil or a lid. If you are adding the alcohol, do it after the cranberries have cooked for an hour. While it's baking, uncover the dish occasionally to stir. Bake for 1½ hours, or until cranberries are soft and surrounded by a thick syrup.

Remove and immediately pour cranberries into a bowl to cool. Let come to room temperature before serving. The sauce will seriously thicken as it cools. Cranberries will keep refrigerated for up to 2 weeks.

Hog's Back Son of a Seacook

This wonderful title is salty dog speak for "boiled salt cod cooked with pork pieces." The Duxbury source here, Mrs. Helen White, admits that this recipe was originally made with salt cod, but she gentrifies it with fresh fish to equal success. This is an easy weeknight dinner, as delicious as it is fun to say.

SERVES 4-6

2 pounds cooked cod, haddock, or hake

1 tablespoon + 4 tablespoons butter, divided

1 onion, sliced

Salt and freshly ground black pepper

3 medium potatoes (about 1 pound), in ¼-inch slices

6 medium to large sliced fresh tomatoes or 1 (28-ounce) can crushed (not pureed) tomatoes

3 slices (about 3 ounces) raw salt pork, chopped

½ cup white wine

2 cups fresh bread crumbs

Chopped parsley for garnish

Lemon for garnish

Preheat oven to 400°F.

In a bowl that will hold all the ingredients, flake the fish gently.

In a medium skillet melt 1 tablespoon butter and sauté onion just to soften. Add to fish. Season well with salt and pepper.

Butter an 8 x 11-inch baking dish. Lay down ⅓ of the fish. Cover with ⅓ the slices of potato. Sprinkle with salt and pepper, and then spread ⅓ the tomatoes, and ⅓ the pork. Continue with these layers until the dish is full. Pour in the wine, and cover dish with foil. Bake for 30 minutes.

In a skillet, melt remaining butter and lightly toast bread crumbs to brown. Sprinkle on the casserole and bake uncovered for 40 minutes longer, or until the potatoes are completely soft. Cover the dish again with foil if the crumbs get too brown but the potatoes are not cooked. Odd for a fish dish, but this one actually improves if it sits for 15 minutes before serving. It is even delicious the next day, the way the flavors in lasagna need to meld and improve.

Spoon dish into warm bowls; garnish with parsley and lemon.

Apple Pandowdy

"We left the pudding steamer in England!"

That seems to be the colonial issue that gave birth to Apple Pandowdy. Without their pudding steamer, early colonists had to adapt old recipes to what they owned in the New World. "It's baked in a pan and looks kind of dowdy," seems to be how the colonists considered the results of their New World apple pudding experiments.

Four hundred years later we think this "broken" topped apple pie an alchemical combination of warm, sweet, crunchy, and crumbly.

SERVES 6-8

For the piecrust:

1½ cups all-purpose flour

1 tablespoon sugar

½ teaspoon salt

½ cup (1 stick) cold butter, cut into ¼-inch pieces

2 tablespoons vegetable shortening

3 tablespoons ice water

For the pandowdy:

4 Granny Smith apples, peeled, cored, and sliced

Juice from 1 lemon

2 teaspoons cornstarch

Pinch of salt

½ cup molasses or maple syrup

¼ teaspoon ground nutmeg

½ teaspoon ground cinnamon

To make the piecrust:

In a food processor fitted with a steel blade, mix flour, sugar, and salt. Add butter and shortening and mix until it resembles coarse crumbs. Add 2 tablespoons ice water, and mix to form a ball. Add the additional tablespoon of water only if the mixture is still too dry to come together. Form dough into a disk, wrap in plastic wrap and chill.

To make the pandowdy:

Preheat oven to 400°F.

Warm a large ovenproof skillet to medium low heat.

In a large bowl combine apples, lemon juice, cornstarch, salt, molasses or syrup, nutmeg, and cinnamon. Toss very well to combine. Pour into heated skillet.

On a lightly floured surface, roll the crust out to a circle ⅛-inch thick. Transfer the crust to cover the apples. Trim crust flush with the edge of the skillet. Cut several steam vents in the crust. Place in oven and bake for 30 minutes.

Remove pan from oven, and reduce temperature to 350°F. Using a metal spatula, cut the crust into 1-inch squares, and press them down beneath the surface of the filling.

Return pandowdy to oven, and bake for 30 minutes longer. Allow to cool for at least 20 minutes before serving.

Serve warm in bowls topped with vanilla ice cream.

Miss Rowe's Old Timey Cake

Another Duxbury recipe too charming and too antique to omit (it is said to be over 250 years old), Miss Rowe's Old Timey Cake is, yes, plain, but it is therefore a wonderful vehicle for fooling around. This would be a divine dessert beneath a few thick, golden tablespoons of Ojala Farms Fruit Soup. Toasted slices of Miss Rowe's would be an equally lovely breakfast beside a glass of Spiced Buttermilk.

MAKES 1 LOAF CAKE

1 cup sugar

½ cup sour cream

¼ teaspoon baking soda

1½ cups flour

2 eggs

½ cup raisins, chopped

Preheat oven to 350°F. Butter and flour an 8½ x 4½-inch loaf pan.

Dissolve sugar, sour cream, and baking soda in a medium mixing bowl. Add remainder of the ingredients, and mix gently. Pour into prepared pan and bake for 45 minutes, or until a toothpick inserted comes out clean. Cool on a wire rack for 15 minutes before inverting pan. Then cool completely on rack.

Island Creek Mignonette

Sharp, bracing, with a little sparkle, this mignonette is an oyster's runner-up choice of sauce in which to be doused; the first choice is the waters of Duxbury Bay.

MAKES ½ CUP

½ cup dry champagne or sparkling wine

2 shallots, minced

1 tablespoon red wine vinegar

¼ teaspoon freshly ground pepper

2 dozen oysters, shucked

Shaved ice or rock salt, for serving

In a small bowl, stir together the wine, shallots, vinegar, and pepper.

Place oysters on a bed of chunked ice or rock salt, snuggling them in to keep from tipping. Spoon mignonette onto oysters, and slurp.

The mignonette can be prepared up to 6 hours in advance. Keep chilled.

Oyster Melts

Make this on a Friday night when you want something wonderful without fuss. Eat Oyster Melts right from the muffin tins, at your kitchen counter, with chunks of warm, crusty bread. Pour champagne.

MAKES 12, A DINNER FOR TWO

1 loaf French bread

Butter for tins

1 dozen large oysters

12 slices good quality cheddar cheese

Preheat oven to 350°F.

Put bread in oven to get warm and crispy. Keep it warm wrapped in foil until oysters are ready.

Turn the oven to broil. Butter a set of muffin tins.

In each tin, place an oyster topped with a square of cheddar cheese. Broil until the cheese melts and gets slightly bubbly.

Eat the oysters straight out of the pan, placing each on a chunk of warm French bread. Serve with dry sparkling wine.

Duxbury Sunday Morning Oyster Omelet

Said to be a great cure for a hangover, an oyster omelet, made with freshly harvested Duxbury oysters, is a great way for someone with an oyster passion to express themselves. If it's Sunday, and you're in Duxbury, boldly shuck the oysters, beat the eggs, and stir a Bloody Mary.

SERVES 1

1 slice bacon

4 fresh oysters, quartered

2 eggs

1 teaspoon cream

Salt and freshly ground pepper to taste

1 teaspoon butter

Fresh parsley

In a small skillet, fry the bacon until brown. Dot dry on a paper towel and crumble the slice.

Reduce heat to medium high, pour off most of the fat from the skillet, and add chopped oysters. Cook for 1 minute, and add the crumbled bacon. Set this pan aside.

Heat a new skillet to medium high.

In a small bowl beat eggs with cream, and season with salt and pepper.

Add butter to skillet, and bring to foamy, swirling to cover the pan.

Pour in the eggs, and swirl to cover. Let cook for 30 seconds, and then lay the oysters and bacon mixture on top of the eggs. Cook until eggs are set, about 3 minutes. Fold omelet in half, cook for 1 more minute, and then slide onto a plate.

Garnish with fresh parsley. Serve with buttered toast.

Duxbury Oyster Stew

There is nothing so comforting on a dreary winter day as a bowl of oyster stew, the simplest of soups, a luscious combination of plump, briny oysters and hot, creamy broth. Ladle it into mugs for brunch on a winter's Sunday or pour it into wide soup bowls for a Christmas Eve dinner. Put another log on the fire, and you will be channeling two hundred years of fine Duxbury meals. Serve Duxbury Oyster Stew with a glass of something chalky and sparkling—perhaps a Westport Rivers Vineyard choice—and one of the world's great pleasures is re-created with ingredients all sourced from the Massachusetts coast.

MAKES 4 AMPLE DINNER SERVINGS, 6 FOR AN APPETIZER

2 quarts whole milk

1 bunch (about 12) scallions with 2 inches of their greens

¼ cup (½ stick) butter

2 pints (about 48) oysters

Salt and pepper

Paprika

In a large saucepan, heat milk to very hot, but not boiling.

While the milk is heating chop the scallions and their leaves thinly.

Melt butter in a saucepan large enough to hold the chowder, and sauté scallions until soft and golden.

Add oysters and their liquid, and spoon them around very gently, just until they begin to plump, and their edges ruffle.

Pour the very hot milk over the oysters, and heat again. The oysters will finish their cooking as the milk returns to just below a simmer.

Taste for salt and pepper. Ladle immediately into warmed soup bowls, and sprinkle liberally with paprika.

Chicken Smothered in Oysters

The chicken in this recipe first roasts with a little broth of its own juices. In the last fifteen minutes of bronzing, plump oysters and a pour of cream join the bird, resulting in a simple velvet sauce of ruffled Wellfleets, or Duxburys, or Cotuits. It's not necessarily the best thing to happen to an oyster, but it's definitely one of the best things to happen to a chicken.

SERVES 4-6

1 small, young chicken, about 4 pounds

3 tablespoons butter, softened

Salt and pepper

1 cup boiling water

1 cup cream

1 pint small oysters, drained

Chopped parsley for garnish

Preheat oven to 425°F.

Split the chicken down its back. With poultry shears or a sharp knife, remove backbone. Flatten chicken, and lay it skin side up in a roasting pan that has a lid. (Or use aluminum foil to cover the chicken when roasting.)

Rub the chicken with the softened butter, and sprinkle liberally with salt and pepper. Pour the boiling water around the chicken, and cover closely with lid or foil. Roast for 1 hour, or until tender.

Pour cream over the chicken. Then cover the chicken in oysters. Cover the dish again, and roast for 15 minutes.

Remove the chicken to a cutting board, reserving oysters and cream in the pan. Cut chicken into pieces. Lay the pieces on a warmed serving platter, or plates. Give the cream and oysters a stir, and briefly rewarm them in the roasting pan. Taste for salt and pepper. Pour this oyster-cream sauce over the chicken. This dish is rather brown, but delicious; don't hesitate to strew parsley. Serve with white or wild rice.

Mussels Mariniere

A little French cooking steers this recipe away from the usual garlicky-brothed dish. A roux is made in a second saucepan beside the steaming mussels. When the shellfish is cooked, the hot mussel broth is poured into the roux saucepan, creating a voluptuous sauce to ladle back over the mussels. The resulting bowl of hot shellfish and rich sauce makes a mussel course with finesse, very Duxbury.

SERVES 6 AS AN APPETIZER

8 tablespoons (1 stick) butter, divided

4 tablespoons flour

1 teaspoon salt

¼ teaspoon pepper

¾ cup onion, chopped

6 small buds garlic, crushed

¾ cup celery, chopped fine

3 pounds mussels

1 cup white wine

4 tablespoons chopped parsley

1 teaspoon lemon juice

French bread

In a large saucepan melt 4 tablespoons butter until it's bubbly. Stir in flour and stir with a whisk or wooden spoon over medium heat until the paste is pale and looks like cornmeal, about 5 minutes. Season with salt and pepper. Set aside.

Sauté onion, garlic, and celery in the remaining 4 tablespoons butter. Lay mussels on top. Pour wine over the mussels. Steam until shells open.

Strain liquid into the pot with the roux. Add parsley and lemon juice. Cook 1 minute or so. Divide the mussels into individual bowls, and pour sauce over the mussels. Serve with toasted French bread.

Herbed Mussels Brasucade

Starring mussels roasted over an open fire and soused in a lusciously herbaceous olive oil, this recipe is one of the most delicious things you can do to that shellfish as beautiful as a blackbird's wing.

We should all be eating more mussels. Their list of virtues—from being inexpensive to being aquatic purifiers—is long. Mussels are good for you and they're good for the world. They're full of iron, vitamin B-12, and omega-3 fatty acids, and as filter feeders they're nature's purifiers. Unlike other aquacultures, mussel farms are known to actually improve water conditions because the small purple-shelled workhorses remove excess algae, nutrients, and sediment from the water as they filter plankton. The Duxbury mudflats are famous for their mussels as well as their oysters.

This preparation can be done in a large, wide sauté pan set on a grill or in a similar pan in your kitchen. It requires heating the mussels on an open pan with no liquid, then pouring a cup of fragrant olive oil, in which tarragon, shallots, garlic, and rosemary have steeped for hours, over the hot, freshly opened orange meats. Plunk the steaming dish in the center of a table with a little pomp. Mop up that sauce with chunks of warmed baguette.

SERVES 6 AS AN APPETIZER

2 large shallots, minced

2 garlic cloves, minced

3 tablespoons minced fresh rosemary

4 tablespoons minced fresh tarragon

Red pepper flakes to taste

1 cup olive oil

5 pounds mussels, scrubbed

1 cup white wine

In a bowl, combine the shallots, garlic, rosemary, tarragon, pepper flakes, and olive oil. Set aside to infuse for at least 3 hours. This can be done a day ahead.

If using a grill, bring it to a high temperature.

Place a large paella pan or a shallow sturdy pan that can take the heat, on the grill. Add mussels to the pan and cook, stirring once in a while until the mussels start to just open and release their first water. Remove pan from heat and carefully discard the water. Return pan to the heat, and add white wine. Continue cooking and stirring until the mussels are fully opened and cooked.

Remove from the heat and pour over the herb sauce, shaking the pan to distribute evenly. Serve as an appetizer with drinks while grilling the rest of the meal or as a main course.

Zarzuela

(Massachusetts Jubilee)

Begin with Duxbury oysters, add New Bedford scallops, Marblehead mussels, Ipswich clams, Gloucester lobster, and Hingham crabs. All these shelled creatures are easily found in so many waterways along the Massachusetts shore. Squid and shrimp find their way in here, too. This is a gorgeous extravaganza of the Massachusetts coast, but without the salt pork and cream routine. The seafood snuggles into saffron, brandy, and white wine, and is crowned not with the reliable buttered bread crumbs, but with toasted almonds, parsley, and garlic. The lid-lifting moment when it is ready to be served releases a shellfish-wine-parsley-and-almond steam that is like releasing a school of Neptune's tipsy sprites.

Make this for a special occasion. Start with bags of quahogs, steamers, and oysters in your sink needing to be shucked. Make it with at least one friend; you chop the onions, and peel and devein the shrimp; they shuck; it all goes quickly and happily.

SERVES 6

24 littlenecks

24 oysters

24 mussels

24 steamer clams

½ cup, plus 2 tablespoons olive oil, divided

2 cups chopped onion

2 tablespoons minced garlic, divided

½ cup chopped scallions, whites and green leaves

8 tablespoons chopped parsley, divided

1 pound squid, bodies chopped into ⅓-inch rings and tentacles to 1-inch pieces

1 cup chopped tomatoes, canned or fresh

Freshly ground black pepper

1 cup slivered almonds, lightly toasted

½ cup oyster crackers

½ teaspoon saffron threads, ground to a powder

½ cup tomato puree

2 cups white wine

⅛ cup brandy

24 shrimp, peeled and deveined

½ pound lobster meat

½ pound crab meat

Shuck the littlenecks and oysters, saving all their liquid together in one large measuring cup or a small bowl. Reserve the meats in separate small bowls.

Strain the juices through triple layers of cheesecloth, and reserve.

Scrub mussels and steamers. Fill a large skillet with a ½ inch of water, and steam open mussels and steamers. Reserve liquid, and strain it through cheesecloth. Add to reserved littleneck and oyster juices.

Shuck the steamer and mussel meats, removing the beard from the mussels. With scissors or a knife snip off the toughened neck of the clams. Reserve the meats together.

Heat ½ cup olive oil in a large skillet or dutch oven to smoking. Add onions and 1 tablespoon garlic, and cook until soft and golden, about 12 minutes. Add scallions, 3 tablespoons parsley, squid, and chopped tomatoes. Season with pepper. Cook for 30 minutes or until the squid begins to soften and the tomatoes cook. At this point the dish may be prepared a day in advance, to be completed an hour before serving time.

About an hour before serving, put the toasted almonds, oyster crackers, remaining 1 tablespoon garlic, and remaining 5 tablespoons parsley in a food processor. Process to a crumbly paste. Add remaining 2 tablespoons olive oil, and process again. Set aside.

Bring the base to a simmer. Add the saffron powder, the tomato puree, white wine, and brandy. Cook for 15 minutes or until the alcohol is completely evaporated.

Add littlenecks, clam and mussel meats, shrimp, lobster, and crab, and stir them in gently.

Lastly, add oysters and stir them in very carefully.

Add reserved, strained shellfish juices to the pot.

Sprinkle the almond/parsley crumbs over the whole dish.

At this point, taste the broth. Much of its flavor will depend on the broth you have collected from the shellfish. If it tastes a bit too strong of clams, add more white wine right here. Be generous, up to another full cup, if you have to. Taste for salt and pepper, also.

Cover, and simmer heartily for 15 minutes. The topping will mix into the soup, thickening it and flavoring it a bit.

Bring the covered dish to the table. Ladle it into warm soup bowls.

Mincemeat and Brown Bread Pudding

If you have any doubts about mincemeat, make this pudding. It includes a short list of iconic Massachusetts ingredients—mincemeat, brown bread, and rum. Discovered in a historic Scituate cookbook, this pudding recipe will fill your kitchen with the aromas of cider, rum, and raisins. The result is a moist, heady dessert, draped in a sweet, almond-scented Hard Sauce. Enjoy spoonfuls of this rummy pudding in January, as the snow accumulates, the wind chill drops, and the seas rise.

SERVES 6–8

1 recipe or 1 (16-ounce) can brown bread

1 cup sugar

½ teaspoon salt

2 teaspoons baking powder

3½ cups or 1 (28-ounce) jar mincemeat

2 tablespoons melted butter

2 eggs, beaten

3 tablespoons rum

½ cup apple cider

Slice the brown bread into ½-inch slices, and allow it to dry out or put it in a 200°F oven. When dry enough, process in a food processor to crumbs. Add sugar, salt, and baking powder to the crumbs.

Preheat oven to 325°F. Butter a 2-quart glass or ceramic baking dish.

In a large bowl combine mincemeat with melted butter and eggs. Add crumb mixture. Stir in rum and cider, and mix well. Pour into buttered baking dish, and bake for 1–1¼ hours, or until the pudding "gives" just slightly when pressed on top. Serve with a small scoop of Hard Sauce (below) on top or on the side.

Hard Sauce

MAKES 1 CUP

½ cup (1 stick) butter

½ cup sugar

1 tablespoon brandy

1 teaspoon almond extract

In a medium bowl, cream together butter and sugar. Beat in brandy and almond extract until all is fluffy.

Old-time Blueberry Grunt

Since Richard Prouty arrived sometime in the mid-seventeenth century, Proutys have been raising families in Scituate for at least eleven consecutive generations. Dick Prouty, perhaps generation number thirteen or fourteen, now lives in Gloucester, but he remembers his grandmother, Edna Gardner Prouty, in the Prouty homestead kitchen. Prouty generously shares Edna's particular Blueberry Grunt recipe and his memories:

"My grandmother, Edna Gardner Prouty, used to cook this blueberry recipe for our family. I have vivid memories of going blueberry-ing with my grandfather on the farm we lived on with Grandma and Grandpa. Then my grandmother would make great tart blueberry pies, but my favorite blueberry dish was this blueberry grunt recipe. Grandma died in 1957 when I was just thirteen, but I still have strong memories of her working with her apron on, and exhaling those long Yankee 'ayaas' when she was satisfied or wanted to affirm you. She had a wonderful warm smile and was always happy, it seemed to me. She was always cooking or getting ready to cook. Thanksgivings were two-week preparation affairs, and the kitchen smelled especially wonderful when she was getting ready for Thanksgiving."

SERVES 8, BUT EASILY DOUBLED OR TRIPLED

2 cups of blueberries

½ cup sugar

1 cup water

I stick cinnamon

2 tablespoons lemon juice

½ teaspoon salt

4 slices, about ¼ pound, good quality whole wheat bread, torn into 1-inch chunks

Cook berries in saucepan with sugar, water, cinnamon, lemon juice, and salt, for about 5 minutes. Drop in whole wheat bread and simmer for a few more minutes. Allow to come to room temperature then put in the "icebox" until chilled.

CHAPTER SIX

Hingham, Cohasset, Hull

Swallows know the route up the Massachusetts coastline from Cohasset to Hull by the white-washed church spires that have punctuated this stretch of Massachusetts shore for more than three hundred years. From the First Parish Church in Cohasset to the Old Ship's Church in Hingham to the sweet little Saint Nicholas Methodist Church in Hull, history has been made in the spaces between these steeples. It's a coastline rich in the beginnings of Massachusetts and of America.

History still clutches Cohasset, Hingham, and Hull, as local cookbooks and the towns' active historical societies attest. Dinners in these communities are still old New England classics.

In Cohasset, a town that celebrates the pristine simplicity of white clapboard and black shutters, of sweeping hydrangea-hemmed lawns, and picket fences, the food is as simply, historically as beautiful as the architecture. Cohasset Punch, a recipe developed for a wealthy Cohasset resident long before World War I, is an exquisite cocktail with half a chilled local peach; mounded with crushed ice; swathed in peach syrup, sweet vermouth, and rum; and served in a champagne saucer.

Deadhead the roses and polish the silver. Bacon-Filled Cherry Tomatoes is a recipe worth snitching from a Cohasset garden party. What may seem dated is simply so good it cannot be retired. A tray of hollowed cherry tomatoes refilled with chopped crisp bacon, green onions, parsley, and Parmesan cheese will always be the first cocktail tray returned empty to the kitchen.

There is no need to alter Hake Baked in Buttermilk. Serve this with new potatoes rolled in melted butter and fresh parsley, and you have a delicate Massachusetts dinner for a spring night.

Old-fashioned Hingham, incorporated in 1635, whose motto is "History and Pride," whose Main Street was declared by Eleanor Roosevelt to

Roosevelt to be "the most beautiful Main Street in America," home to the oldest continuously-worshipped-in church in the country, and still home to generations of Boston Brahmins, epitomizes old-fashioned Yankee Massachusetts that hasn't quite realized it is old-fashioned. Recipe collections are delightfully authentic, sometimes surprising, with many treasured versions of what looks like the same old Yankee thing, but is in fact a well-tuned recipe with years of testing. Take Apple Scrapple for example, a crumbly apple pudding encouraged by Hingham ladies to be served as a start to the day, a fine start indeed.

A platter of Hingham Pickled Shrimp, rosy shrimp laced with lemon and onion slices and studded in bay leaves, looks like a Matisse painting and is a delightfully fresh-tasting first course. For a wonderful secret lunch alone, have these beside a thick slice of toasted Hingham Brown Bread. About that brown bread: spread it with Quince Honey or Cranberry, Date, and Ginger Chutney for breakfast; serve it with Pork Chops and Cranberries from Cape Cod; even with the rustic Azorean kale soup, Provincetown's Soup of the Holy Ghost. The hint of sweetness and molasses in the brown bread is a great counter to savory flavors. Leave the baked beans behind (or serve them with a crunchy toasted baguette.)

As shipping trade in Boston, and farther north to Salem, increased in the nineteenth century, so did ship wrecks off this South Shore Coast, particularly involving ships trying to navigate the treacherous Nantasket Road shipping channel into Boston. A long, narrow peninsula with a putter-like end, the city of Hull points northwest into the Boston Harbor entrance. It is the fourth smallest town geographically in the state of Massachusetts, but it holds a mighty place.

In 1890 the Point Allerton Livesaving Station was erected in Hull, answering the much needed call of the ever-increasing Boston commercial shipping trade, made so vulnerable in the diabolically rocky waters. But Joshua James, the most famous lifesaver of all, had already been saving shipwrecked lives since 1876. (Joshua James was also famous at a very young age for being able to "hear the land speak," distinguishing among shorelines in Hull and its surrounding islands by the different sounds of waves washing against their rocky shores and shoals.) By the time he died in 1902, minutes after a life-saving operation, James had already saved a documented one thousand lives. He lived and led his crews by these words: "You have to go out, but you don't have to come back." The Hull Lifesaving Museum describes James and his crewmates as "men of profound courage, skill, and compassion, true models of heroism in their time and ours."

The very best recipe to be rescued from Hull is for Hermits: gooey, rich molasses planks with those telltale hermit wrinkles across the top, the perfect soul-nourishing snack for the rescued.

Hingham, Cohasset, Hull Index

Apple Scrapple

Almost anything that happens to an apple in an oven evokes goodness, but this simple "pudding," yet another version of a scrapple, becomes a little more special, if only because the Hingham recipe suggests serving it for breakfast with a pour of cold cream, indeed. Cortland and Golden Delicious apples work well in this recipe, but I recommend Roxbury Russets if you can get them. They're available at Russell Orchards Farm Store and Winery in Ipswich.

SERVES 6

6–8 apples, peeled and sliced

½ cup (1 stick) butter, softened

¾ cup brown sugar

1 cup flour

1 teaspoon cinnamon

Preheat oven to 350°F.

Distribute apple slices evenly in a buttered 9-inch square baking pan.

In the bowl of an electric mixer, cream butter and brown sugar. Add flour and cinnamon, and mix until it is the consistency of cornmeal. Spread evenly over apples.

Bake for 1 hour, or until the top is brown and bubbling.

Mildred Justice's Golden Pudding

Mildred Justice's "Golden Pudding," a recipe found in the Hingham Historical Society cookbook, is a mosaic of golden vegetables—carrots, corn, and butternut squash—bound together with a light cornmeal batter. A rumor of mace and orange run through it all, a reminder of the spice trade's omnipotent rule over coastal Massachusetts.

Maybe it's the humility of a pudding. Maybe it's the comforting sweetness of corn. Maybe it's the gentle restraint of New England cooking, but Mildred Justice's Golden Pudding, for a special weekend breakfast, is as celestial as it is unique. Serve it warm (not piping hot, the flavors need to cool a little to be recognized) with a side of Canadian bacon and a drizzle of maple syrup to make breakfast miracles. A poached egg on top would be luscious.

SERVES 8

3 cups ground carrots (ground with the steel blade of a food processor)

2 cups fresh corn (if you can't use fresh, use canned; frozen isn't quite as good)

3 pounds butternut squash, peeled and cubed

1 cup milk

3 eggs beaten

½ cup flour

½ cup cornmeal

1 teaspoon baking powder

1 tablespoon sea salt

2 tablespoons sugar

2 teaspoons mace

Peel from 1 orange

Preheat oven to 350°F. Butter a large glass baking dish.

In a large mixing bowl, combine carrots, corn, and squash.

In a small bowl, lightly mix together milk and eggs.

In a medium bowl mix together flour, cornmeal, baking powder, salt, sugar, and mace. Add milk and egg mixture, and stir to incorporate.

Pour this mixture over the vegetables, and mix well.

Pour the mixture into the prepared dish, and shave the orange peel over the top to lightly cover.

Bake for 45–50 minutes, or until firm to the touch. The dish may be finished under the broiler to brown a little crisper if you like. Allow to cool for 15 minutes.

Serve drizzled with maple syrup, crispy bacon, or roasted sausages on the side.

Hingham Pickled Shrimp

This shrimp dish is the perfect starter to a large holiday meal, flavorful enough to support that first toast, but light enough not to ruin the turkey or the tenderloin to follow. The pink shrimp, canary-yellow lemon slices, and green bay leaves make this platter look like a Matisse painting; more points for Hingham, the town whose cultural bells are never out of tune.

SERVES 12 AS AN APPETIZER, BUT IS EASILY HALVED

5 pounds shrimp

3 large onions, sliced thin

2 lemons, sliced thin

1½ cups vegetable oil

1 cup white vinegar

1 tablespoon salt

12 peppercorns

1 tablespoon celery seed

1 teaspoon sugar

6 bay leaves

Cook shrimp in lightly salted water just to cover. Drain and then peel. Toss gently with onion and lemon slices, then lay out in a shallow ceramic dish.

Combine the remaining ingredients and shake together in a quart container to create a marinade. Pour over the shrimp. This is best made two days in advance, regularly tossing the shrimp in the marinade.

To serve, put the whole recipe in a large, shallow bowl, showing off the lemon slices and bay leaves. Or, you can also make individual servings, placing some shrimp, onion, and lemon slices in a Boston lettuce leaf, making a platter of lettuce cups.

Hingham Baked Tomatoes

With recipes like United States Senate Bean Soup, Chiffonade Dressing, and Poached Swordfish Chablis, the undated cookbook, *Hingham Recipes Old and New,* compiled by New North Alliance reflects a culture of wellbeing that thrived for generations in Hingham. People were cultured enough to make cakes frosted with fondant and rum, nostalgic enough to remember the simplicity of March Meeting Cake, and modern enough to include recipes for "Hors D'oeuvres, Party, and T.V. Snacks." Hingham was old Yankee and a little blue blood; the recipes in this town reflect basic good ingredients cooked well.

I love this recipe—roasted tomatoes layered with baguette toasts—for acknowledging that when tomatoes are roasted a long time (four hours) they become sublime. The toast softens to pudding within the tomatoes; on top the toasts just get crispier. The contributor, Rhodes Lockwood, writes, "We have always served rice first, to have something to place the tomatoes on, which is sometimes too thin in texture to stand alone." I love her formality; it's so Hingham. But my family has made a wonderful winter meal of these tomatoes and 1768 Baked Beans, two dishes that linger in a warm oven for hours.

SERVES 6

½ a baguette, approximately ⅓ pound bread

2 (28-ounce) cans plum tomatoes, with their juices

6 tablespoons butter

2 tablespoons brown sugar

Sea salt and freshly ground pepper

Preheat oven to 350°F.

Slice baguette into ⅓-inch slices. Lay them on a baking sheet and bake until they are toasted light brown, about 25 minutes.

Butter a 2-quart glass or ceramic baking dish.

Crumble ⅓ of the toasts onto the bottom of the pan. These can be roughly crumbled, but don't leave anything larger than a ½-inch chunk.

Spread the first can of tomatoes over the crumbs. Dot with ½ the butter, 1 tablespoon brown sugar, and sprinkle liberally with salt and pepper. Crumble ⅓ of the toasts over the tomatoes.

Repeat with the next can of tomatoes, topping with the remaining butter, brown sugar, salt, pepper, and topping with the last of the crumbled toasts. Press the whole down, so that the top evens out. Dot with extra butter if it looks bare on top.

Cover the dish with foil, and bake for a total of 4 hours, but remove the foil after the third hour to achieve that brownness.

Hingham Brown Bread

Most people in Massachusetts define brown bread by two narratives: it is the only bread anyone has ever known that arrives in a can and, besides a hot dog, it's what goes beside baked beans.

Since 1869 B & M has been producing bread in a can; that's the brown bread that most people know. But, not only is it charming to bake your own bread in a can, the toothsome and mellow results are hugely gratifying.

This recipe is from Hingham, and I'm keeping it there, far from Rowley's 1768 Baked Beans recipe, because I don't think either has to stay attached to the other. Brown bread belongs in Hingham, where fine tastes still reside among honest Boston Brahmins, but I encourage you to travel with this recipe. With its touch of cornmeal and molasses, this brown bread is surprisingly delicious with Wampanoag Turkey Sobaheg. Try it with the Lanesville Finnish recipe, Pork Roast with Apples, Prunes, and Cranberries. Even the simple Cohasset Hake Baked in Buttermilk would be better served with a slice of allspice-scented brown bread.

MAKES 2 LOAVES

½ cup sifted all-purpose flour

½ cup rye meal

½ cup graham flour

½ cup yellow cornmeal

1 teaspoon baking powder

1 teaspoon baking soda

½ teaspoon salt

½ teaspoon ground allspice

1½ cup buttermilk

¾ cup molasses

1 teaspoon orange zest

1 cup raisins (optional)

The bread can be steamed either in a stockpot on top of the stove or set in a pan of water in the oven. If using the oven, preheat to 325°F.

You can either steam it in cans or in small loaf pans. Grease cans or pans with butter. Begin a kettle on the stove for boiling water.

In a large bowl, mix together flours, cornmeal, baking powder, baking soda, salt, and allspice. Add buttermilk, molasses, orange zest, and raisins if you're using them.

Fill the greased tins ¾ full of batter.

Set a baking rack if it will fit, or a basket steamer, in the bottom of a large stockpot or soup pot. Set cans on rack or steamer and fill pot with boiling water that goes half-way up the coffee cans. Cover cans with foil, held tight by a rubber band. Cover pot, and steam on top of stove for 1 hour.

OR, put foil-covered cans or pans in a roasting pan filled with water. Set pan carefully in the oven, and bake for 1 hour, or until bread begins to pull away from sides of the pan. Watch the water level, adding more if necessary.

Remove cans from water, and allow to cool on racks for 15 minutes before removing bread. If loaves do not fall out easily from the pans, remove bottoms of cans and push them through.

Cohasset Punch

Cohasset Punch was created by Marshall Williams supposedly to be served at the estate of another Cohasset resident, comedian William H. Crane.

A freshly stewed peach is served in a champagne saucer with crushed ice on top, and peach syrup, rum, and sweet vermouth poured over all. It's as pretty as it is quaffable.

MAKES 6 COCKTAILS

4 cups water

1 cup sugar

3 very ripe peaches

1 cup syrup

1 cup light rum

¾ cup sweet red vermouth

¼ cup fresh lemon juice (from 2 lemons)

6 dashes bitters

Crushed ice

In a large saucepan, bring water and sugar to a boil. Simmer until sugar dissolves, about 5 minutes. Add peaches. Reduce heat, and simmer until tender, 5–7 minutes. Using a slotted spoon remove peaches to a plate. Reserve 1 cup syrup.

When peaches have slightly cooled, peel them, and slice into halves.

Pour the syrup into a medium mixing bowl or a pitcher, and add rum, vermouth, lemon juice, and bitters. Stir to combine.

Set out 6 saucer champagne glasses. Place a peach half on the bottom of each glass, then fill with crushed ice. Pour syrup over all.

Bacon-Filled Cherry Tomatoes

Yes, this appetizer, from the pages of the Community Garden Club Cookbook of Cohasset, is slightly tedious, but the rewards—tasting like an inside-out, miniature BLT—are great. Make these at the peak of cherry tomato season, when it's practically raining Sungolds and Super Sweet 100s.

MAKES 36

1 pound bacon, cooked to crisp, then crumbled

¼ cup finely chopped green onions

2 tablespoons chopped parsley

2 tablespoons grated Parmesan cheese

½ cup mayonnaise

36 cherry tomatoes

In a bowl, combine bacon, onions, parsley, cheese, and mayonnaise. Blend well.

Remove stems from tomatoes. Place tomatoes stem-side down on a cutting board. Cut a thin slice off the top of each tomato. Using a small teaspoon, carefully hollow out the tomatoes. Invert tomato shells onto paper towels, and let drain.

Fill tomatoes with mixture. Refrigerate several hours before serving.

Cohasset Chocolate Mousse Cake
with Whipped Cream Frosting

Not one's ordinary chocolate mousse cake, this recipe has the added indulgence of the deflated baked cake being filled with more chocolate mousse, then frosted with whipped cream. Make this a day in advance and the flavors and textures "temper" together. This was certainly the crowning glory of many a Cohasset dinner party.

SERVES 6–8

For the cake:

½ cup (1 stick) unsalted butter

7 1-ounce squares semi-sweet chocolate

7 eggs, separated

1 cup sugar, divided

1 teaspoon vanilla extract

⅛ teaspoon cream of tartar

For the frosting:

1 cup whipping cream

⅓ cup sifted powdered sugar

1 teaspoon vanilla extract

Chocolate curls

To make the cake:

Preheat oven to 325°F.

Combine butter and squares of chocolate in top of a double boiler. Bring water to a boil, then reduce heat to low; cook until butter and chocolate melt.

Combine egg yolks, ¾ cup sugar, and vanilla in a large bowl. Beat at high speed until light and fluffy. Gradually add chocolate mixture. Beat well and set aside.

Beat egg whites (at room temperature) and cream of tartar at high speed for 1 minute. Gradually add remaining ¼ cup sugar, 1 tablespoon at a time, beating until stiff peaks form. Fold into chocolate mixture.

Pour ¾ of the batter into ungreased 9-inch spring-form pan. Cover remaining batter and refrigerate.

Bake for 35 minutes. When done, cool completely on wire rack. Cake will fall as it cools. Spread refrigerated batter over cake and refrigerate overnight.

To make the frosting:

Beat whipping cream until foamy. Add sugar and vanilla, beating until soft peaks form.

Remove sides of springform pan, spread or pipe frosting over top and sides of cake. Garnish with chocolate curls.

Hermit Cookies

The definitive hermit cookie—caramel complexion, fudgy interior, wrinkly lines on top—these molasses-dense cookies might have made great nourishment for a rescue team and its beneficiaries at the famous Hull Lifesaving Station, the first of its kind in the nation.

Hull's most famous lifesaver, Joshua James (1826–1902), and his crew are said to have rescued more than one thousand people from shipwrecks in his time. This cookie, now a staple in New England grocery stores, first appeared in cookbooks around 1890, a little late for Joshua James, but not for rescuers who followed him. The hermit's true debut was in Fannie Farmer's 1896 *Boston Cooking-School Cook Book*.

Hermits, along with clam chowder and Indian pudding, are New England soul food. This particular recipe gets the texture, spice, and sweetness exactly right, delicious after school or after rescue.

MAKES ABOUT 50 LARGE COOKIES

1½ cups (3 sticks) butter

2 cups sugar

2 eggs

½ cup molasses

4 teaspoons baking soda

½ teaspoon salt

4 ½ cups flour

2½ teaspoons cinnamon

1½ teaspoons ginger

1½ teaspoons ground clove

2 cups raisins

Preheat oven to 375°F.

In the bowl of a standing mixer, put butter, sugar, eggs, and molasses. Beat on medium for 3 minutes, or until well combined.

In a separate bowl, mix together dry ingredients. Add to the butter and eggs mixture, and stir on low to combine thoroughly, about 2 minutes. Add raisins, and stir gently with a wooden spoon to combine.

Wet hands, and use them to make sure the whole dough is mixed together. Empty dough onto board.

Divide dough into 3 parts. Roll each part into a 1½–inch wide log that is the length of a cookie sheet. With your fingertips, press logs down gently to flatten just slightly.

Lay 2 logs parallel to each other on an ungreased cookie sheet. Lay the third log on a separate cookie sheet, as they will not all fit on one. (The cookies expand considerably.) Bake for 20–25 minutes, or until cracked on top. (Do not overbake!)

Let cookies cool for a minute, and then slice the logs into 3-inch lengths. Cool these cookies completely on a rack. If the cookies are too large, slice each length in half again crosswise to make squares. These will keep in a closed container for up to 3 weeks.

CHAPTER SEVEN

Marblehead, Salem, Beverly

Marblehead, looking a bit like a batard with a chunk ripped off laying in the Atlantic Ocean, is like a tiny country all its own. Of the twenty square miles to this town, three-quarters of it is water, much of that a deep, protected harbor. The Old Town, with its cobbled colonial architecture piled like barnacles upon granite, can feel as tightly packed as a ship's berth. Dense with seventeenth- and eighteenth-century streets, it was built for not much more than an ox cart to pass. A slim sandbar unites Marblehead proper to The Neck, that piece of land that looks like a torn chunk of the loaf laying to the east. Home to Marblehead's six yacht clubs, The Neck is the fancy address in town. The whole is a blend of salty bars and sailor culture happily integrated with this yacht club set. They all check the weather obsessively; they all love a Dark and Stormy; they share the sea.

From the origins of Marblehead's colonial history in 1629, fishing couldn't help but be an industry; that protected harbor made it easier for men to go to sea. But the first real Marblehead fortunes were made in privateering, when fishermen and sailors were given permission to patrol and board British ships, acting as what was then a very successful guerrilla navy, and what emerged as the origins of the present US Navy. If you owned a ship for fishing or for trade, you were given a wink to go to sea and attack the British. As payment you were allowed to keep the contents of the vessels you defeated. Many a ship captain became a rebel, and fortunes in Marblehead were made. Today, a descendent of privateers, Andrew Cabot, is back making rum. His distillery is just up the coast in Ipswich, but six generations back his family was boarding British ships and brewing rum on Water Street in Beverly.

What did a Marblehead privateer snack on when stalking the British? Marblehead's most famous nourishment, the Joe Frogger cookie of course.

The Joe Frogger tale is cemented in Marblehead history: In the early eighteenth century an African-American man named Joe lived on the edge of "Black Joe's Pond." His wife made cookies in a skillet. When she poured the batter, it ran across the pan in the shape of a fat, leggy frog. Whether it's true or not, the cookie is real, and there isn't a cookie on Earth like it. As large as a lily pad and originally baked with seawater, rum, and molasses, a Joe Frogger is purely Marblehead. It is said that long fishing voyages to the Grand Banks out of Marblehead were fueled by Joe Froggers, as were parts of the American Revolution.

Two recipes here, discovered in a Marblehead community cookbook, speak of the "blow yer man down!" good taste in this town: Beef Stew with Gin is a classically delicious beef stew, but, if you can't add seawater you may as well add gin. It's a brilliant move. A little gin to finish a Marblehead Fish Chowder tastes like you've added a half-cup of a bracing nor'easter to the pot. Again, brilliant.

Those six yacht clubs in Marblehead keep the cocktail shrimp business healthy, but one restaurant, Rosalie's, closed since 1995, was the place that made this rocky promontory of sailors' bars and sail lofts a foodie town.

Through the 1970s Rosalie's was where Boston concierge sent guests begging for a good dinner in the land of over-done baked beans and potato-ey codfish cakes. For years many joked that the best restaurant in Boston was actually in Marblehead. To this day, people get misty at Rosalie remembrances: the oysters Danielle, the veal Marsala, that angel hair pasta. The recipe for Rosalie's angel hair pasta—pasta tossed in a marinara sauce laced with cream, prosciutto, shallots, and peas—is here; the original recipe is yours to prepare.

Salem, the next city along this northern coastal route, is and will always be the city linked to the witch trials, and therefore witchcraft, but it's also the city along the Massachusetts coastline that knew best the Far East. The grand wedding-cake-like homes lining Salem's waterfront attest to fortunes made in Sumatran pepper, along with cod to the West Indies, molasses, sugar, and tea from China. The ingredients in Salem kitchens in the nineteenth century, like those of Nantucket, were aromatic and exotic, reflecting the cargoes of Salem ships returning from the Far East. Salem residents were as familiar with the streets of Ceylon as they were with Boston.

In Salem history is alive, as they say, and the recipes are not dull. Even in Pioneer Village, a replica of a 1630 Indian and Puritan encampment, they make a delicious braised chicken with pears, sherry, cider vinegar, and raisins. This recipe may come with historical parentheses, but it's a delicious dinner today—moist and loaded with good flavors. West Indies Fish Cakes, made with salt cod and sweet potatoes, finished with a squeeze of lime and toss of cilantro, are the fish cakes to have with a glass of ale, even better, a Dark and Stormy.

The city of Beverly is dappled with cultures, but more or less defined by a divide: the coastal hamlets where families like Cabots and Lodges keep addresses and the rest of the city.

Rantoul Street and Cabot Street run parallel through the Beverly's eclectic downtown; each is a blend of thrift shops and hipster cafes,

Walgreens and Irish pubs, a movie theater for arty films, town hall, The Organic Garden Cafe, and a Papa Gino's.

Drive north a few miles and the houses get larger, the trees taller, the road windier. This is Beverly's "Gold Coast," a magnificent Olmsted-groomed coastal stretch named Prides Crossing and Beverly Farms. Soon, only glimpses of winged, turreted estates are visible from the road through stands of hundred-year-old pines. Sparkling Beverly harbor is a thread that weaves in and out of view. Watch carefully for Misery Island and Little Misery Islands (New England history had such a cheerful way with words!) off

the coast that briefly housed a resort, but are now wilderness reserves.

But let's turn back for a moment, back to downtown Beverly, and then a little west. It's early in the morning, and the bakers at Henry's Grocery are cutting pastry lids for the hundreds of chicken pot pies they bake every day (nine hundred pounds of chicken every day!) The store's butchers are busy trimming fat from rosy roasts, and wrapping the gleaming meats in caul fat for flavor. Warm donuts, fresh from the oil, are being filled with blackberry jam.

Started in 1941 by Henry Swanson, Henry's Market bridges the Beverly divide. After a couple of years in the war, Swanson returned to Beverly with his friend Leo Marquis. Together they infused youthful energy into this little grocery store, promising "quality, cleanliness, and service." But Swanson also endeared himself to the cooks and butlers in the great homes of Prides and The Farms. Fresh everything was scarce after the war, but somehow Henry found ways to provide the meats and produce those kitchens so desired. Today, the children and grandchildren of those families push carts down the still immaculate Henry's aisles.

Local culinary legend gives Henry's Chicken Salad the largest of blue ribbons; it's a favorite choice for Crane's Beach picnics, tailgate parties at the polo matches down the street, bridge luncheons, and kids' lunch boxes. Proof of chicken salad sales are declared in this statistic: Henry's is the largest consumer of Hellman's mayonnaise in the northeast. (The bones from all those chickens are sent every day to The Myopia Hunt Club to feed the hounds; that's North Shore.)

Henry's Market Bean Dip may sound ordinary, but, just remember how many Beverly Sunday afternoons—either in front of the Patriots football game, at the beach, or at the polo match—include a bowl of this dip. It's a favorite in this city, and now you have the recipe.

Marblehead, Salem, Beverly Index

Henry's Market Bean Dip

The ultimate North Shore side dish, Henry's Market Bean Dip is a favorite from football season through beach season. This makes a large amount; feel free to reduce it, but keep in mind the bowl empties quickly.

MAKES 7 CUPS DIP

2 cups mayonnaise

3 tablespoons sliced scallions

2 cups Sweet Pepper Relish

1 teaspoon Worcestershire sauce

½ teaspoon kosher salt

½ teaspoon white pepper

½ teaspoon dry mustard

3 tablespoons white horseradish

1 tablespoon fresh white bread crumbs

6 cups kidney beans, drained and rinsed

In a very large bowl, mix together first 9 ingredients. Stir well, then add beans, and mix gently. Serve chilled.

HENRY'S MARKET

People still drive distances for Henry's meat. Everyone smiles. The place is still as clean as a whistle.

The real Henry's magic happens in the puzzling warren of seemingly infinite kitchens beyond the perfectly tuned aisles of groceries and smiling checkout staff. Pastry rolling, soup building, salad tossing, and meat cutting are just some of what's going on back there. Carts of platters and boxes with lunch orders are parked in any space available, every nook as clean as a whistle.

ROSALIE

In 1973 a beautiful brunette mother of four created a small shop in Marblehead that sold take-out food and baked goods. Inspired by this storefront success, Rosalie Harrington went on to establish a restaurant in an old brick building with cuisine inspired by the basil, prosciutto, and real Parmi-giana Reggiano of Northern Italy, a romantic dining environment that couldn't be touched by the old Boston school still cooking from Fannie Farmer. People in Boston and the North Shore were hungry for the vibrancy and finesse of Parma and Lombardy. A self-taught cook, with a few lessons from her Italian grandmother, Rosalie seemed to have a magic panache with veal, chicken, pasta, and ambiance. People loved her and her honest, beautifully prepared dishes. The camera loved her, too. Rosalie ultimately had her own television show on the Food Network, and was the food editor of a weekly local television magazine called *Look*. A beauty with innate style, Harrington even spent a semester at the famous Lee Strasberg School of Acting in New York City.

Rosalie's Chilled Strawberry Soup

Rosalie Harrington, chef-owner of Rosalie's in Marblehead, learned from her Italian grandmother the panache of al fresco dining. Chilled soups are one of Rosalie's favorite dishes to serve on a warm terrace with stars overhead.

SERVES 4

1 quart strawberries, cleaned

Red wine

1 cup sugar

Dash cinnamon

Peel from 1 lemon

Mint as garnish

½ cup heavy cream or yogurt (full-fat or non-fat)

Cover a quart of cleaned strawberries with red wine, 1 cup sugar, a dash of cinnamon, and the peel of a lemon. Allow to come to a boil, then cover and simmer until strawberries are soft. Set aside to cool.

With a slotted spoon, transfer the berries only, not the liquid, to the food processor or use a burr mixer to puree. A blender will do as well. Add heavy cream or yogurt and blend again. Serve chilled with fresh mint garnish.

Angel Hair Alla Rosalie

Rosalie placed this pasta, an invention of hers that she considered typically Northern Italian, on her menu in 1973; it never left. It proved to be the most popular appetizer ever offered.

SERVES 4 AS AN ENTREE, 6–8 AS AN APPETIZER

¼ pound prosciutto, finely chopped

2 tablespoons olive oil

2–3 shallots, chopped

2–3 garlic cloves, chopped

1 cup medium mushrooms

2 cups marinara sauce

¼ cup Italian flat-leaf parsley

10 basil leaves, chopped

1 cup peas, fresh or frozen

1 cup heavy cream

1 pound angel hair pasta, fresh or dried

Parmesan cheese

Freshly ground pepper

If possible, buy the prosciutto in a large piece, unsliced, so that you can grind it in a food processor or chop it more easily.

Sauté prosciutto over low heat in 2 tablespoons oil. Add shallots and garlic and cook over medium heat until softened.

Toss in the mushrooms and cook for 5 minutes. Add the marinara sauce, parsley, basil, and cream. Simmer for about 10 minutes.

Just before serving, add the peas and simmer 5 minutes more.

Serve with plenty of Parmesan and fresh ground pepper.

Cook angel hair (fresh or dried) pasta. Drain, and top with sauce and extra Parmesan cheese.

Marblehead Beef Stew with Gin

In one Marblehead community cookbook, there is a recipe for "Marblehead Fish Chowder, with Gin." In another there is this slow-cooked beef stew recipe, brimming with wild mushrooms, finished with that seemingly favorite local spirit, gin.

Maybe the ghosts of privateers haunt the knobby kitchens of eighteenth-century homes on Front Street, inspiring the bottle to tip into more than just a bar glass. Or maybe the sunset salutes, capped by cold cocktails upon the decks of Marblehead's multiple yacht clubs have encouraged gin in Marblehead pots. Or maybe Marblehead folks just know how to freshen a recipe. One guest thought a faintly cold, clean taste came through the three hours of simmering red wine, beef, carrots, and mushrooms. That would be the gin. Gin in evidence or not, this is decidedly the ideal meal to say "pshaw!" to a Massachusetts nor'easter.

SERVES 6

¼ cup olive oil

½ cup flour

1 tablespoon plus 1 teaspoon salt, divided

1 teaspoon pepper

3–4 pounds chuck beef, trimmed and cut into 1-inch cubes

3 cups onions, cut into ½-inch wedges

3 cups carrots, peeled and cut on the diagonal into 1-inch chunks

3 cups wild mushrooms roughly chopped

1 (28-ounce) can tomatoes, undrained

4 teaspoons chopped garlic, divided

½ teaspoon thyme

½ teaspoon dried basil

1 teaspoon dried oregano

1 teaspoon red pepper flakes

½ cup gin

2 cups red wine

½ cup chopped fresh parsley

Freshly ground pepper

Preheat oven to 250°F.

In a large ovenproof casserole dish or soup pot, add the oil.

In a shallow dish, mix flour, salt, and pepper. Dredge the meat through this and lay into the pot. (There is no browning.)

Add onions, carrots, mushrooms, and tomatoes to the pot. Sprinkle with 3 teaspoons garlic, the seasonings (including remaining 1 teaspoon salt), gin, and wine.

Cover and bring to a simmer on stove.

Once simmering, remove pot to the oven, and let cook for 3 hours.

This is best made a day in advance. When reheating, add the last teaspoon of fresh garlic, parsley, and taste for salt and pepper.

Marblehead Fish Chowder with Gin

If one could include a little bracing nor'easter as an ingredient in a chowder, it would taste all that much more like the coast of Massachusetts, which takes its nor'easters face forward. Anyone who lives here knows the taste of bracing salt air in the nostrils.

The gin in this chowder is not just a gimmick—it's as close as one can get to a pinch of nor'easter. Great chunks of haddock or hake reside in a salty, creamy broth finished with a cold, sharp slap.

SERVES 6

⅛ pound salt pork, cut into ¼-inch cubes

3 medium onions, chopped

2 medium potatoes, cubed

1½ cups water

Salt and pepper to taste

2 pounds haddock (skinned) or hake

1 (12-ounce) can evaporated milk

1 quart whole milk

4 ounces gin

In a large saucepan, enough to hold the chowder, sauté salt pork over medium heat until it yellows, about 10 minutes. Add onions and cook until softened, 10–15 minutes. Add potatoes and water. Cover and simmer for 10 minutes more.

Salt and pepper the potatoes. Lay the whole fish on top. Add ½ cup more water if it looks very dry. Cover again, and cook for another 10 minutes.

Add the evaporated milk and the whole milk, and bring to a simmer. Do not disturb the fish; let it break up gently and naturally; the larger the pieces of fish the better in this chowder. Cook at a gentle simmer for 12–15 more minutes, or until the fish flakes.

Add the gin, and heat just to let the flavors meld. Serve very hot in heated bowls with crusty French bread.

Joe Froggers

As wide as lily pads, baked with seawater and rum, Joe Froggers are Marblehead's mascot cookie. There are almost as many Joe Frogger legends as there are versions of the recipe, but the one below seems to be the royal Joe Frogger.

As for the legend? Here are the Joe Frogger stories most often told:

Joseph Brown, an African-American man, lived on the edge of "Black Joe's Pond." Joe's wife Lucretia baked cookies in a skillet. When the batter landed in the pan, it ran to form shapes like a frog. Seawater, rum, molasses, and spices were the critical ingredients in these cookies. It's no mystery why Joe Froggers were very popular in Marblehead in their day. When Joe died, his daughters continued the tradition. As it seems Joe Froggers had become a healthy business, something about those special preservatives—seawater and rum!

Marblehead fishing boats apparently packed Joe Froggers on long voyages to the Grand Banks. While other towns on the Massachusetts coastline were learning about the keeping qualities of hermits, Marblehead, a town ever marked with salty character and the gritty independence born of being a rocky peninsula, was measuring lily pads, hauling in seawater, and baking Joe Froggers.

Minus the seawater, this recipe is as Joe Frogger as it gets. The recipe is easily halved and the dough also freezes well.

MAKES 4 DOZEN LARGE COOKIES

¾ cup hot water

¼ cup rum

2 teaspoons baking soda

2 cups molasses

7 cups flour

1 tablespoon salt

1 tablespoon ginger

1 teaspoon ground clove

1 teaspoon nutmeg

½ teaspoon allspice

1 cup (2 sticks) butter

2 cups sugar

In a medium-size bowl, combine hot water, rum, baking soda, and molasses.

In a separate bowl mix flour, salt, ginger, clove, nutmeg, and allspice.

With an electric mixer cream together butter and sugar.

Starting with wet ingredients, add them alternately with dry ingredients to the creamed mixture.

Chill for at least an hour.

Preheat oven to 375°F.

Roll out dough to ¼-inch thick. If possible, cut cookies with a 4-inch round cookie cutter. A wide drinking glass may work, or some people use a coffee can.

Place on greased cookie sheet (or cookie sheet lined with parchment), and bake for 10–12 minutes, or until golden brown. Remove immediately from pans and cool on racks.

1630 Salem Chicken

In 1630 Salem, Massachusetts, sandy paths ran through woodland to marsh, where early settlers and natives shared the burgeoning shellfish beds. Rough-cut board homes with thatched roofs clustered protectively together. Smoke rose gently from a stand of native wigwams along the shore. Medicinal plants were nurtured in kitchen gardens, which looked weed-run by today's standards. Sparks flew from the blacksmith's workshop. An ominous set of stocks warned against deviance.

This chicken stew is an adaptation of the one served at Pioneer Village, a living history museum that recreates this Salem settlement of 1630. A fine example of colonial cooking, this braised chicken, raisin, and Bosc pear stew tastes delicious four hundred years later. It is particularly wonderful served with Sweet Pickled Limes, which may not have been available in Salem in 1630, but recipes indicate they were a favorite all along the coast of Massachusetts in the next hundred years, probably a way of preserving the citrus shipments that arrived with the first global whaling trips.

SERVES 4-6

1 chicken, 4–6 pounds, cut into pieces

Salt and pepper

1 tablespoon butter

1 tablespoon cooking oil

4-5 Bosc pears, cored and quartered (skin on)

1 cup golden raisins

½ cup cider vinegar

½ cup brown sugar

½ cup sherry

2 cups water

Chopped parsley

Rinse chicken, pat dry. Season well with salt and pepper.

In a large dutch oven, heat butter and oil to medium high. Add chicken, and brown on all sides. This will take 15–20 minutes.

Add pears, raisins, vinegar, sugar, sherry, and water. Simmer for 1 hour, stirring occasionally, and adding more water if the liquid level gets too low.

Remove chicken pieces to a warm serving platter. Pour the sauce over all. Sprinkle with chopped parsley, and serve with Sweet Pickled Limes (page 84).

East India Crab Cakes

More Salem fortunes were made carrying spices—most importantly pepper—back from the East than any other good, including the West Indies rum and sugar traded earlier in the eighteenth century. These crab cakes make a gem-like presentation, and represent the cargo on those spice ships.

In this recipe hot-out-of-the-pan, feathery crab cakes meet mango salsa, wedded by a sweet chutney sauce. Toasted coconut and almonds add crunch, and just in case you forget the spice trade's colonial roots, a pool of green on the plate reminds you that this is still Salem.

SERVES 6–8 AS AN ENTREE

3 tablespoons plus ¾ cup mayonnaise, divided

2 eggs, lightly beaten

½ teaspoon curry powder

1 teaspoon red pepper flakes, divided

Salt and pepper to taste

2 pounds lump crab meat

½–¾ cup panko crumbs, or just enough to bind crab (don't make them too bready)

2 tablespoons coconut oil (add more if pan gets too dry)

¾ cup mango chutney

2 cups chopped mango

½ red onion, sliced into thin arcs

1 cup chopped cherry tomatoes

1 cup chopped cilantro

Juice of 2–3 limes, divided

2 cups fresh or frozen peas, if desired

6 cups leafy greens plus more chopped cilantro if desired

2 tablespoons olive oil

1 cup toasted unsweetened coconut

½ cup slivered almonds, lightly toasted

In a medium mixing bowl stir together 3 tablespoons mayonnaise, beaten eggs, curry powder, ½ teaspoon red pepper flakes, salt, and pepper.

Gently stir in crab, being careful not to shred the meat. Stir to combine all. Then fold in bread crumbs.

Shape into 8 cakes, approximately 3 inches in diameter. Let sit for 10 minutes so that the bread crumbs absorb some of the mixture, and they hold together better.

Preheat oven to 350°F. Heat a large frying pan to medium high. Add coconut oil. When heated, add crab cakes and cook until golden brown on the bottom, 4–5 minutes. Turn, and brown the other side. Remove cakes to a baking sheet and finish cooking in the oven, 10–15 minutes, or until firm when pressed on the top and very hot.

Meanwhile, in a small bowl stir together the ¾ cup mayonnaise and chutney. You will have enough to serve extra on the side if you like. Set aside.

In a medium bowl stir together the mango, onion, tomatoes, ½ teaspoon red pepper flakes, and cilantro. Squeeze ⅓ the lime juice over all, tasting to get the right amount and proper moistness.

The right moistness will depend on how ripe your tomatoes and mango are. Don't worry too much, this can be a very wet salsa or dry.

Cook the peas as directed, and toss with another ⅓ lime juice, ½ teaspoon sugar, salt, and pepper. Keep warm.

Toss the leafy greens with the olive oil, remaining ⅓ lime juice, and salt.

When ready to serve, put a handful of greens on each plate. Lay 2 crab cakes on top of these. Add a tablespoon or so of the chutney mixture on top of the crab cakes, and tumble the mango salsa on top of that. Top with coconut and almonds. Serve peas on the side. This is delicious with a toasted tortilla wrap, which serves well to combine mouthfuls of all the ingredients, including those rolling peas.

CHAPTER EIGHT

Cape Ann

Manchester, Gloucester, Rockport

The iconic Gloucester Fisherman statue stands gripping a ship's wheel, chin jutting at the sea, sou' wester pushed slightly back on his forehead. It's clear what's before him, water. But what's behind him? Gloucester. He's left Gloucester, its harbor rimmed by Rogers Street, the address of The Crow's Nest, the bar George Clooney made famous in the movie *The Perfect Storm*, and which is still known to serve a better-than-decent hamburger. More bars line Rogers Street, bars popular with the salty crowd. Some are said to serve the best haddock sandwich in town. The Causeway Restaurant down the road also has a great haddock sandwich, and great everything else that comes from the sea. Gloucester fishermen eat in these places, and where a Gloucester fisherman eats, the fish is the freshest; that's what makes the haddock sandwich or the chowder, or anything else from the sea, the best—freshness. Follow the fishermen, however endangered their species is; that's where the kitchens are serving the best seafood.

Just off of Rogers Street is the Harbor Loop, where Gino Mondello has his dory shop, a small shack so jammed with carpentry materials and always a whole boat in progress, that a visitor has to talk to Gino shouting over the half-built vessel. There's a woodstove in the front, and room for a few chairs. In the fall, when the air gets chilly, Gino, who also operates a lobster boat, invites anyone (and I mean anyone—tourists walking by, old friends and new) to come by and sit by the fire. Some people bring instruments, so there's music, and always something cooking. Sometimes there's an enormous pan of paella on the fire; sometimes it's Gino's legendary codfish cakes. You're lucky every time.

Just across Rogers Street and around the corner, is bread as good as anything in Paris. I'm not exaggerating. Alexandra's Bread, a tiny, tin-ceilinged storefront owned and operated by Alexandra Rhinelander and Jonathan Hardy, bakes bread that would crack a smile on the iciest Parisian fashion model.

Their cobbles and baguettes balance crust with true chew, not a soft crumb that falls apart in your mouth, but one that requires a good tug with the teeth to rip off a bite. The ratio of natural wheat sugars to a faint sour tang honeymoons in one's mouth with a smear of sweet butter.

But, Alexandra's Olive Branches, baguettes burgeoning with olives so delicious people at the dinner table dive for a stray, are beyond bread perfection. And don't think for a second this can't be eaten for breakfast with sweet butter and rich black coffee. Until you've tried it, you have no idea.

Take a right out of Alexandra's Bread and walk a few doors down to Halibut Point, a pub so popular that when owner Dennis Flavin tried to pass it down to his daughter and her husband, the patrons wouldn't let him. "What?! You can't do that! What if they change the burger!" they said. Flavin kept Halibut Point, but here's another uniquely Gloucester kind of thing: Halibut Point serves two kinds of chowder: a traditional, milk-based quahog chowder and a tomato-based Portuguese chowder. In Gloucester, you're a real native when you sit at the Halibut Point Bar, order both chowders, and pour one on top of the other.

Lobster is big in Gloucester. Mortillaro's Lobster Company is a multimillion-dollar business that ships all over the world. Vince Mortillaro is still horrified at the idea of someone making macaroni and cheese with his lobster, although that's what they did at Farm Aid recently. Neil Young and the late Pete Seeger tucked into Mortillaro Lobster Mac and Cheese backstage thanks

to a caterer who only sources locally, organically, and sustainably. Mortillaro's is a local family business operating the old-fashioned way—with lobster tanks filled with seawater pumped in from the harbor ten feet away, not lobsters in a building twenty miles from any ocean, kept in chemically balanced water. So eat your Lobster Mac and Cheese in Manchester, where they are a little less lobster-rigid. In Manchester they make a "gourmet" Lobster Mac and Cheese that includes butternut squash and a touch of vanilla. When you're in Gloucester, bake and stuff your lobster. Vince Mortillaro's recipe is definitive.

Gloucester is a wildly colorful place. The Sicilians still rule the waterfront, and some of the best recipes and traditions have been made in their kitchens. Getting back to bread: Virgilio's, a classic Italian grocery, bakes not only the fluffiest Scala bread and the most tender Semolina loaf, but it sells its own herbed olive oil in which to dip them. Order a "St. Joseph"—Genoa salami, German bologna, mortadella, salami, provolone, oil and vinegar on a St. Joseph's Roll—and sit down at one of the two tables outside to watch life on Main Street, Gloucester, Massachusetts roll by. That's one of the best seats on the planet.

In March, when the rest of the Northeast has resigned to just suffering the last of winter, Gloucester Sicilians are happily building altars to Saint Joseph, the patron saint of fathers, carpenters, real estate, workers, and hopeless cases, in their living rooms. It's a wonderful time for the Tarantinos and other Sicilian families. It begins with nine days of novenas, also an excuse to travel around the city to friends' homes where the novenas are being held, and to share pastries and coffee. The last day, March 19, is the feast day, and the cooking gets serious. Some families make lunch for a hundred guests passing through

that day. People come for the octopus salad, the special Saint Joseph's Day pastries, breads, and cookies, but most of all for the pasta—homemade egg fettuccini with fennel, cauliflower, and chickpeas. All through the day, as families prepare the pasta and the goranza, or sauce, as they ladle out servings, family and guests let out the cry, "Viva San Guiseeeeeep-PE!"

But Gloucester also includes the wooded northern tip of the Cape Ann peninsula, where the quarries attracted immigrants from Finland. The village of Lanesville is shy Gloucester, quietly facing northwest to Ipswich Bay, turning away from the open sea, away from the bars, restaurants, and squawking seagulls of Rogers Street, and facing sunsets. Its woods are puzzles of shadowy granite quarries and their smaller siblings, small basins of water (havens for spring peepers) called "motions." Descendants of those original Finnish immigrants still live in Lanesville; the

saunas still get stoked on Sunday afternoon. The woods of Lanesville are dotted with saunas. An hour or two in the hot, wood-fired steam is still considered essential by Lanesville Finns to get the heart pumping and the blood flowing.

If you know it well, you might find the air in Lanesville tinged with dissent and cardamom. Opinions are strong in this community. Finns, nature-loving, athletic people, seem to have activism built into their strong hearts. The coffee is strong here, but that's okay because there is always a slice of gently provocative cardamom bread, nisu, unofficially the national bread of Finland, to go with it.

Along with Finns, a community of nationally known artists settled in Lanesville. Walker Hancock created an altar at The National Cathedral in Washington, DC. (As national poet laureate, Robert Frost came to Lanesville to pose for Walker Hancock. While he was there he was

lucky enough to have local celebrity Barbara Erkkila bake his birthday cake.) Paul Manship created the golden Prometheus sculpture in Rockefeller Center in New York City. Virginia Lee Burton won a Caldecott Award for the children's book *The Little House*. She also created a nationally known guild of printmakers called The Folly Cove Designers. All theses artists made Lanesville their home; it was a time when the Lanesville woods hummed with as much important cultural activity as Montmartre.

There is a collection of recipes here from this gilded who's-who of American artists, proving that, even though the generals are coming to review the World War II monument, or Lord &

Taylor in New York awaits a shipment of Folly Cove textiles, dinner also needs to be made.

Swedes, quarries, lobstering, and quaint seaside vacations could be the words on a banner flying high over the town of Rockport, the tip of the Cape Ann Peninsula. While Finnish families settled across the border in Gloucester's Lanesville to work in the quarries, stoneworker Swedes settled in Rockport.

One of Rockport's signature buildings is Spiran Hall, the Vasa Order No. 98, or the Swedish Club of Rockport. In mid-December the chosen "Saint Lucia," a young Swedish Rockport girl, walks the hall bearing the symbolic wreath of candles at the Jul Fest. Tinseled tables sell

Tomten-like Christmas decorations, and hundreds of other Scandinavian knick-knacks, along with Swedish sausage, pickled herring, rice pudding, grape nut pudding, fruit soup, and nisu. Spiran hosts a Swedish pancake breakfast in the spring and fall, and a summer festival featuring strawberries and cream in early June. That's the kind of fun they have in this seaside town.

Indeed, innocence here has been official since 1856, when an angry Rockport wife, Hannah Jumper, gathered together one hundred of her fed-up housewife friends and marched down Main Street swinging hatchets, destroying rum barrels all over town. "The gutters ran with rum," it is said of that night, and Rockport husbands learned to enjoy a cup of coffee with dinner.

Rockport is no longer a "dry" town. Wine, beer, and even a martini can be enjoyed with your lobster roll, but somehow—maybe it's the window boxes on Main Street fluttering with seasonal flowers, maybe it's the smell of fresh donuts rising from The Brothers Brew, maybe it's the prettiest candy canes in the world being made in a window at Tuck's candy shop—innocence is still winning in Rockport.

These days local Rockport foods are having a party. At HarvestFest in October, T-Wharf in the center of town is draped in an enormous tent under which is served the best of local foods, from homemade nisu to Willow Rest pulled pork sandwiches to Roy Moore lobsters, and there's always a local beer truck, so you can enjoy a cold IPA with your Rockport innocence.

A discussion of Rockport cuisine must include Anadama Bread. This cornmeal and molasses loaf is said to have originated here when a Swede with a wife named Anna got fed up (yes, another angry Swede; this time a husband) with cornmeal mush for dinner again. "Anna, damn her," the Swede declared in lore, and made the Scandinavian polenta famous with molasses, flour, and yeast. For years an Anadama Bread factory in Rockport trucked the loaf all over New England, and even as far as Texas. Melissa Abbot, granddaughter of the bakery owner, is keeper of the recipe, but she shares.

In Rockport, lobster is the menu item of choice; it's the best town to stroll with a lobster roll in your hand. But the best meal in this town is still a picnic on Cape Hedge Beach. Cape Hedge Chicken Salad served in Mason jars, eaten in a beach chair, is as good as it gets. Stay past sunset, pull out the sweatshirts, and drag up some driftwood to build a fire. That's when some of Rockport's finest cooks show their stuff, under the shooting stars, their toes in the cold sand, cheered on by their sun-weary friends. Serve that chicken salad with Cape Hedge Beach Do Chua—Vietnamese-style pickled vegetables—for a flavor-packed meal that just gets better in a jar. It's all easy to transport—for centuries civilizations have successfully packed foods in jars, clay and otherwise, and gone on picnics or voyages—and easy to keep free of sand. Add Beach Banana Bread Brownies and sip from your jars of Summer Water. That is Cape Hedge living.

Cape Ann Index

Cape Hedge Chicken Salad in a Jar

In Rockport, besides Spiran Hall, HarvestFest in October, and the Saturday morning Farmers' Market, the best food scene is on Cape Hedge Beach, where serious Rockport cooks pack Pinterest-worthy coolers.

It looks like the palm of a great hand catching the Atlantic Ocean waves. Cape Hedge Beach is a hidden gem. Just north of Gloucester's popular Good Harbor Beach, which is a mecca for city daytrippers, Cape Hedge gets the same waves and none of the crowds. Rockporters love it, and many spend their whole summer there.

Here is a Cape Hedge Gourmet picnic that will translate to any beach, any picnic, anywhere.

A rosemary-layered chicken salad simply marinated in lots of olive oil, salt, and pepper, and packed into a jar will be the easiest "gourmet" beach food you can take out of a cooler. This chicken salad's list of virtues is long: It can—and must—be made ahead so that the flavors infuse. It is flavorful, not something easily achieved in room temperature picnic food.

SERVES 8

5 organic chicken breasts halves, bone-in

1 carrot, chopped coarse

1 onion, quartered

2 garlic cloves (for the broth)

Fine sea salt to taste

Freshly ground black pepper to taste

½ cup fresh rosemary leaves, chopped, reserving 2–3 sprigs for decoration

10 garlic cloves, chopped loosely in a food processor

1–1¼ cups extra virgin olive oil

4-cup Ball jar, or similar glass jar with a lid

In an 8- to 9-quart kettle, combine chicken, carrot, onion, garlic, salt, pepper, and enough water to cover chicken completely. Bring mixture to a boil, skimming any foam that rises to surface, and simmer, covered, just until chicken is tender, about 25 minutes.

Remove kettle from heat and let chicken cool completely, uncovered, in poaching liquid. Remove chicken from liquid and shred, discarding bones. Put meat into a large bowl.

Toss chopped rosemary, garlic, salt, and pepper all over the chicken. Drizzle some good glugs of the oil over all, and toss to distribute the ingredients equally. Taste the salad. It will definitely need more salt and oil, so keep drizzling and tasting. It needs much more oil and salt than you realize, so keep adding, tossing gently, and tasting until it's delicious.

When you are ready to spoon the salad into the jar, put about ½ cup chicken into the bottom. Stand the reserved sprigs of rosemary up so they press against the jar sides, pressing the stems into the first layer of chicken to hold them in place. Spoon in the remaining chicken to fill the jar, making sure the rosemary stays attractively against the sides.

Drizzle a last tablespoon of olive oil over all, and close it up.

Chill for at least 1 day and up to 3 days, turning the jar occasionally to distribute the oil. Let jar stand at room temperature at least 1 hour before serving.

Cape Hedge Beach Do Chua

Cape Hedge Beach Do Chua is a Rockport interpretation of the aromatic way the Vietnamese make pickles. Fresh farm stand vegetables, as easy to find as carrots and daikon radish (which are also almost always in grocery stores), are salted and left alone for about a half hour. This releases much of the moisture in them—moisture that naturally causes the vegetables to break down. Removing the moisture with salt allows the vegetables a quick cure, and is thus a quick way to preserve them and keep them crisp. Just like this, the vegetables will remain crisp in your refrigerator for up to two weeks. Try other vegetables this way, too: cucumbers, radishes, onions, even thinly sliced kohlrabi.

After the salting, the vegetables are tossed in a dressing of sesame oil, rice wine vinegar, ginger, and cilantro. Pack these into Mason jars and chill until ready to pack into the beach cooler. Along with the chicken salad, this is a beautiful, if not cool, aromatic meal on a beach towel—perfect beach food. Don't forget your Summer Water and Banana Bread Brownie.

SERVES 8

3 cups julienned daikon radish

2 cups julienned carrot

Salt for curing

3 tablespoons finely shredded fresh red chilies, such as serrano

One bunch scallion, thinly sliced

1 cup chopped fresh cilantro

½ cup finely chopped mint (optional)

For the dressing:

½ cup rice wine vinegar

3 tablespoons sesame oil

2 tablespoons sugar

2 cloves garlic, finely minced

In a large strainer, begin layering radish and carrots, sprinkling each layer with a heavy shake of salt, about ½ teaspoon per layer. This is not a meticulous process, simply put down some vegetables, and shake salt. Do that again, and again, until the vegetables are all layered. Set strainer over a bowl, and set aside for at least 30 minutes, or up to 3 hours, unrefrigerated.

Mix together dressing ingredients until sugar is dissolved.

There will be a considerable amount of water drained from the vegetables, but press them to release any more. The vegetables will be crisp, but more limp than before.

Put them into a bowl, and add the fresh chili and scallion. Toss with dressing. Add cilantro and mint.

Pack into Mason jars, and keep in refrigerator, turning them occasionally to distribute the dressing. Vegetables will keep up to a week, getting better all the time.

Summer Water

In Rockport the term summer water is slipping into history. From a time when many Rockport cottages were only summer homes, summer water meant water pipes that hooked up to the town water from these seasonal houses, but were only turned on in summer months. The spindly oxidized pipes can still be seen running through an overgrown ivy patch here and there, along the sides of many properties.

I think it is fitting to offer this recipe for a different Summer Water. It's an easy, beautiful, and refreshing drink to pack in individual Mason jars for a day at the beach. Summer water, evocative by any definition, need not be forgotten in Rockport.

SERVES 6–8

1 cucumber, peeled, cut in half lengthwise with
   seeds scooped out, sliced thin

1 lemon, thinly sliced

10 sprigs fresh mint

3 sprigs fresh cilantro

Fill a pitcher with 6 cups cold water. Add all ingredients and let steep refrigerated for 6–8 hours.

To take to the beach, fill 6–8 lidded Mason jars halfway with ice cubes. Pour Summer Water over the ice, and close lids tightly. Pack in a cooler.

Beach Banana Bread Brownies

The nicest people you know bake banana bread. The smell of that kitchen is one of the most tangible, instantly sentimental memories you have. It hits a place in your brain where butterflies, school vacation, swing-sets, pajamas, and ponies archive.

Take these bars to the beach. They are not beautiful looking bars, but something about a banana bread bar beneath sweet frosting makes these particularly compatible with beach breezes and squawking seagulls.

MAKES ABOUT 30 BARS

For the bars:

1½ cup sugar

1 cup sour cream

½ cup (1 stick) butter, softened

2 eggs

1¾ cups (3 or 4) ripe bananas, mashed

2 teaspoons vanilla extract

2 cups all-purpose flour

1 teaspoon baking soda

¾ teaspoon salt

½ cup chopped walnuts (optional)

For the frosting:

½ cup (1 stick) butter

4 cup powdered sugar

1½ teaspoon vanilla extract

3 tablespoons milk

Heat oven to 375°F. Grease and flour a 15 x 10-inch jelly roll pan.

To make the bars:

In a large bowl, or in a standing mixer, beat together sugar, sour cream, butter, and eggs until creamy. Blend in bananas and vanilla extract.

In a separate bowl mix together flour, baking soda, and salt. Add to butter and eggs mixture, and blend for 1 minute. Stir in walnuts.

Spread batter evenly into pan. Bake 20–25 minutes or until golden brown.

To make the frosting:

Heat butter in a large saucepan over medium heat until boiling. Let the butter turn a delicate brown, then remove from heat immediately.

Add powdered sugar, vanilla extract, and milk. Whisk together until smooth (it should be thicker than a glaze but thinner than frosting). Using a spatula, spread the brown butter frosting over the warm bars (the frosting will be easier to spread while the cake is still warm).

Pack in an attractive tin with parchment paper between the layers. Keep the Summer Water close!

The Original Anadama Bread

Just beyond the train station on Railroad Avenue in Rockport, a large bakery once turned out warm loaves of Anadama Bread. Inside were huge vats of dark molasses and steamed cornmeal mush ready for flour to be added, turning Massachusetts porridge into beautifully scented bread loaves. The Anadama factory produced 2,600 loaves an hour. A fleet of forty Ford F600 trucks stood solidly outside ready to make deliveries to all of New England. Bill and Melissa Smith opened the Anadama Bread Factory in 1956. The bakery closed shortly after Bill Smith's death in 1970.

Lore says the bread was born out of a Finnish fisherman's temper tantrum when his wife Anna served him the same cornmeal and molasses dinner, and he turned it into a loaf of bread, cussing Anna as he kneaded.

Anadama Bread stories rise like the loaves themselves in Rockport. A favorite tale is about the day the pigs in the large piggery at the foot of Great Hill got loose. Smelling the aroma of baking Anadama Bread, the animals "shuffled and snuffled all the way up to the bakery. What a mess! It took a while to get the pigs back home again," so says Rockporter Sam Coulburn.

Anadama Bread is still baked by many home cooks in town, but this is Bill and Melissa Smith's original recipe, offered by their daughter, the third Melissa Smith, also a great cook.

MAKES 2 LOAVES

2 cups boiling water plus ¼ cup warm water, divided

½ cup coarse cornmeal

2 tablespoons butter

½ cup unsulphured blackstrap molasses

1 teaspoon salt

1 package active dry yeast

5 cups unbleached flour

In a double boiler, bring 2 cups water to a boil in the upper pot. Slowly stir the cornmeal into the boiling water. Let steam covered in the double boiler for an hour. To the warm cornmeal add 2 tablespoons butter, molasses, and salt. Stir to melt the butter in, and let cool a bit. This can be done a day in advance and set aside in the pot, but it is an important step.

Dissolve the yeast in ¼ cup warm water. Add to the lukewarm cornmeal mixture.

Put the mixture into a large bowl, and add enough flour to make a stiff bread dough. Knead for 10 minutes, or until smooth and shiny.

Put dough into a lightly buttered bowl, and turn to coat the dough. Let rise until doubled in bulk, about 1½ hours. Shape into 2 loaves, and place in buttered 8 x 5-inch loaf pans. Let rise until double in bulk again, about 1 hour.

Preheat oven to 400°F. Bake loaves for 1 hour, or until brown on the top and hollow sounding when tapped.

Remove baked loaves from tins, and allow to cool on wire racks. That molasses and little bit of warm, crunchy cornmeal may make Anadama Bread the best breakfast toast in the world. With butter and Spiced Pear Jam it's definitive.

Lee Natti's Cape Ann Blueberry Cake

Everyone on Cape Ann seems to love this blueberry cake; it is listed in many local cookbooks, always with references to it being "a very old recipe," originally from the 1700s, found in Ruth Holberg's recipes. Lee Natti, a Folly Cove designer, children's book author, and editor, says of the cake, "It may seem silly to use a roasting pan for a blueberry cake, but to take it to a potluck, it works very well."

SERVES 32

1 cup shortening

2½ cups sugar

3 eggs

1 cup milk

5 teaspoon baking powder

1 teaspoon salt

5 cups flour

3 cups blueberries

¾ cup cinnamon-sugar

Preheat oven to 350°F. Spray a roasting pan with cooking spray.

In a large bowl with a wooden spoon, cream shortening and sugar together. Beat in eggs one at a time. Add milk.

Sift together the dry ingredients. Add to batter and mix well. Stir in blueberries. Sprinkle all with cinnamon-sugar and bake for 50 minutes if berries are fresh and you are using a convection oven. In a regular oven with frozen berries bake for 55–60 minutes.

Mudiga Steak

Mudiga is a seasoned bread crumb mixture used throughout the Gloucester Sicilian community. No one really knows the origins of the word, but the blend coats chicken, steak and fills meatballs in many a Sicilian Gloucester kitchen. There are still some Gloucester fishermen who rise for work at 3:00 and 4:00 a.m., and are looking for something hearty by 7:00. In Gloucester, Mudiga Steak served on a Virgilio's roll is their favorite breakfast.

SERVES 4

For the mudiga:

1½ cup bread crumbs (toast your own or you can use the regular store-bought type)

½–¾ cup grated Parmesan cheese

½ medium white or yellow onion, chopped very small

¼ cup chopped flat-leaf parsley

3–4 cloves garlic, chopped fine

Salt and pepper to taste

For the steak:

2 cups flour (seasoned with salt and pepper)

4 eggs

1 cup milk

2 cups mudiga or Italian bread crumbs (recipe above)

3 tablespoons olive oil (more may be necessary to add to the pan)

1 top of the round roast, about 3 pounds, sliced into 10 slices, each gently pounded out to tenderize

Fresh lemon

10 slices provolone cheese

To make the mudiga:

Mix all together and taste for salt and pepper. This makes about 2½ cups; you can freeze any you don't use in a plastic bag.

To prepare the steak:

Lay out three bowls: Fill one with the seasoned flour. Fill the second with the eggs and milk, beaten together. Put the mudiga or Italian breadcrumbs in the last bowl.

Heat a large skillet to medium high. Add the oil, and heat. Working in batches, dip the first steak in the flour, shaking to remove excess. Then dip in the egg wash, again shaking to remove excess. Lay in the the breadcrumbs to coat both sides, and put in the hot oil. Repeat with as many steak as will fill the pan without crowding. Cook steaks until beautiful golden brown on each side. Drain on paper towels. Remove steaks to a baking sheet, and squeeze a bit of fresh lemon over each one. Cover each steak with a slice of provolone cheese. Put baking sheet in a warm oven. This keeps the steaks warm while you cook the rest, and melts the cheese. Continue like this with all the steaks.

Serve on a crusty Italian roll with lemon wedges and hot sauce on the side.

FIESTA AND SAINT JOSEPH'S DAY IN GLOUCESTER

Fiesta in late June is the festival everyone knows about, when the carnival rolls out and muscled Gloucester boys hang their reputations on trying to walk a greasy pole hanging over Gloucester Harbor. It's a hallowed circle of men who have grabbed the flag at the end of the walk before landing in the cold ocean. Fiesta is all bawdy celebration of color, noise, and walking the streets eating roasted sausages.

In March there is another celebration just as important to the Gloucester Sicilian community: Saint Joseph's Day, the time to honor Jesus's "foster father," as they say.

As the protector of the Holy Family, a carpenter, and the world's most famous dad, Joseph is the saint of workers, of the unemployed, of houses, deals around houses, and fathers. It's common legend that burying a statue of Saint Joseph, ideally blessed by a priest, on a property will get it sold.

Sicilian history ties itself closely to Joseph: In the Middle Ages, a drought threatened the island, and Sicilian lore credits prayers to Joseph for the rain that finally saved the fava beans.

In Gloucester, the novenas for Saint Joseph begin nine days before his feast day, March 19. Gloucester's Sicilian women gather afternoon and night to sing the rosary and pray to Joseph for sick friends and family, for relatives lost at sea, to help them in times of distress, and quite specifically to help with work.

All over Gloucester, people build altars to Saint Joseph in their living rooms. Traditionally, on the day before the actual feast day, durum wheat flour, and oranges are placed on these family altars, and the local priest comes around to bless them. The next morning the women start the dough for the Saint Joseph's rolls and the fettuccine for the Saint Joseph's Pasta with the blessed flour. The baked rolls are placed back on the altar for visiting friends, traveling around the city from altar to altar, to collect along with a blessed orange.

At the end of the nine days, on the actual feast day, these same women come together to prepare the great luncheons.

The dishes are very specific and traditional. Saint Joseph's Day comes during Lent, so the celebration is meatless. In Gloucester, there is always Saint Joseph's Pasta, the pasta handmade that morning, with a goranza (a Gloucester Sicilian word for sauce) of chickpeas, fresh favas, cauliflower, and fennel fronds. There's always a selection of fried fish—whiting, smelt, and haddock—the Saint Joseph's rolls, and for dessert the crowns of zepolle, an egg-rich, custard filled pastry.

Imagine going out every night for nine days in a row with your friends to pray for everyone else, and then grocery shopping and cooking for a hundred people, with probably twenty of your favorite friends there beside you to help? I think all this fits elegantly into Joseph's description of work.

Octopus Salad

A Saint Joseph's Day feast in Gloucester is not complete without a bowl of chilled Octopus Salad on the table, a stack of roughly cut, crispy baguette slices beside it to soak up the delicious garlicky vinaigrette. In fact, I'm told that octopus salad makes an appearance at every Sicilian holiday table; Gloucester men insist on it.

If you are cooking the octopus yourself, here is how they do it in Gloucester: Bring a large pot of salted water to a boil. Hold the octopus with the tentacles down. Dip the tentacles down into the pot; make the sign of the cross on your chest while saying, "In the name of the Father, the Son, and the Holy Spirit," and lift it out. Do that two more times, the third time leaving the octopus in the water. This makes the tentacles curl and easier to drop into the pot.

SERVES 6–8

2 pounds frozen octopus, thawed and rinsed

3 large carrots, peeled and cut into 1-inch lengths

1 cup celery, cut into ½-inch pieces

1 tablespoon finely chopped garlic

1 tablespoon chopped fresh parsley

1 pinch red pepper flakes

¼ cup olive oil

6 tablespoons red wine vinegar

½ teaspoon salt

½ teaspoon black pepper

Cut off and discard head of octopus, then cut tentacles into 1-inch pieces. Generously cover octopus with water in a heavy medium pot and gently simmer, uncovered, until tender, 45–60 minutes.

Drain octopus in a colander and cool to room temperature, then transfer to a bowl with carrots, celery, garlic, parsley, and red pepper flakes.

Mix oil and vinegar with salt and pepper in a jar and shake well. Pour over octopus mixture and toss well.

Marinate 5–6 hours in refrigerator. Serve cold or at room temperature with crusty bread.

Saint Joseph's Pasta:
Fettuccini with Cauliflower, Fennel, and Dried Beans

The Saint Joseph's Day celebration in March is dear to the Gloucester Sicilian community. Because Saint Joseph's Day comes during Lent, the grand luncheon served on March 19, after nine days of evening novenas in homes all over the city, is always meatless. The flour, which has been blessed the night before by a priest, is used to make the special Saint Joseph's day bread and the fettuccini for the Saint Joseph's Day pasta. The pasta is handmade that morning, with a goranza of chickpeas, favas beans, cauliflower, and fennel fronds, clearly a dish to be eaten on the cusp of winter and spring.

Each Gloucester family has its own variation on Saint Joseph's Pasta; this recipe comes from the Tarantino family. Generations and branches of them come together early in the morning to begin making the Saint Joseph's Day Feast. By 7:00 a.m. the chanting begins: "Como siamo tutti mute?!" (What are we all mute?!) The family responds in unison, "Viva, Jesus, Maria, Giu-seeeep-PI!"

The flavors in Saint Joseph's Pasta are subtle. Serve this on March 19, whether you are Gloucester Sicilian or not, and you will understand why it is the perfect soul-salve for a cold early spring day.

SERVES 6–8

For the goranza:

1¼ cups dried fava beans

1 (19-ounce) can fava beans

⅔ cup dried lentils

⅔ cup yellow split peas

Salt and pepper to taste

1 tablespoon plus ¼ cup olive oil, divided

1 small cauliflower

1 (15-ounce) can chickpeas, rinsed

Stems and fronds of 1 fennel bulb, sliced thinly

For the pasta:

4 cups sifted all-purpose flour

½ teaspoon salt

4 eggs

6–8 tablespoons cold water

To make the goranza:

Wash dried fava beans and let soak over night.

Rinse the canned fava beans and peel.

Drain soaked fava beans, cover in fresh water, and simmer in a very large pot until tender. This pot will hold all the sauce.

Wash lentils and yellow peas and pick out any small stones. Place in a medium-size pan with water to cover, and cook until slightly tender. Add salt, pepper, and 1 tablespoon olive oil while cooking.

Wash and cut up cauliflower and place in a medium to large pan covered with salted water, cook until slightly tender.

Add lentils with their liquid, peeled fava beans, chickpeas, cauliflower with its liquid, and chopped fennel into the pot with the now cooked dried fava beans. Mix everything together. Pour in ¼ cup oil, and taste for salt and pepper. Simmer for ½ hour

or until the fennel is tender and the flavors mingled. This will be very soupy; don't be alarmed.

To make the pasta:

Sift flour and salt into a large bowl.

Make a well in the center of flour. Add eggs, one at a time, mixing slightly, using your hands, after each addition.

Gradually add cold water. Still using your hands, mix well to make a stiff dough. Turn dough onto a slightly floured surface and knead into a ball. Knead for approximately 20 minutes. Allow dough to rest.

Cut off small portions of dough, the size of a small egg, and shape them between your hands into a football shape.

Roll each of these shapes through a pasta machine first set on 3 to slightly flatten, and then set on 6 to flatten more. Allow to rest again on clean dish towels. Then, cut a final time into fettuccini shapes. Spread pasta ribbons out again on a clean surface so that they can dry slightly and won't stick together.

Bring a large pot of salted water to boil. Add pasta, and cook for 8 minutes. Drain.

Ladle pasta into the prepared goranza, which will still have a lot of liquid; it's more soupy than a traditional pasta dish. Allow pasta and sauce to "marry," letting it sit on a low temperature together for 15 minutes before serving. When serving, stir up from the bottom to make sure you get all the goranza, and serve in warmed bowls.

Cuccia alla Ricotta

(Sicilian Wheat Berry Pudding)

A version of this wheat berry pudding is served in Sicilian Gloucester households in December, typically for Saint Lucia's Day. Soft piles of ricotta cheese studded with earthy wheat berries, all flavored with that uniquely southern Italian combination of candied fruits, chocolate, orange, and cinnamon, make a luxurious, Old World dessert for any holiday. This recipe is from the Italian food stylist, John Carafoli.

The legend that accompanies the dish goes like this: During a famine hundreds of years ago in Syracuse, Sicily, Saint Lucia arrived on her feast day—December 13—with ships bearing loads of wheat, thus saving the city from starvation, and promising she would be forever enshrined in a wonderful dessert. Where Sicilians travel, wheat berry pudding is created, even in the fishing town of Gloucester, Massachusetts.

SERVES 4-5

1 cup wheat berries

½ teaspoon salt

1 cup of ricotta

4 tablespoons of sugar

½ cup of assorted candied fruits

¼ cup chopped chocolate or chips

Zest of ½ orange

2 drops vanilla

1 teaspoon of sugar mixed with a pinch of cinnamon powder

Soak wheat berries covered in cold water overnight in the refrigerator. In the morning, drain and place in a 3-quart saucepan along with salt and enough water to cover by 2–3 inches. Cook at a slow simmer, partially covered, about 1 hour, or until tender. Drain and set aside.

Combine ricotta, sugar, candied fruits, chocolate, orange zest, and vanilla. Blend ingredients thoroughly.

Add the boiled wheat berry mixture and keep mixing until smooth and creamy. If it is too dry, add some milk and adjust the sweetness by adding sugar to your taste. Pour into an attractive serving dish, and dust with cinnamon sugar.

Kropsua

(Baked Finnish Pancake)

Kropsua is the heavenly baked pancake that rises like a golden bowl out of a buttery pie pan. So easy and beautiful a breakfast, it's easy to understand why every Lanesville Finn remembers it fondly. What worked in Lanesville in 1954, works today. Take this golden puff out of the oven in the morning, fill it with cooked apples, blueberries, or just pour a little maple syrup over it, and that breakfast—weekday or holiday—will certainly become a happy memory.

SERVES 4-6

2 tablespoons butter

2 eggs

2 cups milk

1 cup flour

1 tablespoon sugar

¼ teaspoon salt

Preheat oven to 400°F. Put butter into a 10-inch ovenproof skillet (or one approximately that size). Put the pan in the oven to melt the butter. Get the pan very hot.

In a large bowl beat eggs and milk together.

In a medium bowl combine flour, sugar, and salt.

Add flour mixture to eggs, and beat until smooth, about 1 minute.

Pour batter into hot skillet. Butter will come up the sides, and on top of batter.

Bake for 40–45 minutes, or until the pancake is puffed and golden.

Allow to cool slightly. The pancake will deflate, but the custardy center is still delicious. Serve in wedges from the skillet with maple syrup, or fill the sunken center with cooked apples or blueberries.

Finnish Rice Pudding

Rice pudding is as dear to Finnish culture as fruit soups and lingonberries. At Spiran Lodge Number 98, the Cape Ann organization of Vasa, the national Scandinavian club, rice pudding and grape nut pudding are served in great batches at every December Jul Fest. Every local Finnish cookbook includes rice pudding recipes.

What I have learned trying to reproduce the best rice pudding is that something I dismissed as "grandmother food," too plain for me, and something too obviously easy to create, isn't either of those things. The rice must be very tender, but not completely mushy. Much of the flavor, I learned, comes from the milk as it cooks down and caramelizes. Made properly, it is a mythologically delicious dessert; the Norse gods must have spooned it greedily.

The ladies at Spiran confirmed my findings: Rice pudding is a little tricky to prepare, mostly requiring some watching. The best recipes require a quart of milk to just one-quarter cup of rice and one-half cup of sugar, so you can see that the milk must reduce a lot. With such little sugar added, you can also see how healthy a dessert this is, like so many Finnish dishes.

The rice pudding is cooked slowly in the oven with the lid off so that the milk simmers away. You will have to skim the unattractive skin as you go, but that isn't too trying. In the last half hour of cooking, the milk turns pale brown, the same caramelization that happens with dulce de leche. The rice plumps into the small pool of thickened milk. Serve this divine reduction as is, or chill it and stir in one cup of fluffy whipped cream. This simply turns something delicious for dessert or even breakfast into something more snowy and festive. The creamy version is delicious for dessert topped with Ojala Farms Fruit Soup. Serve the fluffier version chilled in a glass bowl, with Blueberry Soup poured over all.

SERVES 4-6

1 quart whole milk

¼ cup long grain white rice

½ cup sugar

½ teaspoon salt

1 teaspoon vanilla

¼ teaspoon nutmeg

1 cup cold heavy cream, whipped (optional)

Preheat oven to 325°F.

Mix milk, rice, sugar and salt in a 6-cup buttered casserole dish. Bake uncovered for 2 hours, stirring, and skimming off the skin that forms on top every ½ hour. At first it will seem as if the rice will never absorb the milk, but it all comes together in the last ½ hour. Be patient.

Add vanilla and nutmeg, and mix carefully. Bake for another ½ hour without stirring.

Serve warm or cold, plain or with fruit soup on top.

For a fluffier rice pudding, allow pudding to cool, then fold in whipped cream. Serve it like this in an attractive glass bowl, or pour Blueberry Soup over all.

Finnish Beet Salad

This is an easy, interesting Finnish treasure of a salad, just the right balance of sharp (the horseradish), smooth (the cream), and suave (the roasted beets).

    With Fish Cakes from Lobster Cove, this beet salad is delicious; beside Codfish Scrapple, it's amazing. The fuchsia-colored salad with the golden yellow cornmeal is a stunner.

SERVES 6–8

5 medium beets, about 1 pound

2 tablespoons olive oil

Salt and pepper to taste

1 tablespoon horseradish

Juice from ½ lemon

1 teaspoon caraway

½ cup heavy cream, whipped

Preheat oven to 350°F. Toss beets with olive oil, salt, and pepper. In a covered dutch oven or wrapped in foil, roast them for 30–45 minutes, or until cooked through. Remove from oven, and let cool. This may be done a day in advance.

Shred beets with the shredding blade of a food processor. You should end up with about 4 cups.

In a large bowl toss together the beets, horseradish, lemon and caraway. Fold in whipped cream. Chill for ½ hour or longer before serving. Dish can be prepared up to 2 hours in advance.

Vasa Nisu

Nisu. Kaffeeleippaa. Pulla. By any name, this cardamom-flecked buttery loaf means sweet, nostalgic comfort to even the oldest, most outspoken Lanesville Finn. Nisu and coffee are the stuff of life here. This recipe is the one baked by the dozens for sale at Vasa Order in Rockport, Spiran Lodge Number 98. Many people consider this nisu their favorite; the dough is so flecked with cardamom that it is almost brown. These braids shimmer with an egg wash that "cooks" on the hot bread, which is then dusted with sugar. The loaves sell out almost as quickly as they come out of the oven, and for good reason.

In *The Lane's Cove Cookbook*, it says that when the Finnish people first came to Lanesville no one knew what the early-morning hammering in the kitchen was. People learned it was Mother, or Aiti, pounding the cardamom for a new batch of nisu.

MAKES 4 LOAVES

2 cups whole milk

1 cup (2 sticks) plus ¼ cup (½ stick) butter, divided

1½ packages active dry yeast, or 3 ¼ teaspoons

¼ cup warm water

7 eggs

1¼ cups sugar, divided

1 teaspoon salt

4 heaping teaspoons cardamom seeds, ground in a spice grinder or small coffee grinder

15–18 cups all-purpose, unbleached flour

Heat milk and 1 cup butter until butter melts. Pour into a low 11 x 13-inch pan to cool. (Leave remaining ½ stick of butter out to soften.)

Dissolve yeast in warm water.

In a very large bowl, beat together 6 eggs, 1 cup sugar, salt, and cardamom. Add cooled milk mixture to egg mixture and beat with an electric hand mixer. (This could be done in a stand mixer, but once you add the flour you will have to transfer the dough to a larger bowl.) Add yeast and beat well, about 5 minutes.

Add flour a little at a time. Use mixer to work in the flour, beating well after each addition, until the dough is too stiff. Then continue adding flour, but use your buttered hands to work it in. Keep scraping the bowl with a little bit of dough as you mix.

When dough no longer sticks to the bowl and is smooth and elastic, it is done. But caution, dough will still be soft.

Using your hands, spread softened butter all over the top and sides of the dough, then turn the dough over in the bowl and butter the bottom side.

Cover dough with a cloth towel, and let rise until double in bulk, about 2 hours.

Punch dough down and form into a ball again. Using your hands, spread butter again all over the top and sides of the dough, then turn dough over in bowl and butter the bottom. Cover with a cloth towel and let rise until it doubles again, about another 2 hours.

Beat remaining egg in a small bowl with a fork to create an egg wash.

Divide the dough into 4 equal portions by cutting with a large sharp knife. Divide each dough in half.

Squeeze the air out of each portion, then roll into rolls about 15 inches long. Repeat with all sections.

Cross two rolls over each other at their centers like an x. Pick up each end of the bottom length of dough. Holding each end in your hands, cross your hands over each other and drop the ends of the dough. You should have made the bottom dough begin to "knot" the top dough. Now pick up the other two ends of dough. Holding each end, cross your hands over each other and drop the lengths where your hands arrive. Now you have knotted the other length. Now, pick up the lengths that you didn't just touch, and cross your hands over each other, and drop the lengths to create a new knot. Continue doing that, always picking up the lengths that you didn't just touch, until the loaf is

completely knotted. Tuck the spare lengths under the loaf attractively. Do this to create the remaining 3 loaves of dough.

Spray 2 cookie sheets with cooking spray.

Put braided loaves on pan, and brush each loaf with egg wash. Cover with cloth towel and let rise 1 hour.

Preheat oven to 350°F.

Bake for 30 minutes. Remove from pan to cooling racks immediately.

While loaves are still hot, brush again with egg wash and then sprinkle with sugar. Cool thoroughly. Nisu can be served sliced and spread with sweet butter. After a few days in the bread box, it makes wonderful toast. Extra loaves freeze well in plastic bags.

Lanttulaatikko

(Finnish Rutabaga Casserole)

This rutabaga casserole is one of the Cape Ann Finns' favorite dishes. Rutabagas have a welcoming, haunting note of cinnamon and cayenne that just gets lovelier in this casserole with bread crumbs, cream, and nutmeg. Sadly, rutabagas seem under-appreciated by those of us non-Scandinavians, but the way Lanesville Finns wax over this baked rutabaga dish, almost as passionately as they do their beloved nisu, should turn heads. If anyone thinks they have hit their limit of root vegetables— roasted, blah, blah—it's time to reconsider this nutmeg-y example. A holiday in a Finnish home in Lanesville is not complete without Lanttulaatikko. It would be pitch-perfect at anyone's Thanksgiving or Christmas dinner.

SERVES 8

2 pounds rutabagas, peeled and cubed (or substitute turnips)

½ cup soft bread crumbs

2 tablespoons butter, melted

1 cup cream or milk

1 teaspoon salt

½ teaspoon nutmeg

Pepper to taste

1 tablespoons sugar

2 eggs slightly beaten

Place rutabagas in a saucepan. Cover with water and bring to a boil. Lower heat and simmer 25–30 minutes or until tender. Allow to cool slightly.

Preheat oven to 350°F.

Put rutabagas into a food processor to blend to smooth. Pulse butter in to melt, and add remaining ingredients.

Turn into a buttered 1½-quart baking dish. Place this dish into a roasting or baking pan filled with 1 inch of water.

Bake for 45 minutes or until a knife inserted in the center comes out clean. Serve warm. Dish can be made 1 day in advance, and reheated.

Mike's Hamburg

So many children gazed at the whimsical images in children's book *Mike Mulligan and His Steam Shovel* by Caldecott Award–winning author Virginia Lee Burton, that they may recognize the literary reference if you announce dinner as "Mike's Hamburg." It's worth making this just to find out.

Burton was one of the more beloved residents of Lanesville and Folly Cove. A dancer who later went to art school, Burton brought not only her joie de vivre to the community, but her profound talents.

Along with being an award-winning children's author, Burton created The Folly Cove Designers. She invited local residents to join a guild that elaborately carved linoleum blocks—with images from nature, local scenery, and whimsy—to print on linens, producing a beautiful line of textiles that were sold at Lord & Taylor in New York City.

Burton submitted "Mike's Hamburg" to a local Rockport church cookbook. In the recipe she says, "cover and cook for ¾ of an hour. The length of time is not so important; it may cook longer if you are busy. If you are in the studio printing Folly Cove designs, your mind won't be bothered with food burning, and your children will enjoy their dinner."

A recipe for all time.

SERVES 4

2 pounds lean ground beef

1 cup finely chopped onions

1 cup chopped carrots

½ cup roughly chopped parsley

1 tablespoon Worcestershire sauce

Salt and pepper

2 tablespoons olive oil

1 (28-ounce) can crushed tomatoes

In a medium bowl, mix together beef, onions, carrots, and parsley. Season well with Worcestershire, salt, and pepper, and shape into one large patty.

Heat a large skillet to medium high. Add olive oil, and heat. Set patty in the pan and cook until the bottom browns, 5–7 minutes.

If the patty is too cumbersome to turn over, divide it with a knife or spatula into 4 parts. Turn over each quarter, and then shape the meat back into a whole patty. Allow this side to brown, 5–7 minutes.

Pour the tomatoes over the patty, allowing them to run down the sides. Cover, and cook for 45 minutes. As mentioned above, this is a very simple dinner, and perfect for children. Serve the meat and sauce over rice or buttered noodles.

Folly Cove Lamb Dinner

The sculptor George Demetrios, trained by a student of Rodin, studied at the Ecole des Beaux-Arts. Later he taught at the Boston Museum of Fine Arts School, and was awarded both the Thomas R. Proctor Prize for the best portrait in sculpture at the National Academy of Design as well as the 75th Medal of the National Sculpture Society for outstanding achievement.

Demetrios and his wife, the writer and artist Virginia Lee Burton, who wrote the Caldecott Award–winning book *The Little House*, settled in Folly Cove, the far north village of Gloucester and Rockport. They opened their arms wide to this artistic and Finnish end of Gloucester. Like his fellow sculptors Paul Manship and Walker Hancock, Demetrios almost ferociously made Folly Cove and Lanesville home; his life-drawing lessons here were legend. Statuesque Finnish children and adults posed for his world-renowned sculptures. Burton and Demetrios have been deceased for over sixty years, but the stories of the dancing, the song, the joy, and the food at their summer feasts are so clear it sometimes seems as if you can still hear the laughter and music through the woods in Folly Cove.

In the same cookbook with Virginia Lee Burton's Mike's Hamburg, Demetrios submitted Folly Cove Lamb Dinner. Demetrios' words show a little of that spirit with which he created both sculpture and dinner:

"First, raise your own lambs. Feed them on Folly Cove grass and they will far surpass Western lambs raised on tough Buffalo grass. . . . Serve this on buttered rice with red wine. My sister makes the best wine, but have red wine with this dinner."

This is Folly Cove Lamb Dinner rewritten in a more organized recipe form. The only adaptation is a bit of that wonderful red wine goes into the dinner, too. But, heed Demetrios and pour some with the meal. The onions stew to manna-like sweetness, and the lamb melts into the tomatoes. Folly Cove could be famous for this recipe alone.

SERVES 8–10

5-pound leg of lamb or 4–5 lamb shanks

Salt and pepper

2 onions minced, plus 4 pounds onions, peeled and quartered

1½ (28-ounce) cans whole tomatoes (about 5 cups)

½ cup chopped parsley

2 bay leaves

3 teaspoons paprika

1½ cups red wine

1 pound carrots, peeled and sliced in rounds

½ cup chopped parsley for garnish

Season the meat well with salt and pepper.

In a large skillet or a heavy roasting pan set on top of the stove, brown the leg whole, or the lamb shanks. There is no need to add any fat or oil.

When brown on all sides, remove meat from pan, and place in a large dutch oven with a cover. (If the

meat is too large to cover with a lid, you can use tight-fitting foil.)

Preheat oven to 300°F.

In the same pan in which the meat browned, cook the 2 minced onions until soft and yellow, about 10 minutes. Add the tomatoes, parsley, bay leaves, paprika, red wine, and more salt and pepper to taste. Bring this to a simmer.

Lay the carrots and quartered onions over the meat in the dutch oven. Pour the tomato liquid over all.

Cover and bake for 4 hours. If you need longer to cook it, you can—up to 5 hours—but lower the temperature to 250°F. The meat should be very soft but still in pieces when it is done.

Once it's done, remove the meat to a heated platter. Cover it all with the sauce, and sprinkle with parsley. It is critical to serve this with something that catches the wonderful sauce. I prefer wide buttered egg noodles or crusty bread—a good baguette, a loaf of Gloucester's Virgilio's Scala, or Portuguese Broa recipe.

Kitty Recchia's Hardscrabble Apple Cake

Rockport artist Kitty Parsons Recchia lived with her husband, also a sculptor, in a Summer Street Rockport home named "Hardscrabble." Kitty was a founding member of the Rockport Art Association, behind which stands one of her husband's sculptures, a classic nude poised in diving position. The sculpture was originally situated beneath a large magnolia tree; when the blossoms fell, the woman appeared ready to plunge into a pool of flowers.

Printed in the *Saint Mary's Episcopal Church Cookbook*, "Hardscrabble Apple Cake" is an unusual translation of apple pie. Apples are piled high in a pie dish with a layer of brown sugar and butter on the bottom. A unique macaroon-like batter tops it. After it's baked, the cake is turned over; that macaroon becomes a crust while the rivulets of brown-sugar glaze run down through the slices of apple. The name refers to Recchia's home, but it's also a fitting tribute to this delicious, tumble of apples and "hardscrabble" crust.

SERVES 8

1 cup brown sugar

⅓ cup unsalted butter

5–6 apples, peeled and cut into thin slices

1 tablespoon plus ¼ cup water, divided

2 egg yolks, beaten

1 cup sugar

1 teaspoon vanilla

1 cup flour

1 cup plus 2 tablespoons wheat bran

¼ teaspoon salt

2 teaspoons baking powder

Preheat oven to 375°F.

Spread brown sugar on the bottom of a 9-inch pie plate. Dot with butter. Layer apples on top. Sprinkle 1 tablespoon water over apples.

In a medium bowl, mix together ¼ cup water with egg yolks. Add sugar and vanilla, and mix.

In a separate bowl, mix together flour, bran, salt, and baking powder. Add this to the egg yolks, and stir gently, only to mix.

Spread mixture over apples.

Bake for 45 minutes. When done, allow to cool in the pie pan. When ready to serve, heat gently in the oven to warm. Remove from oven, and invert dessert onto a serving plate immediately, allowing the brown sugar and butter from the bottom to pour down through the apples.

White Cake for Robert Frost

For years Barbara Erkkila, fine-boned and lively with a beautiful head of thick curly hair, "got the story" for the *Gloucester Times*. She covered Cape Ann news from her early days as a teen journalist reporting on new boats arriving in Lane's Cove, to covering the first Gulf of Maine shrimp landing in Gloucester Harbor, to interviewing the fishermen playing cards in the Lane's Cove fish shacks. Erkkila could tell by the position of the building if a fish shack was older than the pier in front of it. She saw the sweetness in the fishermen who got dressed on Sundays for church and ended up down at the cove in their good clothes playing cards.

Erkkila emerged as an authority on Cape Ann for the outside world. When someone asked how wide the gap was at Lane's Cove, she called the Coast Guard: "You don't know?" she cried. "But I've seen your boats in Lane's Cove; you must know how wide it is to get them in!" They didn't, so resident George Morey measured the gap for Erkkila. It's fifty-two feet wide.

"I called the Coast Guard and told them," Erkkila made clear.

When the Holland Tunnel was being worked on, and two large blocks at the entrance had been ruined, the New York authorities called Erkkila. They described the granite's color to her, and she said, "Oh, that's from the Blood Ledge quarry."

"You know where it came from?!" they exclaimed.

"Of course," Erkkila answered. And to their amazement she was able to find someone to quarry new pieces of the "Lanesville gray with a little green" colored granite from the exact source.

Erkkila lived in Lanesville in the golden age when the number of great sculptors living there equaled the number of those shingled fish shacks. She lived down the street from nationally renowned sculptor Walker Hancock, and as a result ended up baking Robert Frost's birthday cake when he was posing for his bust carved by the sculptor.

"White cake with white frosting," Hancock decided when Erkkila asked him what flavor. "Just put "Happy Birthday" on it," he added, as opposed to "Happy Birthday, Frost or Bob."

Erkkila received a hand-written note, including a freshly written poem, from the poet for her efforts. In her later years she claimed to be too busy to cook, but Erkkila's recipe files are as dense and carefully annotated as her files on quarrying, for which she wrote the definitive book, *Hammers on Stone*.

MAKES 2 ROUND 8-INCH PANS OR 1 13 X 9 X 2-INCH RECTANGULAR

For the cake:

2 ¼ cups all-purpose flour

1⅔ cups sugar

3 ½ teaspoons baking powder

1¼ cups milk

⅔ cup shortening

1 teaspoon vanilla

5 egg whites

For the lemon filling:

¾ cup sugar

3 tablespoons cornstarch

¼ teaspoon salt

¾ cup water

1 teaspoon grated lemon peel

1 tablespoon butter

⅓ cup lemon juice

For the White Mountain Frosting:

½ cup sugar

¼ cup light corn syrup

2 tablespoons water

2 egg whites

1 teaspoon vanilla

To make the cake:

Preheat oven to 350°F. Grease and flour 2 round 8-inch pans or a 13 x 9 x 2-inch rectangular pan.

Beat flour, sugar, baking powder, milk, shortening, and vanilla in a large mixing bowl on low speed, scraping bowl constantly, for 30 seconds. Increase speed to high, and mix for another 2 minutes, scraping bowl occasionally.

Beat in egg whites on high speed, scraping bowl occasionally, for 2 minutes. Pour into pans.

Bake until wooden toothpick inserted in center comes out clean, or until cake springs back when touched lightly in the center. Layers will take 30–35 minutes; a rectangle will take 40–45 minutes. Cool layers for 10 minutes. Remove cake from pans. Cool completely. Fill layers with lemon filling and frost with White Mountain Frosting.

To make the lemon filling:

Mix sugar, cornstarch, and salt in a saucepan. Stir in water gradually. Cook, stirring constantly, until mixture thickens and boils. Boil and stir 1 more minute. Remove from heat. Add lemon peel and butter. Stir in lemon juice. Cool. If filling is too soft, refrigerate until set.

To make the White Mountain Frosting:

Mix sugar, corn syrup, and water in a saucepan. Cover. Heat to rolling boil over medium heat.

Remove cover and boil rapidly to 242°F on candy thermometer or until the small amount of mixture dropped into very cold water forms a firm ball that holds its shape until pressed.

As mixture boils, beat egg whites until stiff peaks form.

Pour hot syrup very slowly in a thin stream into egg whites, beating constantly on medium speed. Add vanilla. Beat on high speed until stiff peaks form.

Rockport Lobster Roll

Politics behind lobster rolls are ugly. There are people in Gloucester who will not come to Rockport, one town away, because they dare add celery to their lobster rolls here. One teaspoon of finely minced celery. You can choose celery or not, but there are two other laws upon which everyone agrees: You must use Hellman's mayonnaise and a toasted, square-sided hot dog roll. Use sliced bread or add lettuce under penalty of law. On Cape Ann, the lobster roll police are watching.

MAKES 1 ROLL

¼ pound lobster meat, chilled

1 tablespoon Hellman's mayonnaise

Juice of ¼ lemon

1 teaspoon small dice celery (optional)

Salt and pepper to taste

Unsalted butter

New England–style hot dog roll, the kind with flat
   sides

In a small bowl gently mix together lobster, mayonnaise, lemon, celery, salt, and pepper.

Butter the flat sides of the hot dog roll. Toast both sides to golden brown in a warm skillet. Fill with cold lobster salad. Stroll down Bearskin Neck.

THE FORT AND MORTILLARO'S LOBSTER

For generations The Fort was where each new immigrant population came when they first landed in Gloucester. It was here that a new arrival found work and shelter in one place, working in the fishing industries just down the street, packing into the wooden homes at the end of the point. The Fort was a dead end of Gloucester no one else wanted, but generations of Gloucester citizens grew up there. They sardined into houses with cousins, aunts, and uncles. Some moved out, but often an aunt or grandmother stayed behind. Today that elderly aunt's relatives might still squeeze into her home again for Saint Joseph's Pasta. The Fort had its own cuisine, rooted in the Sicilian villages these most recent immigrants left behind.

The Fort was crowded and noisy, almost tree-less, a blend of working houses, processing plants, fish, sea, sky, and squawking seagulls. In a small building they called The Boat Shop, Vince Mortillaro's father worked as a woodworker servicing wooden boats in the harbor. When fiberglass replaced wood, Mortillaro the woodworker found a new economy. He was the first to produce six-foot wooden crates in which blue fin tunas, which Gloucester fishermen were paying to dump because there was no market, could finally be shipped long distances, i.e., Japan. For years Vince, his brother, and his father built a lucrative business out of these crates, the actual origins of long-distance fishing commerce. Cardboard came to replace the crates, but Mortillaro's recovered again, this time with a fish and lobster business.

That wooden boat shop is still there, but now houses tanks that can hold fifteen thousand pounds of live lobsters. It's called The Tin Building now, for its corrugated metal sides, but the phone line still reads The Boat Shop in the phone book. Directly across Commercial Street is the large Mortillaro Lobster Company building, the business which has adapted, with the true resilience of a scrappy Italian family, into this now thirty-million-dollar-a-year business.

In 2013 Willie Nelson, Neil Young, Jack Johnson, and John Mellencamp sang their hearts out on behalf of the small family farm at that year's Farm Aid Concert in Saratoga Springs, New York. For lunch, the stars relaxed backstage, spooning into creamy, hot bowls of lobster mac and cheese, made with thirty pounds of sweet Gloucester lobster meat, compliments of Mortillaro's Lobster.

All Farm Aid's meals—from snacks to backstage dining—are provided by Homegrown Concessions, the Farm Aid catering company promising "that all food products served in concessions and catering are sustainably produced by family farmers, identified as local, or organic, or non-GMO, or humanely raised, or utilizing other ecological practices, along with a commitment to a fair price for producers," as stated by the Farm Aid Concessions Criteria. Farm Aid promises to source as locally as possible.

Thus, Mortillaro's lobster received a special kind of crown by being included in the Farm Aid chafing dishes. Mortillaro lobster quality—locally fished, kept in pure seawater tanks without chemicals, and processed humanely—was duly acknowledged.

Mondello's Cod Cakes

These are the fresh cod cakes that lobsterman Geno Mondello cooks in a large pan on his woodstove in The Dory Shop right on Gloucester's harbor. Fall and winter Saturday afternoons, anyone is welcome to wander into this wooden workshop, where Mondello builds wooden dories. Mondello cranks up the woodstove and pulls out the large frying pan. Other people bring food. The wooden dory being built in the middle of the room gets turned over, and the bottom is used for a table. Musical instruments come out, and soon the captain of Gloucester's herring fleet is playing his squeeze box, another fisherman strums a guitar, and the Celtic music shimmers out the front door, calling at passersby. Mondello begins his cod cakes with a homemade bechamel sauce; he's no slouch in the kitchen.

MAKES 18 3-INCH CAKES

For the béchamel sauce:

2½ tablespoons butter

⅛ cup all-purpose flour

2 cups milk

1 teaspoon salt

¼ teaspoon nutmeg

For the fish cakes:

2 pounds potatoes, peeled and cut into chunks

2 pounds fresh cod

½ cup chopped onion

1 cup béchamel sauce

3 eggs lightly beaten, divided

Salt and pepper to taste

1½ cups Italian bread crumbs, divided

Canola oil

Lemon wedges and parsley for serving

To make the béchamel sauce:

Melt butter in a large saucepan over medium heat. Whisk in flour until smooth. Let roux cook until it is a golden, sandy color, about 7 minutes.

Slowly pour in milk, whisking quickly as you pour. When the milk is incorporated, bring to a gentle simmer. Stirring constantly, simmer for 10–15 minutes, or until the sauce thickens considerably. Season with salt and nutmeg. Béchamel can be made a day in advance. Store in a plastic container in the refrigerator. When using, bring to room temperature and whisk in milk if it's too thick. It should be thick but pourable.

To make the fish cakes:

Put a small colander or vegetable steamer in the bottom of a large pot or saucepan with 1–2 inches of water. Steam potatoes.

When potatoes are almost fork tender, lay cod on top and cook until it is opaque and flakes easily.. Put into a bowl and mash all together.

Add chopped onion, béchamel sauce, 2 eggs, salt, and pepper. Mix together.

Add ½ cup bread crumbs, using more if mixture is too wet, or less if it's stiff enough.

Form mixture into patties, and let sit for at least 2 hours.

When ready to cook, dip cakes into the remaining

beaten egg, and then roll in remaining bread crumbs.

In a wide skillet heat ½-inch of canola oil to medium high, and cook cakes until brown and crispy on each side, adding more oil if it gets low, and adjusting the temperature to keep a hot pan. Finish cakes in a 350°F-oven to warm all the way through. When all the cod cakes are fried and warm, remove to a wide platter, and sprinkle generously with fresh lemon. Garnish platter with more lemon wedges and parsley. For a true coast of Massachusetts dinner, serve Rowley's 1768 Baked Beans on the side. Alternatively, serve two cod cakes on an Italian roll (Gloucester's St. Joseph Roll from Virgilio's is ideal) with a smear of homemade mayonnaise on top. Listen for the seagulls squawking.

Lobster, Fresh Corn, and Bacon Chowder

From sea to farm to table, this chowder represents a late summer day on Cape Ann, when the sweet corn at Marshall's Farm is piled high on tables at the farm stand and Sandy Bay in Rockport is so speckled with lobster pots it looks like a pointillist painting. The beauty of this chowder is the stock, which is made from lobster bodies and corncobs simmered together in milk. The bacon—ahhh, the bacon. This is what happened when all those eighteenth-century chowder recipes that began with salt pork grew up.

SERVES 6–8

3 (1½-pound) cooked lobsters, meat removed and shells reserved

3 ears corn, kernels removed, cobs reserved

For the stock:

5 tablespoons unsalted butter

1 cup chopped yellow onion

¼ cup cream sherry

1 tablespoon sweet paprika

6 cups whole milk

1 cup dry white wine

For the soup:

1 tablespoon olive oil

¼ pound bacon (about 4 slices) chopped into ½-inch pieces

2 cups diced unpeeled Yukon gold potatoes (about 2 medium potatoes)

1½ cups chopped yellow onions (about 2 medium onions)

2 cups diced celery (3–4 stalks)

1 tablespoon kosher salt

1 teaspoon freshly ground black pepper

¼ cup cream sherry

2 teaspoons chopped fresh chives

To make the stock:

Melt butter in stockpot large enough to hold all the lobster shells and corncobs. Add onion, and cook over medium low heat for 7 minutes, until translucent. Add sherry and paprika and cook for 1 minute. Add milk, wine, lobster shells and their juices, and corncobs and bring to a simmer. Simmer this stock over very low heat for 30 minutes.

To make the soup:

In a separate stockpot, heat olive oil and bacon and cook for 4–5 minutes over medium low heat, until browned and crisp. Remove bacon and set aside.

Add potatoes, onions, celery, corn kernels, salt, and pepper to the bacon pot, and sauté for 5 minutes.

When stock is ready, remove largest pieces of lobster shell and corncobs with tongs and discard. Place a strainer over the soup pot, and carefully pour the stock into pot with potatoes and corn. Simmer for 15 minutes, or until potatoes are tender.

Add cooked lobster and sherry, and season to taste with salt and pepper. Heat gently. (For a more elegant presentation warm the lobster separately, put it into the soup bowl, and ladle the chowder all around.)

Serve hot, each bowl garnished with chives and bacon.

Lobster and Butternut Squash Macaroni and Cheese

Lobster mac and cheese may be considered blasphemy in Gloucester, but cross the Cut Bridge and drive south to Manchester-by-the-Sea, where the lobster codices are chucked in the name of "this is outrageously good."

Originally called "Jeffrey's Creek," and then "Manchester," the town distinguished itself from the other Manchester in New Hampshire, too close for comfort, in 1989 by adopting the train conductors way of identifying one from the other, "Manchester-by-the-Sea."

Manchester-by-the-Sea may have once been a fishing village, but 150 years ago the wealthy families in Boston claimed it as their summering spot, building homes along the coast to match their in-town residences of splendor. The trickle-down theory works in the case of good taste, even in the kitchen. A glance through the Manchester-by-the-Sea local cookbooks reveals glorified versions of Yankee dishes. Lobster and Butternut Squash Macaroni and Cheese says all.

SERVES 8

1 pound peeled, seeded, and cubed butternut squash

Salt and pepper

9 tablespoons butter, divided

2 teaspoons vanilla, divided

1 pound cavatappi or elbow macaroni

1 quart milk

½ cup all-purpose flour

½ teaspoon freshly ground black pepper

½ teaspoon nutmeg

1½ pounds cooked lobster meat

4 cups (12 ounces) grated fontina cheese

2 cups (8 ounces) mild Gouda

1½ cups (about 8 ounces) fresh white bread crumbs

Kosher salt

Vegetable oil

Preheat the oven to 425°F.

Cut the butternut squash into ½-inch cubes. Sprinkle with salt and pepper and lay them on a baking sheet. Roast for 40 minutes, or until tender. Allow to cool slightly on the pan.

When just warm, on the pan, use spatulas to toss the squash in 1 tablespoon butter. Sprinkle 1 teaspoon vanilla over all, and toss again. Allow to cool on the pan.

Reduce oven to 375°F.

Prepare pasta according to directions on the package. Drain well and set aside.

In a small saucepan, heat milk on medium low.

In a large pot, melt 6 tablespoons butter and add flour. Cook over low heat for 2 minutes, stirring with a whisk. Add hot milk, whisking at the same time, and cook for another 1–2 minutes, until thickened and smooth. Remove from heat. Add 1 teaspoon salt, pepper, nutmeg and remaining teaspoon vanilla to the milk.

In a large bowl mix together the cooked macaroni, butternut squash, and lobster. Mix very gently. Pour the warm sauce over all. Add the cheeses. Place the mixture in an 11 x 16-inch glass or ceramic baking dish, or 8 individual gratin dishes.

Melt the remaining 2 tablespoons butter, combine them with the fresh bread crumbs, and sprinkle on the top. Bake for 30–35 minutes, or until the sauce is bubbly and the macaroni is browned on the top.

LOBSTERMAN GINO MONDELLO

Lobstering is the oldest continuous business in Massachusetts. With eight legs, twenty-one body segments and a brain the size of a grasshopper's, a lobster inhales through its legs and exhales through its head, extracting oxygen on the way through its gills.

Lobsters can smell. While officially they don't hear, it is said that traps are usually empty on July 5, leaving many to believe lobsters hear enough to hide from the fireworks the night before.

Since almost nothing in the world is the same as it was years ago, I asked Geno Mondello, the captain of The Western Edge to compare lobstering in 1967, when he first started with twenty lobster traps, to lobstering now. After a long pause, Geno said, "Lobstering was very romantic then—being out on the water, no traffic. Lobstering today?" Another long pause, and then, "It's too much like a business now; too much competition."

Mondello works out of a small wood-framed building called The Dory Shop right on Gloucester's inner harbor. When he's not out on the water lobstering, Geno builds wooden dories, originally used by schooner fishermen to catch cod on the Grand Banks. In June, Gloucester hosts the International Dory Races. A dory in progress almost always hangs gracefully in the Dory Shop amid the dark, oily clutter of old tools like a sleek, fluid sculpture in an artist's muddle of chisels and dust. Work benches are so piled with tools it's hard to find a place to sit down.

"Lobstering today. . ." Geno repeated. I anticipated more sad news that indeed the entire world had been permanently altered, more lifestyles and cultural landmarks lost, like oyster-shell driveways, rotary telephones, and homemade bread. "Lobstering today." Geno said again, "I still get excited about it."

Geno lives in East Gloucester, 347 steps from his skiff. He can see The Western Edge, a traditional Beals Island, Maine, lobster boat, from his dining room. He has two hundred traps. What's striking about that is the official limit is 880. Geno doesn't fish with more traps, although he could. "Everyone's in a hurry," he says. "I like to take my time."

Many say that over-fishing of cod in the 1970s all but eliminated the serious predator of the lobster, which, they say, has largely contributed to the lobster industry flourishing. But, also, simple industry measures have helped. Lobstermen uniquely regulate themselves; a committee of local fisherman, scientists, and policy managers make up committees called Lobster Conservation Management Committees. They report to the Atlantic States Marine Fisheries Commission, so local fishermen have an active voice in federal policy.

But keeping lobstering a sustainable business in New England is simpler than that: It's illegal to take female lobsters, which are easily identifiable by the pair of feathery appendages closest to the body on the underside of the lobster. Lobstermen are required to notch a female's tale before they toss it back, to further distinguish a breeding female. A special door is now required in all traps to allow young lobsters to escape easily. Not only that, lobster traps are basically inefficient. It's believed that only 10 percent of the lobsters who approach a trap actually enter, and 6 percent remain caught.

Take care of the mothers and children, make greed harder than playing fair; there's a recipe for sustainability.

Mortillaro's Baked Stuffed Lobster

Great chefs around the world translate plump, sweet lobster meat into everything from mousse to moo-goo-gai pan, but in Gloucester there are only a few acceptable ways of preparing lobster; the rest are considered an abomination. So, save your lobster mac and cheese (actually delicious) for another town. This version of baked stuffed lobster, Vince Mortillaro's favorite, is definitive. The dual flavors of a buttery cracker and saltine crackers make just the right combination of fat, salt, and crunch without letting the stuffing get too wet or too dry. A last word of warning: the lobsters are split and cleaned here while still alive; you may find a brave friend to assist.

SERVES 4

1 pound fresh lobster meat

1 tube butter crackers, roughly pounded to crumbs, not ground fine

10 rounds unsalted saltines, roughly pounded to crumbs

1 cup (2 sticks) butter, melted

3 dashes Worcestershire sauce

2 dashes hot sauce

Dash of pepper

Dash of oregano

Dash of dried parsley

2 live 1½- to 2½-pound hard-shell select lobsters

Salt and pepper

3 tablespoons butter, melted

Parsley

Lemon wedges for garnish

Preheat oven to 425°F.

In a large bowl mix together the first 9 ingredients. Mix well to combine, breaking up any large pieces of cracker crumbs.

With a cleaver or chef's knife, split the lobsters in half lengthwise. Remove and discard the head sac and intestine. Remove the tomalley and the roe if present and place in a small bowl. Break into small pieces using a fork. With the back side of a knife, crack the center of each claw on one side only. Season the lobsters lightly with salt and pepper. Place the halves, cut side up, on a large roasting pan or baking sheet.

The tomalley and roe are optional for the stuffing. If you want to include them, mix them into the stuffing mixture. Divide the mixture evenly between the 4 lobsters halves. Do not pack the stuffing tightly, or it will affect the even baking of the lobster. Place any leftover stuffing in a buttered casserole dish or ramekins to bake separately.

Brush melted butter over the exposed meat tail, stuffing, and claws. Bake until the lobster is cooked through and the stuffing is crisp and golden. Bake 17 minutes for a 1½-pound lobster and 24 minutes for a 2-pound lobster. This makes a dramatic presentation. Serve one lobster half on a platter-size plate. I have a collection of various antique platters I use for this. You want a roomy plate! Serve this with chilled Nantucket Cold Slaw and lemon wedges on the platter.

CHAPTER NINE

Essex, Ipswich, Rowley, and Newburyport

Clams. Not quahogs, clams. *Mya arenaria*. The fragile oblong mollusks that, shucked, dipped in batter, and fried, are so finely balanced between salty and sweet, crunchy and soft, that even Howard Johnson needed them on his menu. Clams and rolling farmland define the Massachusetts coastline from Essex north to Newburyport.

The Essex River looks like a ribbon snaking past town, through acres of golden or green salt-marsh, depending on the season. Main Street in Essex is antiques shops and restaurants doing their best to keep the tide out. Salt marsh is both in front and behind. Often enough water creeps up to make shop, restaurant, road, and river one and the same.

Along this stretch of Route 133, wooden shack-like buildings with bare lightbulbs hanging from the ceiling sell some of the most sought after foods in the world: Essex Fried Clams may be world famous, but clams were already famous in Essex before Chubby Woodman fried one. In fact, along with vegetables, homemade pies, and the new craze of "fried potato slices," Chubby Woodman was selling Essex clams from

his store on the side of the road one hundred years ago when one of his bored buddies suggested Chubby throw a clam in the potato oil to see what would happen. The first clam, shell and all, exploded. Chubby's wife Bessie said, "It needs a batter." She tossed a (shucked) clam in evaporated milk, then corn flour, and into the oil. It came out to change the lives of now three generations of Woodmans, and plenty of other Essex folks. Clams and Woodmans are a culture all their own.

Did you notice Lufkin Road as you drove through Essex? The Lufkins are almost as well known in Essex as the fried clam, and have been here longer. Laurie Lufkin, an inspired home-cook-turned-competitive-cook, has both the talent and the ancestry to offer the definitive "North of

Boston Clam Chowder," meaning it's made with clams, not quahogs. Generations of Lufkins have put rake to mudflat. Sue Lufkin, Laurie's mother, organizes the Essex Clam Chowder Festival every year. Laurie has also won enough cooking contests to fill a garage with blenders (and to put ten thousand dollars from Hood Milk in her bank account for her New England Buttermilk Pumpkin Cakes with Sour Cream Apple Caramel and Dried Cranberries). She owns clam chowder here.

Leaving Essex heading north, we arrive in Ipswich, where clams are no less honored.

But Ipswich has other histories: dairy cows, apple trees, and a Greek community that came here to work in the mills, and stayed. Their Hellenic Center graces Ipswich with classical Greek beauty. It's a favorite wedding reception site, that even offers a Greek catering option. Best of all, for seventy-five years they've been throwing a Greek festival in mid-July. There's a roasted lamb dinner, souvlaki, and the special Greek smoked pork sausage, locanico, flavored with orange rind, wine, and spices. Of course there is spanakopita, dolmathes, pastitso, tiropita (triangles of cheese-filled pastry). For dessert, local women produce loukoumathes (the Greek version of a beignet), trays of baklava, and the butter cookies, koulouria and kourambiedes. Someone always makes the wonderful rich cookie, melomakarona, with semolina and soaked in honey. Isn't the coast of Massachusetts great? As soon as you think there may be too many clams and too much salt cod, someone hands you a melomakarona.

The fields of Appleton Farms roll for acres and acres along Route 1, 658 acres exactly. The Appleton family has continuously run this farm as both working and gentleman's since 1636; that's twenty-three years before Tristam Coffin wrangled Nantucket from the Wampanoag.

In 1998 Mrs. Appleton, heir-less, deeded those beautiful acres to the Trustees of Reservations, a non-profit group that is again making a working farm of the property. They have crops, including a CSA, and they have cows, a herd of Jerseys that produce the best milk you will ever drink, and the butter and cheese that come with it.

Along Argilla Road, the road to Ipswich's glorious Crane Beach, is Russell Orchards. Apple picking on Argilla Road has a long history. A hundred years ago the road was lined with orchards; the Russell fruit trees alone, once Goodale's, still stand. Autumn on the North Shore isn't autumn without a drive to Russell Orchards to load up on cider donuts, cider, apple pies, and apples, not to mention marveling at how fat the pigs are.

The Ipswich food discussion isn't complete without a mention of probably its most famous story of all: "A&P" by John Updike. Almost every high school student reads this short story, about a young checkout boy working at the local grocery store. He indignantly quits when a trio of beautiful girls is told to leave because they're barefoot. The A&P is a Walgreens now, but the building still stands in Ipswich, representing local shopping, local roots, local relationships, and a little buttoned-up Yankee morality, elements that, like twisted old apple trees on Argilla Road, will probably never be completely removed from this stretch of coastline.

Driving north through the town of Rowley toward Newburyport, the landscape changes. The sides of the road open up to wide, open spaces. Sometimes this is tidal marsh, where clammers have raked clam beds for generations, swooping in from the east, and sometimes it is remnants of farmland. On the way to Newburyport a few farms still stand. Farming here was rockier, colder, more difficult than on the South

Coast. The recipes that mark this stretch of coastline recall long winters and hearty dinners by a woodstove.

George Oldmixon contributed his family's tomato soup recipe to the *Rowley Grange Anniversary Cookbook*, circa 1989, adding a note that "the 3rd generation of my family is now using this recipe." We may be on number four now. Made with clove, cinnamon, celery, and brown sugar, Oldmixon's recipe tastes like the homemade version of the Campbell's Soup with which so many of us define childhood lunch.

The baked bean recipe in Rowley dates to 1768, the last time, as far as I'm concerned, that baked beans were delicious. Without the syrupy blandness of what people consider baked beans today, this version is sweetened only because when you bake tomatoes and Roman beans for six hours they become wonderfully caramelized. The best ingredients here are tomatoes and time.

This is the land where farming and baking go hand in hand. Green Tomato Apple Pie is a bonus deliciousness, something just wonderful to do with the last unripened tomatoes on the vine. Argilla Road Apple Pie is the best blue-ribbon finish to a day of picking at Russell Orchards. If you are lucky enough to pick strawberries at Russell Orchards in the spring, rush to make the Warm Ipswich Strawberry Shortcake. You have not had strawberry shortcake unless you have had biscuits straight out of the oven, filled with fresh strawberries and poured with cream. You may never go back to cold whipped cream again.

In Rowley there is a treasure chest of tea bread recipes. Farm wives and friends must have once relished these quick loaves with the chameleon-like ability to be both bread and cake. Golden Kumquat Bread is one of the tea bread treasures discovered in Rowley recipe boxes. Sliced in small squares and spread with Shy Brothers cloumage, any of these would make wonderful delicate sandwiches for an elegant lunch, perhaps with a cup of George Oldmixon's Rowley Grange Tomato Soup.

Newburyport sparkles at the end of this rural stretch. Situated at the mouth of the Merrimac River, its history reads like a to-do list for a city on the Massachusetts coast. There was whaling here, shipbuilding, privateering, rum making and a Crown Pilot Crackers factory. Yup, Crown Pilot Crackers, New England's favorite carbohydrate to float on a chowder, were once baked in Newburyport. A small, beautiful city has risen up through and around all that history. Street after street of eighteenth- and nineteenth-century homes cluster around a busy downtown, with packed restaurants on Friday and Saturday nights. The local farms and fishermen have noble positions on many of the Newburyport restaurant menus. One of my favorite salads, and my daughters' favorite meal ever, is a brussels sprout panzanella, a Newburyport restaurant's attempt to create a panzanella-type salad with winter Massachusetts ingredients. There's no need to imagine panzanella; just know this: Blanched brussels sprouts are tossed in a pancetta-molasses vinaigrette with roasted wild mushrooms, toasted bread, and finished with the squares of candied bacon. This is North Shore farm food; it says winter on coastal Massachusetts the way a panzanella says summer in Tuscany. It's a beautiful testament to what creativity can do with honestly local Massachusetts ingredients. Maybe new traditions will be started here. Here's to making this salad as "Massachusetts North Shore" as baked beans someday.

Essex, Ipswich, Rowley, and Newburyport Index

Clam Dip—The Real Deal

The name says it all—this is not the stuff in the small plastic tub. This is the fine recipe from whence that stuff in the plastic tubs was born. Real clams, with real ocean in their little souls, are blended with cream cheese and sour cream to be the best thing that ever happened to a Massachusetts potato chip.

SERVING/YIELD?

2 dozen steamer clams and their liquid

2 cloves garlic, minced

½ cup grated onion

1 tablespoon lemon juice

Hot sauce

Salt and freshly ground black pepper

2 cups sour cream

1 (8-ounce) package cream cheese

Scrub clams lightly, and let soak in a bowl of salted cold water for 30 minutes.

In a wide skillet or sauce pan, steam the clams in ½-inch of water. Strain, but reserve ½ cup of the broth.

Shuck clams, and cut off their siphons with scissors. Rinse the clams under a faucet to remove any traces of sand. Put in a strainer and drain well.

Place the clams, and ½ cup of liquid in a blender or food processor. Add garlic, onion, lemon juice, hot sauce, salt, and pepper. Pay attention to how much salt you need, as the clams may be salty. Cream to blend.

Add sour cream and cream cheese. Blend everything together. This dip is best made at least a day in advance, allowing the flavors to truly expand. If you taste it right away, the dip will taste quite bland, so please make ahead. The results are significantly different. It can be made up to two days in advance and is best stored in a glass jar or bowl in the refrigerator.

This dip deserves the best quality potato chips.

Chubby and Bessie's Fried Clam Recipe

Of course, the best recipe for Woodman's Fried Clams begins with grabbing your car keys and sunglasses, and driving to the causeway in Essex, where Woodman's looks almost the same as it did when Chubby and Bessie first opened their roadside stand.

But, should you be inspired to re-create the first fried clam in your kitchen, here is Chubby and Bessie's recipe, unchanged since that fateful clam one hundred years ago.

SERVES 8 AS AN APPETIZER

5½ cups lard or vegetable shortening

12 ounces evaporated milk

26 ounces whole belly clams

4 cups corn flour

Salt to taste

In a 4-quart saucepan, melt lard or vegetable shortening to a depth of 2 inches in the pan. Using a cooking thermometer to gauge, heat oil to 350°F.

Pour evaporated milk into one bowl, and corn flour into another.

In small batches put clams in a hand-held strainer, and submerge in the bowl of evaporated milk to coat. Remove strainer from bowl and shake off excess milk.

Next dredge clams through corn flour until well coated. You may want to use a clean, dry strainer to shake off the excess flour.

Carefully place clams into hot lard or oil. Be careful because lard will spatter. Cook in small batches, turning to cook both sides, until they are golden brown. Clams will take approximately 1½ minutes to cook. Using a slotted scoop, remove clams from oil. Shake gently to remove the excess oil. The color is the most important indicator, and should be golden brown. Drain briefly on paper towels, and shake with salt. Serve immediately with lemon, ketchup or even hot sauce. Of course, tartar sauce is good, too.

CLAMBAKES

Both the Agawam on the North Shore and the Wampanoag on the South Shore of Massachusetts had been preparing festive clambakes for thousands of years, although their clambakes didn't involve just clams. Usually a feast of lobsters, mussels, scallops, crabs, striped bass, and alewife steamed between a pile of moist kelp and a bed of red-hot stones was featured. Clambakes for Native Americans were special occasions, usually built to honor a member of the community. The site of a clambake was one of the most important elements, and time would be taken to stake out exactly the right place. Next the stones that would line the bed were chosen, almost as important an effort. The stones had to be the right size and shape to conduct the heat. Stones could not be used a second time, as they became "tempered," and would not heat.

Clearly, the English settlers adopted this festive shore-side cooking. Even today, a clambake creates a special kind of energy—part picnic, part feast, part the anticipatory fun of preparing food outside. And that seaweed! Who doesn't love the mystery of lifting off the steaming seaweed to reveal brilliant red lobsters and gaping clams!

Woodman's in Essex is probably the world's expert on clambakes. By 1923 Woodman had streamlined the clambake process and made it transportable; "We Come to You and Cook" was his signature line. In the summer of 1923, Woodman held his first commercial clambake for the Caleb Loring family at his oceanfront estate in Beverly Farms. To this day, the Loring family has a Woodman's Clambake every June beneath a "Strawberry Moon."

To become a Woodman's baker is not easy; a long internship is required. It takes a combination of hard work—loading the extremely efficient Woodman's trucks, setting up at the sight where there might be all kinds of challenges, starting with bad weather, bugs, and uneven ground, preparing the food, and understanding the steaming techniques, not to mention being friendly, and then packing it all up again. It makes for a long day, but being a baker at Woodman's is an honor.

In his way, Chubby Woodman understood when he began producing clambakes that he was offering authenticity, culture, and *terroir*. Today a Woodman's Clambake is the gold standard of summer dining fun, and Harvard University's favorite way to throw a class reunion. How Yankee is that?

Baked Stuffed Clams from Doug Woodman

Doug Woodman, grandson to Chubby, knows baked stuffed clams. Woodman doesn't bother putting his bacon, crumb, and clam manna back into its shell. He knows that even the most delicious filling can dry out, or crumble out if put back in the shell. Sentencing the stuffing back to "its room" is not the best way to stuff a clam, as odd as that sounds. Instead, Woodman creates this magnificent celebration of all things that go great with clams, and bakes them together in a baking dish. It's all stuffing; it stays moist and the flavors honestly marry. I might pile a stack of washed clamshells beside this baking dish, and spoon the piping hot stuffing into the shells to serve.

MAKES 10 SERVINGS

¼ pound bacon

¼ cup (½ stick) butter

3 large cloves garlic, minced

½ red onion, minced

1 quart minced clams

2 ounces Parmesan cheese

2 sleeves Ritz crackers, crushed

Preheat oven to 350°F.

Fry bacon in a frying pan until crispy, and set aside to drain on paper towels. Discard bacon grease.

In a large pan over medium heat, melt butter and sauté garlic and onions until the onions are translucent.

Add clams, and cook until tender, about 15 minutes. Crumble bacon into mixture. Add grated cheese, and stir for 1 minute.

Remove mixture from the heat, and add crushed crackers. Stir until mixture is thoroughly combined. Spoon mixture into an 11 x 7-inch baking dish.

Bake for 30 minutes or until tops brown. Spoon into washed clamshells if desired.

WOODMAN'S

The village of Essex is known as the straight of road edged in antiques shops and fried clam shacks, between which extend magnificent vistas of winding creek and tidal marshes. Crane Beach is just a slip of white sand on the far horizon, framed by the pine-dark shapes of Great Bank and Cross Island.

Essex is sixteen square miles in size. Two of those square miles are water, or more correctly, tidal estuary upon which the autumn light smears itself like butter. In spring a delicate green emerges from the marshes looking like old doors painted in lichen-stained milk paint. In winter the marsh's golden, crow-crossed expanse, with the Essex River slipping through like a girl's lost ribbon, warms the starkest New England light. This tidal estuary is where some of the best soft-shell clams in the world call home.

For thousands of years the Agawam Native Americans moved from their inland settlements to the banks of Ipswich Bay and the Essex River each summer, taking advantage of the abundance exposed when the tides retreated from these muddy banks. The next most significant thing to happen to an Essex clam is recorded by Chubby and Bessie Woodman in the Woodman Family Bible, just beneath the birthdates of their two eldest children: "We fried the first fried clam in the town of Essex, July 3rd, 1916."

This is perhaps the most famous North Shore food story, and the happiest. In 1914 Chubby Woodman and his wife Bessie were running a roadside stand along the Essex causeway. They sold chewing gum, cigarettes, fresh fruit, homemade pies, and, of course, Essex clams (probably dug by Chubby himself). Most people took these clams home to steam, turn into chowder, or use for bait. Fried Potato Chips were the latest craze, and Chubby had set up a deep fryer to offer this new treat hot and fresh.

One day a bunch of Essex guys were sitting around Chubby's stand. As a Woodman family member noted in the *100th Anniversary Woodman's Cookbook,* it must have been high tide, otherwise these guys would have been out clamming. Someone suggested, as a joke, that Chubby throw a clam into the hot lard used for the potatoes. The first one went in, shell and all, and exploded! A shucked clam went in next, which didn't taste so good. As author Winslow Pettingell tells the tale, Bessie stepped forward and said, "It needs a batter." She dipped the clam in canned milk, which is what people had around in those days without much refrigeration, and then corn flour. The clam descended into the hot lard, and came out a golden, crispy nugget of history. So much depended upon that clam.

The Woodman family—generations and extended lines of them—have come to make that fried clam an empire, an icon, a symbol of the best roadside food in America. To top off a day at the beach with a visit to Woodman's for fried clams is about as American a thing to do as climbing the Washington Monument, as standing on the edge of the Grand Canyon, as watching the Red Sox play the Yankees.

Laurie Lufkin's North of Boston Clam Chowder with Handmade Oyster Crackers

If Woodman's is the temple of the Essex clams, Laurie Lufkin is its goddess. Lufkin grew up along the clam flats of Essex, as did her parents, grandparents, greats and great-greats, maybe even farther back than that. The Lufkin name is as Essex as it gets. Lufkin Road winds down along the eastern edge of the salt marsh that banks the Essex River. And all those Lufkins have been great cooks along the way. Laurie credits her mother, Sue Lufkin, who runs the Essex Clam Festival, for her talents in the kitchen, which are many. Laurie hosts her own local cooking program, *Inspired Cooking*, and has won a garage full of blenders and toaster ovens in cooking contests.

But, being a Lufkin, Laurie's got Essex clam flat sand between her toes. I wouldn't ask anyone else for a proper soft-shell clam chowder recipe; Laurie Lufkin's is definitive, as are her homemade oyster crackers.

SERVES 8 AS A FIRST COURSE; 12 AS AN APPETIZER

For the clam chowder:

2 pounds Maine red potatoes, diced to ½ inch

8 cups clam broth

4 ounces salt pork, cut into very small cubes

2 cups diced sweet onions

1 teaspoon dried thyme

1 fresh bay leaf

½ teaspoon freshly ground black pepper, plus more to taste

3 (12-ounce) cans evaporated milk

¼ cup (½ stick) butter

3 cups whole milk

1 pint half and half

5 cups cooked steamer clams, shucked and rinsed (black "necks" removed if desired)

Salt and pepper to taste

For the oyster crackers:

2 ¼ teaspoons yeast

½ cup lukewarm water

½ teaspoon sugar

1⅔ cup cake flour

1½ cup all-purpose flour, plus more for rolling surface

1 teaspoon salt, plus more for sprinkling if desired

¼ cup cold shortening, cut in cubes

¼ cup (½ stick) cold butter, cut in cubes

2 tablespoons milk

To make the clam chowder:

In a large stockpot, bring potatoes and clam broth to a boil. Cook until potatoes are fork tender but not soft. Set up a large bowl with a colander inside and strain the potatoes, reserving the broth. Set aside.

In the same pot, sauté finely diced salt pork over medium-low heat until fat is rendered out and the bits of meat left in the pot are deep brown and crispy, 10–15 minutes. Stir occasionally to lift any browned bits off bottom of pan while cooking. With a slotted spoon, remove crispy bits and reserve,

MOBY DICK'S CHOWDER CHAPTER

Fishiest of all fishy places was the Try Pots, which well deserved its name; for the pots there were always boiling chowders. Chowder for breakfast, and chowder for dinner, and chowder for supper, till you began to look for fish-bones coming through your clothes. The area before the house was paved with clam-shells. Mrs. Hussey wore a polished necklace of codfish vertebra; and Hosea Hussey had his account books bound in superior old shark-skin. There was a fishy flavor to the milk, too, which I could not at all account for, till one morning happening to take a stroll along the beach among some fishermen's boats, I saw Hosea's brindled cow feeding on fish remnants, and marching along the sand with each foot in a cod's decapitated head, looking very slipshod, I assure ye. . . . However, a warm savory steam from the kitchen served to belie the apparently cheerless prospect before us. But when that smoking chowder came in, the mystery was delightfully explained. Oh! sweet friends, hearken to me. It was made of small juicy clams, scarcely bigger than hazel nuts, mixed with pounded ship biscuits, and salted pork cut up into little flakes! the whole enriched with butter, and plentifully seasoned with pepper and salt. —Moby Dick, chapter 14

leaving drippings in the pan. Reserve crispy pork for garnish. Add onions, thyme, bay, and black pepper. Cook until onions are transparent, 10–12 minutes, stirring occasionally.

Increase heat to medium high and add clam broth. Bring to a simmer. Reduce heat to low and add evaporated milk and butter. Stir to combine. Add whole milk, half and half, and clams. Re-warm chowder to serving temperature. Remove bay leaf. Re-season with salt and pepper to taste. Serve in individual bowls and sprinkle with crispy salt pork if desired.

Serve with Handmade Oyster Crackers.

To make the oyster crackers:

Preheat oven to 375°F. Cover two baking sheets with parchment paper. Set aside.

In a small bowl, combine yeast, water, and sugar. Stir to combine and set aside until mixture is frothy and yeast is activated.

In the bowl of a food processor, combine cake flour, all-purpose flour, and salt. Process for 1 minute to mix and aerate. Add shortening and butter and pulse until small crumbs form. With processor running, pour yeast mixture through feed tube. Process until a soft dough forms.

Turn dough out onto a floured surface and knead. Add a little flour if dough is sticky. Roll out dough as thin as possible into a rectangle. Fold in the long sides of the dough to the center and repeat with the ends to form a smaller rectangle. Roll out thin again and repeat this procedure two more times.

Roll out one final time to a 9 x 11-inch rectangle. Brush top of dough very lightly with milk and sprinkle very lightly with additional salt if desired.

With a pastry cutter or knife, cut crackers into ½- or 1-inch squares as desired. Place crackers 1 inch apart on prepared baking sheets. Bake for 12–15 minutes until lightly browned.

Slide parchment off baking sheet and allow crackers to cool. Serve with seafood chowder. These can be made days ahead if necessary, as they keep well stored at room temperature in an airtight container.

Wilted Lettuce

A classic spring salad, this is best made with new greens from any of the North Shore farms, from Alprilla to Appleton to Arrowhead. When lettuces in Massachusetts finally arrive, they come by the truckful; lettuce loves the area's cool springs. Spring greens are so lush tasting, and by May we are so starved for the honest taste of chlorophyll, that some nights the new lettuce is all one wants for dinner. A mound of this beside Codfish Scrapple makes a wonderful light dinner or substantial first course. Even with just a good chuck of homemade bread, you have an ethereal meal that will leave you time to enjoy the new spring light in the evening.

SERVES 4-6

3 slices good quality, nitrate-free bacon

8 cups Bibb lettuce, washed, dried well, and torn into 2-inch pieces

2 tablespoons chives

¼ cup red wine vinegar

1 teaspoon sugar

Salt and pepper to taste

Cook bacon in a skillet until crispy. When done, drain on paper towels and set aside. Pour grease from bacon into a jar and reserve. Wipe the skillet clean.

Toss lettuce leaves with chives in a salad bowl.

Heat skillet again, and return 3 tablespoons bacon drippings to it. Add vinegar, sugar, salt, and pepper, and whisk together. When mixture is hot, pour over the greens and toss well. Serve immediately.

1768 Baked Beans

While baked beans mean something symbolically to the coast of Massachusetts, their modern actuality—cans of flavorless pellets packed in syrup—is characterless, not much more than a dismally sweet condiment to a hot dog.

Baked beans were not like that in 1768. Deep in the pages of a Rowley church cookbook this recipe is labeled "1768 Baked Beans." Whatever the truth to that, these are a rich pot of mahogany legumes bound in a caramel-tinged, roasted tomato glaze. The sweetness comes a wee bit from that half cup of sugar, and a lot from what tomatoes do when they're roasted with fat and onions for six hours. (I am not a fan of too much molasses or too much bacon, both of which people tend to pile onto baked beans, probably because flavor in a dried bean is elusive. But that's what baked beans often become: bacon and molasses vehicles.)

The flavors in the 1768 method are extracted from good, simple ingredients, including heat and time, and it produces a more refined, complex baked bean. Don't substitute the salt pork, which releases clean, luxurious fats without overpowering the dish with animal flavor. These are baked beans of which a Massachusetts resident can be proud. This makes a large amount, so make them for an "occasion." For a special 4th of July celebration, or even a Labor Day Party, these beans would make a great Massachusetts meal served with Lobster Cove Fish Cakes or Gino Mondello's Codfish Cakes. Serve leftovers beside Hingham Baked Tomatoes for a beautiful, simple dinner.

[8-10 SERVINGS]

1 medium onion, quartered

¼ pound salt pork, chopped into ½-inch pieces

1 pound Roman beans, soaked overnight and drained

1 (28-ounce) can diced tomatoes, drained

1 teaspoon dry mustard

½ cup sugar

1 teaspoon salt

1 teaspoon ground pepper

2 bay leaves

Preheat oven to 350°F.

On bottom of ovenproof casserole, lay onions and ¼ of the salt pork.

Layer beans and tomatoes with remaining salt pork, topping with last of salt pork.

Add spices, and fill pot with water to cover all.

Bake covered for 5½–6 hours. Stir beans occasionally to make sure top beans don't get too dry as the water evaporates. By the end of the cooking time, tomatoes should have broken down to a thick sauce, and the beans should be well cooked but not too mushy. Remove bay leaves and serve.

Brussels Sprout Panzanella Salad with Candied Bacon

This brussels sprout recipe, from the now-closed Enzo Restaurant in Newburyport, answered the question, "How do we make a panzanella salad—the traditional Italian bread salad made with summery red tomatoes and fresh basil—in New England in the winter?"

The result looks nothing like its parent, and should enjoy its own unique place at the table. Sometimes we poach an egg on top, for the more deluxe, full-dinner version of this salad. Sometimes we don't, but we throw a handful of roasted walnuts on top.

SERVES 4-6

4 cups brussels sprouts, ends trimmed, and the sprouts sliced to ¼ inch

3 cups mushrooms, a mix of shiitake and button is good, cleaned and sliced

6 tablespoons olive oil, divided

Salt and pepper to taste

3 cups cubed bread, semolina or a country-style loaf

2 slices good quality bacon, cut into ½-inch-wide sections

2 tablespoons brown sugar

1 cup, or to taste, Pancetta Molasses Dressing (page 292) at room temperature

4 poached eggs or 1 cup toasted walnuts (only if you are not poaching an egg)

In lightly salted boiling water, blanch brussels sprouts, dropping immediately into ice water. Spread leaves out on paper towels to dry, padding the top layer with more paper towels. Try to get as dry as possible.

Meanwhile, preheat oven to 400°F. Toss mushrooms with 3 tablespoons olive oil, salt, and pepper to taste, and lay out on a baking sheet. Roast for 15 minutes, or until mushrooms begin to turn brown and crispy.

Toss bread cubes with remaining 3 tablespoons olive oil, or more if bread does not look completely coated. Lay out on a baking sheet. Toast in the same oven until brown, about 15 minutes, depending on your bread.

In a small bowl, toss bacon pieces with brown sugar. On a baking sheet lined with parchment paper or aluminum foil, lay bacon, scraping loose brown sugar on top.

With the oven still at 400°F, roast for 15 minutes, or until bacon is brown and crispy. Watch carefully that it doesn't burn. Remove from oven and lay pieces out on a baking rack to "dry."

To assemble the salad: In a large bowl toss sprout leaves with enough Pancetta Molasses Dressing to coat liberally.

Distribute dressed sprouts among large salad bowls. Distribute mushrooms on top of sprouts. If poaching an egg, nest it into the mound of mushrooms and spouts.

Toss croutons and 4–5 pieces of candied bacon on and around the egg. Salt and pepper the egg, and serve immediately.

If not using the egg, simply toss the toasted walnuts over the salad and serve.

Pancetta Molasses Dressing

This dressing, heavily weighted with cold weather New England tastes (that pork, mustard and molasses combination), is sometimes just the right compliment to hearty Massachusetts vegetables. Brussels sprouts, as seen in the Brussels Sprout Panzanella Salad with Candied Bacon, tossed with Pancetta Molasses Dressing become a great winter side dish. Butternut squash drizzled with Pancetta Molasses Dressing and roasted could be a light dinner. Even parsnips would be made luxurious with this dressing poured oven them, or stirred into a puree. Again, this is a dressing for cold weather and sturdy crops, something the farms of coastal Massachusetts know well.

YIELDS ABOUT 3 CUPS

3 ounces pancetta, sliced or cubed

2 tablespoons Dijon mustard

½ cup molasses

¼ cup balsamic vinegar

1 cup oil (I use a blend of olive and canola oils)

Cook pancetta in a skillet until crisp and browned and the fat is rendered out. Cool slightly and place pancetta and all the rendered fat in the bowl of a food processor.

Add mustard, molasses, and vinegar to processor bowl. Turn processor on and let it grind up the pancetta. When mixture looks semi-smooth, pour in oil.

When dressing looks cohesive and smooth, turn off processor and check for seasoning.

Taste for salt, or more molasses or vinegar: Dressing should taste sweet, sour, and salty together. This dressing should be stored in the refrigerator and brought up to room temperature (or heated) before use.

Rowley Grange Tomato Soup

I instantly recognized something nice about this tomato soup, but didn't identify it until I tasted it: Campbell's. It tastes like the homemade version of the Campbell's soup with which so many of us define childhood lunch. Hang that memory on the clove and cinnamon.

Add whole milk and you will be transported back to your childhood kitchen; if that's not compelling, omit the milk for a beautifully spicy, but lighter, tomato soup. Serve it with grilled Asiago cheese sandwiches, and be a real grown-up.

SERVES 6

2 tablespoons olive oil

10 whole cloves

1 small onion, cut in half

3 stalks celery, mostly leaves, chopped

1 cinnamon stick

1 teaspoon red pepper flakes

2 (28-ounce) cans plum tomatoes,

2 tablespoons brown sugar

1 teaspoon salt

Freshly ground black pepper to taste

1½ cups water

1½ cups whole milk

In a large heavy saucepan heat olive oil over medium heat.

Stick cloves into each half of the onion. Add onions halves, celery, cinnamon, and red pepper flakes to the oil. Cook until celery softens and onion begins to get tender, 10–12 minutes, stirring occasionally.

Add tomatoes, brown sugar, salt, pepper, and water. Bring to a simmer, and cook for 30 minutes.

Remove clove-studded onions and cinnamon stick.

Puree mixture with an immersion or regular blender. For a finer consistency, pass through a fine meshed strainer, pushing it through with the bottom of a ladle. Taste soup to check for salt and pepper, adding more if necessary.

Return soup to a clean saucepan, and heat. Add milk, and heat to a simmer. Serve piping hot with grilled cheese sandwiches.

Green Tomato Apple Pie

The Gothic beauty of a late September vegetable garden evokes so much—moldy fruits speak of missed opportunity. Desiccated vines weave around swollen zucchinis no one has the oomph to harvest anymore. Drought-shriveled leaves reveal a rising tide of pumpkins heaving themselves to the finish line of plumpness. Green tomatoes droop from withered stalks, wishing for ripeness, verdant phantoms of their Big Boy brothers.

From Essex to Newburyport—the view from the winding country road is more farmland than sea. In the fall, a drive along Route 1A north is all harvest: from Russell Orchards to Alprilla Farm to Appleton Farms to Tendercrop Farms. Heavy green and not-quite-ripe tomatoes drag their vines to the earth across wide swatches of field. Almost everyone in these farms' CSAs is groaning with tomatoes by late September into early October, but here is a scrumptious alternative to green tomato mincemeat: Green Tomato Apple Pie.

MAKES ONE 9-INCH PIE

A top and bottom piecrust (or just one crust if you choose to omit the bottom)

2 cups green tomatoes, sliced

3 large apples, peeled and diced (Granny Smith apples are preferred, but any good baking apples will do)

1 tablespoon lemon juice (fresh is best)

½ cup sugar

½ cup light brown sugar

2 tablespoons flour

1 teaspoon cinnamon

½ teaspoon salt

2 tablespoons butter

1 egg

1 tablespoon cream

1 teaspoon sugar

Preheat oven to 425°F.

Prepare and chill your favorite double piecrust recipe.

Toss tomatoes and apples in a large bowl with lemon juice.

Add sugars, flour, cinnamon and salt. Mix well.

Roll out piecrusts as directed.

If using a bottom crust, lay it in 9-inch pie pan. Spread ½ of the filling into piecrust and dot with 1 tablespoon of butter.

Spread the other ½ of the mixture on top and dot with remaining 1 tablespoon butter.

Cover with the top crust and crimp the edges with the tines of a fork.

Combine cream and egg for an egg wash, and brush pie all over, including edges.

Cut decorative slits in the top of the crust for steam to escape.

Bake at 425°F for 15 minutes. Then, reduce heat to 350°F and cook for another 45 minutes.

In the last 15 minutes of baking time, sprinkle piecrust with 1 teaspoon sugar.

Argilla Road Apple Pie

There are still people in Ipswich who remember resident Adele Crockett Robinson, who wrote *The Orchard*, a compelling account of her attempts during the Great Depression to save her family's apple orchard on Argilla Road.

Argilla Road in Ipswich is famous for many reasons, mostly because each summer it delivers thousands of flip-flopped visitors to the sea-grassed dunes and sand-dollared sands of Crane Beach. But in the fall visitors drive Argilla Road to Russell Orchards, the last apple orchard of many that flanked this route in the Adele Crockett Robinson years. Russell Orchards, once Goodale's, attracts families in the fall like bees to the "drops" in the orchards. They come for the pumpkins, the cider donuts, to pet the friendly horses, to "just look" at the questionably friendly pig, and for the apples. Russell Orchards makes sure that the Ipswich apple tradition is almost as famous as Ipswich clams. Look carefully when you drive Argilla Road, a sharp eye can spot the last of Robinson's knobby trees on a protected hillside.

Found in an old Ipswich cookbook, this is an old-fashioned apple pie, unusual because the fruit cooks slightly with the spices and butter before it is put into the pastry, resulting in a sweet, juicy filling that tastes like the ingredients have met before. Many apple-pie fillings are a mound of raw fruit tossed with cinnamon and sugar; often the apples are so uncooked they still crunch. While retaining the character of the apple, this filling tastes more finished, more complete.

Adele Crockett Robinson's grandmother said that "Northern Greening" apples make the best pies. I'm sure she wouldn't complain about the splash of Privateer Rum, either. Privateer is bottled in Ipswich by the Cabot family, who were known in the eighteenth century for their privateering success against the enemy British.

MAKES ONE PIE

For the pie crust:

2½ cups flour

1 teaspoon salt

1 teaspoon sugar

1 cup (2 sticks) cold butter, cut in pieces

6–8 tablespoons ice water

For the filling:

6–7 cups peeled and sliced apples, about 7 medium apples

Juice from 1 lemon

¼ cup (½ stick) butter

1 cup sugar

2 tablespoons water

2 teaspoons pumpkin pie spice (cinnamon, nutmeg, ginger, lemon peel, cloves, cardamom)

½ teaspoon salt

2 tablespoons flour

2 tablespoons rum (optional, but Privateer Rum from Ipswich is ideal)

1 beaten egg

1 tablespoon milk

To make the pie crust:

Put dry ingredients in the bowl of a food processor fitted with a steel blade. Pulse to blend.

Add cold butter pieces, and pulse until the mixture is like coarse cornmeal.

Add water, a tablespoon at a time, pulsing after each. Blend until mixture comes into a ball, at around 7 tablespoons.

Divide dough in half, with one half only slightly larger than the other. Gently press doughs into thick disks, wrap in plastic wrap, and refrigerate for at least 15 minutes or until the filling is prepared, and you are ready to assemble and bake the pie.

To make the filling:

In a large bowl, toss apple slices with lemon juice.

In a wide sauté pan heat butter, sugar, water, pumpkin pie spice, and salt on medium heat. Cook for 3–4 minutes or until everything melds and begins to caramelize.

Add apples and flour, and cook, tossing all together, for 10–12 minutes, or until apples begin to noticeably soften. Toss regularly. Do not let them become mushy, just a little cooked. Add rum if desired, and mix in. Allow filling to cool.

Preheat oven to 400°F. Prepare egg wash by mixing egg and milk together in a small dish.

Roll bottom pie dough and place in pie pan. Brush the lip with the egg wash.

Roll out top pie dough.

Fill the pie, and cover with top dough, pressing egg-washed edges so they adhere. Trim pie, and crimp accordingly. Brush the whole pie with the remaining egg wash. Cut attractive slits for steam to escape. Bake for 45 minutes or until pastry is golden brown.

Newburyport Pear Pudding

This pear pudding, sweetly baked fruit coddled in a rich custard, was found in a church cookbook in the Newburyport public library. In France it is called *Clafoutis Aux Poire*. By any name this is sublime. The contributor recommends serving it with a pour of maple syrup, which keeps her version rooted in Massachusetts.

SERVES 6

5 ripe pears, peeled and quartered

Juice of 1–2 lemons

⅔ cup milk

⅓ cup heavy cream

½ cup plus 2 tablespoons sugar, divided

⅓ cup flour

2 eggs

1 teaspoon vanilla

1 tablespoon butter, cut in pieces

2 tablespoons confectionary sugar

Preheat oven to 425°F. Butter a 1½-quart glass or ceramic baking dish.

Toss pears in lemon juice and arrange pears in an attractive pattern in the baking dish.

In an electric blender or food processor fitted with a steel blade, add milk, heavy cream, ½ cup sugar, flour, eggs, and vanilla. Mix together until just combined and pour over pears.

Sprinkle top with remaining 2 tablespoons of sugar and dot with butter. Bake until golden brown on top, and the pudding is set, about 30 minutes.

Remove pudding from oven, and sprinkle immediately with sifted confectionary sugar. Serve warm or room temperature.

Warm Ipswich Strawberry Shortcake

Clearly written in a farmer's kitchen, with a huge bowl of freshly picked strawberries on the counter awaiting purpose, this recipe is all about the best, freshest, most immediate route to dessert for the jammy, ruby berries for which we wait all year.

Bake a biscuit-like shortcake, split it in half as soon as it comes out of the oven, dot the steaming bottom with butter, and smother in fresh strawberries. Pour a little heavy cream over that, and top immediately with the still-hot second half of shortcake. You may never go back to cold biscuit and cold whipped cream again.

SERVES 8–10

1 quart fresh strawberries

3 tablespoons plus 1 teaspoon sugar, divided

½ cup (1 stick) cold and cut into pieces, plus 1 tablespoon butter, divided

4 cups flour

1 teaspoon baking soda

2 teaspoons cream of tartar

2 cups milk

½ cup heavy cream

Clean and halve the strawberries. Toss them in a bowl with 2 tablespoons sugar, or to taste, and allow them to sit for at least 15 minutes to allow the juices to begin to run.

Preheat oven to 450°F.

In a large bowl (or in the bowl of a food processor fitted with a steel blade) cut the butter into the flour. Add in the baking soda, cream of tartar, and 1 tablespoon sugar.

(If using a food processor empty the butter and flour mixture into a large bowl.) Pour milk into the flour, and stir very lightly just to combine. Avoid over mixing.

Pat dough into a circle, and lay on a buttered baking sheet.

Bake until golden brown, 15–20 minutes.

When baked, split cake immediately. Lay bottom half on a cake plate, and dot the hot cake with 1 tablespoon butter cut into pieces. Pour strawberries over cake. Pour cream over berries.

Top with the other half of the shortcake. Sprinkle final 1 teaspoon of sugar over top of cake, and serve immediately while all is warm.

Switchel

Switchel seems to be the drink that hot and thirsty hay-threshers required. The amount of water the overheated workers needed would make them nauseated if consumed by itself; Switchel's tummy-comforting cider, molasses, and ginger made quaffing one's hard-won thirst easier. Add rum, and all those benefits still apply, along with being very tasty. This makes a cocktail for thirsty haymakers of the more metaphorical sort.

SERVES 5–7

1 cup cider

½ cup molasses

1 tablespoon ground ginger

4 cups ice water

1 cup rum (optional)

Combine everything in a tall chilled pitcher. "Serve to haymakers."

Pear Walnut Bread

This sweet old-fashioned recipe is really more cake than bread. Moist and tender, it has melt-in-your-mouth crumb, and the flavor of an autumn day. I found this recipe in an old Rowley cookbook, and immediately imagined this cake cooling in a sunny Rowley kitchen window, the old pear tree in the yard stooped with hanging fruit, children about to run in the door from a day at school. A warm slice of this needs nothing else but a cup of tea or a glass of milk.

MAKES 1 LOAF

½ cup oil

1 cup sugar

2 eggs

¼ cup sour cream

1 teaspoon vanilla

2 cups flour

1 teaspoon salt

1 teaspoon baking soda

½ teaspoon cinnamon

¼ teaspoon nutmeg

½ cup walnuts

1 cup peeled and chopped pears

Preheat oven to 350°F. Butter and flour a 9 x 5-inch bread pan.

In the bowl of a mixer beat together oil and sugar. Beat in eggs one at a time.

Add sour cream and vanilla, and mix in. Then add flour, salt, baking soda, and spices.

Fold in nuts and pears. Pour into prepared pan.

Bake for 1 hour, or until a knife inserted comes out clean. Cool for 10–15 minutes on a wire rack, and then remove from pans. Cool completely on racks.

Rowley Buns

These sweet, fluffy morning rolls called "Rowley Buns" are from a cookbook issued "For the benefit of the Ladies Benevolent Society of the Oldtown Parish of First Church." On the title page is offered this quote from Mrs. Wiggs: "Somehow, I never feel like good things b'long to me till I pass 'em on to somebody else."

I feel that way about these buns; their sweet, light deliciousness, brushed with a milk and molasses glaze, needs to be shared beyond the Rowley town line.

The recipe recommends starting these buns the night before and allowing the first long rise to happen while you're asleep, and finishing them in the morning. If your schedule doesn't allow morning baking, feel free to start the rise in the morning, giving it at least 4 hours.

MAKES 3 DOZEN SMALL ROLLS

For the glaze:

1 tablespoon milk

1 tablespoon molasses

1 teaspoon lemon extract

For the buns:

3 cups milk

1 package active dry yeast

1½ cups sugar, divided

7 cups flour, divided

½ cup currants

½ teaspoon cinnamon

½ cup (1 stick) butter softened

To make the glaze:

In a small bowl, combine milk, molasses, and lemon extract. Stir until mixture comes together as a pourable glaze.

To make the buns:

The night before put milk, yeast, and 1 cup sugar in a bowl. Add enough flour to make a "fritter-like" soft dough, about 4 cups. Let sit overnight.

The next day, add ½ cup sugar, currants, and cinnamon. Work in the softened butter. Add enough flour to make a soft, kneadable dough, about 3 cups.

In a buttered bowl, set dough and turn it to coat lightly with butter. Let rise until double in bulk.

Punch down, and divide dough into pieces about 2½ ounces. Roll into balls. On a buttered baking sheet, set rolls 1 inch apart. Cover with a towel, and let rise until double in bulk.

Preheat oven to 350°F.

Bake until golden brown, about 40 minutes.

Brush rolls with glaze as soon as they come out of the oven.

Golden Kumquat Bread

Slivers of candied kumquats star in this delicious, simple loaf. Not only is it heavenly scented, but the sturdy peel is like having homemade marmalade inside your bread. It would make a wonderful gift loaf, but bake a loaf for home so you know the treat this makes toasted and slathered with butter.

   Candied kumquats can be found in Middle Eastern grocery stores, specialty stores, or you can make them by following the recipe below, which is simply cooking them in a simple syrup. A jar of candied kumquats is a wonderful citrus to keep in your refrigerator in the winter months. Serve them with a roasted chicken, chop and mix them with sweet potatoes, even top a bowl of warm oatmeal with a few of these tiny urns of sunshine.

MAKES 1 LOAF

For the candied kumquats:

2 cups kumquats

¾ cup water

1 cup sugar

For the bread:

2 cups flour

½ teaspoon baking soda

1 teaspoon cream of tartar

½ teaspoon salt

⅓ cup butter

⅔ cup sugar

1 egg

3 tablespoons sour cream

¾ cup slivered candied kumquats

2 tablespoons kumquat syrup

To make the candied kumquats:

Slice the kumquats in half and remove seeds. (This is easier than you think, but don't worry if you miss some, they're edible.)

Heat water and sugar over high heat to a boil. Simmer for 5 minutes, or until sugar is dissolved. Add kumquats, and simmer for 10 minutes.

Drain kumquats through a sieve set over a bowl. Set them aside, and return the syrup to the pan. Simmer to reduce syrup for 5 minutes. Pour ¼ cup syrup over kumquats. Serve or refrigerate. This can be stored in a glass jar for up to 2 weeks.

To make the bread:

Preheat oven to 350°F. Grease and flour an 8 x 4-inch bread pan

In a medium bowl combine flour, baking soda, cream of tartar, and salt.

In a separate bowl, cream butter and sugar. Beat in egg and sour cream. Fold in kumquats and syrup.

Gently mix in dry ingredients, avoiding overmixing. Spoon batter into prepared loaf pan.

Bake for 50–60 minutes, or until a knife inserted comes out clean. Cool 10 minutes, and remove from pan. Let cool completely on wire racks. This beautiful bread could easily be served for dessert, even with a small scoop of vanilla ice cream.

Index

About the Author

Heather Atwood is author of the blog "Food for Thought" and the weekly column by the same name syndicated in a number of Massachusetts newspapers. For the online cooking site Cook123, Ms. Atwood hosts cooking videos featuring regional Massachusetts chefs and cooks. This combined work has created a fine web of connections in the New England food community, allowing Atwood a prized familiarity with Finns in West Barnstable who still make fruit soup, Gloucester Sicilians who bake their own zeppole, and day-boat fishermen who sell pearly scallops from coolers out of the backs of their cars. She reveres the people who preserve and energize the New England food landscape.